C. EDMUND BOSWORTH (1928–2015) was a Fellow of the British Academy, an Honorary Member of the Hungarian Academy of Sciences and, until his retirement, Professor of Arabic Studies at the University of Manchester. He was the British Editor of the second edition of the *Encyclopaedia of Islam*, and wrote numerous books and articles on the history, culture and literature of the Arabic, Persian and Turkish lands of the Middle East and Central Asia in the pre-modern period. For many years he was also the editor of *Iran*, the journal of the British Institute of Persian Studies. He was the recipient of the biennial Giorgio Levi Della Vida Award at the University of California, Los Angeles.

'This is an excellent annotated translation of this important historical text by a most qualified scholar.'

—Farhad Daftary,
Co-Director and Head of the Department of Academic Research and Publications, Institute of Ismaili Studies.

'All in all this is a most useful publication which … makes available one of the earliest examples of Persian historical literature and most important sources for the history of the Khurasan.'

—The Bulletin of the School of Oriental and African Studies

THE ORNAMENT OF HISTORIES

A History of the Eastern Islamic Lands
AD 650–1041
The Original Text of
Abū Saʿīd ʿAbd al-Ḥayy Gardīzī

Translated and with Commentary by
C. EDMUND BOSWORTH

BIPS Persian Studies Series
A Joint Publication with the British Institute of Persian Studies

New paperback edition published in 2018 by
I.B.Tauris & Co. Ltd
London • New York
www.ibtauris.com

First published in hardback in 2011 by I.B.Tauris & Co. Ltd

ISBN: 978 1 78831 112 0
eISBN: 978 1 83860 955 9
ePDF: 978 0 85771 957 7

A full CIP record for this book is available from the British Library
A full CIP record is available from the Library of Congress

Library of Congress Catalog Card Number: available

Camera-ready copy edited and supplied by Swales & Willis Ltd, Exeter, Devon

To the memories of Vladimir Minorsky (1877–1966) and Sir Gerard Clauson (1891–1974), who were always ready to share their expert knowledge on the Iranian and Turkish worlds with a much younger scholar.

CONTENTS

Preface and Acknowledgements xi
Abbreviations of Journals, etc., cited xiii

Introduction 1

TRANSLATION OF THE TEXT
Part One: The Arab Governors 13

[Chapter Ten]Concerning the Table of the Governors of Khurasan 13
Chapter Eleven Concerning the Historical Accounts of the Governors of Khurasan 14
ʿAbdallāh b. ʿĀmir b. Kurayz 14
Umayr b. Aḥmar al-Yashkurī 15
ʿAbdallāh b. ʿĀmir b. Kurayz 15
Jaʿda b. Hubayra al-Makhzūmī 16
ʿAbd al-Raḥmān b. Abzā al-Khuzāʿī 16
ʿAbdallāh b. ʿĀmir b. Kurayz 16
Ziyād b. Abīhi 17
ʿUbaydallāh b. Ziyād 17
Saʿīd b. ʿUthmān b. ʿAffān 18
ʿAbd al-Raḥmān b. Ziyād 18
Salm b. Ziyād 18
ʿAbdallāh b. Khāzim 19
Baḥīr b. Warqā' 19
Umayya b. ʿAbdallāh 19
Ḥajjāj b. Yūsuf 20
[Qutayba b. Muslim] 21
Wakīʿ b. Abī Sūd al-Ghudānī 22
Yazīd b. al-Muhallab 22
Jarrāḥ b. ʿAbdallāh al-Ḥakamī 23
ʿAbd al-Raḥmān [b.] Nuʿaym al-Ghāmidī 24
Saʿīd b. ʿAbd al-ʿAzīz 24
ʿUmar b. Hubayra 24
Khālid b. ʿAbdallāh al-Qasrī 24

Ashras b. ʿAbdallāh 25
Junayd b. ʿAbd al-Raḥmān 25
ʿĀṣim b. ʿAbdallāh al-Hilālī 25
Khālid b. ʿAbdallāh al-Qasrī 25
Naṣr b. Sayyār 26
Abū Muslim ʿAbd al-Raḥmān b. Muslim 28
Abū Dāwūd Khālid b. Ibrāhīm al-Dhuhlī 31
ʿAbd al-Jabbār b. ʿAbd al-Raḥmān 32
Abū ʿAwn ʿAbd al-Malik b. Yazīd 33
Usayd b. ʿAbdallāh 33
ʿAbda b. Qadīd 33
Ḥumayd b. Qaḥṭaba 33
Abū ʿAwn ʿAbd al-Malik b. Yazīd 34
Muʿādh b. Muslim 35
Musayyab b. Zuhayr 35
Abu ʾl-ʿAbbās al-Faḍl b. Sulaymān 36
Jaʿfar b. Muḥammad b. al-Ashʿath 37
ʿAbbās b. Jaʿfar 37
Ghiṭrīf b. ʿAṭāʾ al-Kindī 37
al-Faḍl b. Yaḥyā al-Barmakī 37
Manṣūr b. Yazīd 38
ʿAlī b. ʿĪsā b. Māhān 38
Harthama b. Aʿyan 39
al-Maʾmūn ʿAbdallāh b. Rashīd 40
Ghassān b. ʿAbbād 41

Part Two: The Tahirids and Saffarids **43**

Ṭāhir (I) b. al-Ḥusayn 43
Ṭalḥa b. Ṭāhir (I) 43
ʿAbdallāh b. Ṭāhir (I) 44
Ṭāhir (II) b. ʿAbdallāh 45
Muḥammad b. Ṭāhir (II) 46
The Outbreak of Yaʿqūb b. al-Layth 46
ʿAmr b. al-Layth 49

Part Three: The Samanids **53**

[Chapter Twelve] Concerning the Rule and the Lineage of the Samanids 53
Ismāʿīl b. Aḥmad (I) b. Asad b. Sāmān 54
The Martyred One (*al-shahīd*), Abū Naṣr Aḥmad (II) b. Ismāʿīl 55
The Fortunate One (*al-saʿīd*), Naṣr (II) b. Aḥmad (II) 56
The Praiseworthy One (*al-ḥamīd*) Abū Muḥammad Nūḥ (I) b. Naṣr (II) 60
The Rightly-Guided One (*al-rashīd*)
Abu ʾl-Fawāris ʿAbd al-Malik (I) b. Nūḥ (I) 65

The Upright One (*al-sadīd*) Abū Ṣāliḥ Manṣūr (I) b. Nūḥ (I) 67
The Well-Pleasing One (*al-raḍī, al-riḍā*)
Abu 'l-Qāsim Nūḥ (II) b. Manṣūr (I) 70
Abu 'l-Ḥārith Manṣūr (II) b. Nūḥ (II) 77
Abu 'l-Fawāris ʿAbd al-Malik (II) b. Nūḥ (II) 78

Part Four: The Early Ghaznavids **81**

[Chapter Thirteen Concerning the Historical Accounts of
Yamīn al-Dawla and His House] 81
The Reign of the Most Exalted Amir, Sayyid Yamīn al-Dawla wa-Amīn
al-Milla wa-Kahf al-Islām Abu 'l-Qāsim Maḥmūd, Son of Nāṣir al-Dīn
wa 'l-Dawla Sebüktegin, God's Mercy upon Them! 82
The Meeting of Yūsuf Qadïr Khān and Sultan Maḥmūd,
God's Mercy upon Them Both! 94
A Description of the Celebration and the Feast 94
The Beginnings of the Seljuq Turks 95
The Rule of Amir Jalāl al-Dawla wa-Jamāl al-Milla Abū Aḥmad
Muḥammad b. Yamīn al-Dawla, God Most High's
Mercy upon Them Both! 100
The Rule of Amir Nāṣir Dīn Allāh Ḥāfiẓ ʿIbād Allāh wa-Ẓahīr Khalīfat
Allāh Abū Saʿīd Masʿūd b. Yamīn al-Dawla [Walī]Amīr al-Mu'minīn,
God's Mercy upon Them Both! 102
The Rule of Amir Shihāb al-Dīn wa 'l-Dawla wa-Quṭb al-Milla
Abu 'l-Fatḥ Mawdūd b. Nāṣir Dīn Allāh Masʿūd b. Maḥmūd,
God's Mercy upon Them Both! 112

Notes 115
Select Bibliography 149
Indices 155
1 Persons, peoples, tribes 155
2 Places 163
3 Technical Terms 167
4 Book titles 169

PREFACE AND ACKNOWLEDGEMENTS

Having completed, after some eight years' work on it, my translation of and commentary on Bayhaqī's *Tārīkh-i Mas'ūdī* (see below, pp. 9–10), it seemed to me worthwhile attempting a similar task – one fortunately less arduous – for the other contemporary source for the sultanates of Mas'ūd and his immediate successors in Ghazna, the *Zayn al-akhbār* of Gardīzī. Gardīzī's section on the Ghaznavids actually forms part of an extended history of the successive rulers in Khurasan and the Islamic East from early caliphal days until the author's own time. The translation given here is accompanied by a commentary, one which is, however, on a less detailed scale than that provided for the Bayhaqī translation; nevertheless it will, I trust, be adequate for the comprehension of Gardīzī's narrative and its place in the general history of the Eastern Islamic lands. Ideally, the task of making available in translation the contemporary sources on the early Ghaznavids should be completed by a version of al-'Utbī's recounting of the origins of the Ghaznavid dynasty and the first two-thirds of Maḥmūd's reign, in his *al-Ta'rīkh al-yamīnī*; but tackling al-'Utbī's florid and discursive Arabic must be left to a future labourer in the Eastern Islamic vineyard.

It is especially fitting that this book should appear in the publication series of the British Institute of Persian Studies, for whose journal *Iran* I have acted as Co-Editor for over forty years (surely a record in journal editorship!), and I am grateful for the encouragement of colleagues at the Institute in putting the present book together.

Various other colleagues have helped me by providing items of information, sending me copies of books and articles, etc.; I am much indebted to them all. They include: Mr Mel Dadswell (Chudleigh Knighton, Devon); Dr Farhad Daftary (Institute of Ismaili Studies, London); Professor Geert Jan Van Gelder (Oxford University); Professor Peter Golden (Rutgers University, N.J.); Dr Pavel Lurye (Österreichische Akademie der Wissenschaften, Vienna); Professor Nicholas Sims-Williams (School of Oriental and African Studies, London); Dr Luke Treadwell (Oxford University); and M. Étienne de la Vaissière (ENS Laboratoire d'archéologie, Paris). These are specifically thanked in the appropriate places, but I am especially obliged to Dr Daftary and to Mr François de Blois (School of Oriental and African Studies, London) who have advised on certain problematic words and passages of Gardīzī's text. But as always, the buck stops with the author himself, to whose account any imperfections must be laid.

C. Edmund Bosworth
Castle Cary, Somerset
February 2009

ABBREVIATIONS OF JOURNALS, BOOKS, ETC. CITED

AEMAe	*Archivum Eurasiae Medii Aevi* (Wiesbaden)
AOHung	*Acta Orientalia Academiae Scientarum Hungaricae* (Budapest)
BGA	Bibliotheca Geographicorum Arabicorum (Leiden)
BSOAS	*Bulletin of the School of Oriental and African Studies* (London)
CAJ	*Central Asiatic Journal* (The Hague, Wiesbaden)
CHIr	*The Cambridge History of Iran* (Cambridge)
EI[2]	*Encyclopaedia of Islam*, second edition (Leiden)
EIr	*Encyclopaedia Iranica* (New York)
GMS	E.J.W. Gibb Memorial Series (Leiden, London)
H	Ḥabībī's text of the *Zayn al-akhbār*
IQ	*Islamic Quarterly* (London)
Iran JBIPS	*Iran, Journal of the British Institute of Persian Studies* (London)
Isl.	*Der Islam* (Strassburg-Berlin, Leipzig-Berlin)
IsMEO	Istituto Italiano per il Medio ed Estremo Oriente (Rome)
JESHO	*Journal of the Economic and Social History of the Orient* (Leiden)
JRAS	*Journal of the Royal Asiatic Society* (London)
M	Riḍāzāda Malik's text of the *Zayn al-akhbār*
MW	*The Muslim World* (Hartford, Conn.)
N	Nazim's text of the *Zayn al-akhbār*
RSO	*Revista degli Studi Orientali* (Rome)
SBWAW	*Sitzungsberichte der Kaiserlichen Akademie der Wissenschaften zu Wien* (Vienna)
St.Ir.	*Studia Iranica* (Paris)

INTRODUCTION

The author of the 'Ornament of Histories', Abū Saʿīd ʿAbd al-Ḥayy b. al-Ḍaḥḥāk b. Maḥmūd Gardīzī, is a most shadowy figure. He must have been connected with the early Ghaznavid court or bureaucracy, and he claims to have been present at many significant events involving the military exploits of his masters (see below), although it is strange that neither of his fellow-historians, Abū Naṣr ʿUtbī (who was admittedly of an older generation, probably dying in the last decade of Sultan Maḥmūd's reign), nor Abu 'l-Faḍl Bayhaqī (who died in 470/1077, hence may well have been a fairly exact contemporary of Gardīzī) mentions him. It seems very improbable that he did not know Bayhaqī at least, working as Gardīzī obviously did at the Ghaznavid court.[1] Our Gardīzī may perhaps have been a relative of the Abū Mursil b. Manṣūr b. Aflaḥ Gardīzī who brought back to Nishapur from the caliph al-Qādir's court at Baghdad an investiture patent for Sultan Masʿūd b. Maḥmūd (see below, p. 99). He presumably stemmed from Zābulistān, the Ghazna–Gardīz region of what is now eastern Afghanistan, as indicated not only by his *nisba* but perhaps also by the name of his father (if al-Ḍaḥḥāk is here an arabisation of (Azhi) Zahāka, the tyrant who in Iranian legend overthrew Jamshīd, nevertheless popular in the lore of the far eastern fringes of Khurasan). The only rough dates that we have for Gardīzī's life are those of the reign of Sultan ʿAbd al-Rashīd b. Maḥmūd (r. ?440–43/?1049–52), whom Gardīzī mentions in the historical section of his book as his sovereign, to whom he was dedicating the work; but when Gardīzī was actually born and died is unknown. The book's title *Zayn al-akhbār* is apparently a *kināya* or allusion to ʿAbd al-Rashīd's honorific title *Zayn al-Milla* 'Ornament of the Religious Community'. The only contemporary personal and intellectual connection one may suggest with some confidence is with the great Abu 'l-Rayḥān al-Bīrūnī and his *Taḥqīq mā li 'l-Hind* and *al-Āthār al-bāqiya*, since Gardīzī states that he heard information directly from him[2] and the material for his chronological tables stems largely from the Khwarazmian scholar.[3]

The 'Ornament of Histories' is a *mélange* of information, historical, geographical and ethnographical such as would be of interest to the ruling official and scholarly classes of the Eastern Iranian world; if for nothing else, it would be noteworthy as the first work in New Persian to combine general history with specifically dynastic history.

The Turkish ethnic origins of the house of Sebüktegin and the raids into northern India of the Amirs would explain Gardīzī's appending sections on the Turkish tribes of Inner Asia and Eastern Europe and on the festivals and religious and philosophical sects of the Indians to the more strictly historical part of the book. This historical part plunges *in medias res*, since a presumed preface or exordium has been lost from the manuscripts (on which, see below), with the legendary Persian kings, the Arsacids and the Sasanid emperors. It continues with a sketchy account of the Islamic caliphs up to Gardīzī's contemporary al-Qā'im (acceded in 422/1031) until the author gets to what obviously interested him most, the history of the Arab governors in the East from ʿAbdallāh b. ʿĀmir (governor of Basra and the East 29–44/649–64) onwards and the subsequent rulers there, still nominally agents of the caliphs but in practice increasingly independent. After dealing in some detail with the events surrounding the fall of Umayyad rule in Khurasan, the rise and career of Abū Muslim, and the establishment of the ʿAbbasid Revolution there, the story of the successive governors continues till the time of the civil war between Hārūn al-Rashīd's sons al-Amīn and al-Ma'mūn, with the latter's eventual victory organised from his base in Khurasan. Al-Ma'mūn's rule merges into sections on the Tahirid governors in Khurasan, the Saffarid brothers Yaʿqūb and ʿAmr b. Layth, the Samanid amirs of Transoxania and Khurasan, and the early Ghaznavids.

Gardīzī is thus essentially concerned with the Mashriq, the Greater Khurasan which, as Bert Fragner has stressed, emerged in the early Islamic period as a region in its own right, as against the Western Persia of the 'two Iraqs', sc. the old Media, Persis and Azerbaijan which formed ʿIrāq-i ʿAjam, 'Persian Iraq', and the Mesopotamian lands of the preceding Persian empires from the Achaemenids to the Sasanids forming ʿIrāq-i ʿArab.[4] This Greater Khurasan straddled the Oxus – now no longer seen as a separating and dividing boundary, and never in any case a serious obstacle for the movement of peoples and armies – and included not only eastern Persia and what is now modern Afghanistan, but also Transoxania, with its heartland of the former Sogdia, and regions connected with it culturally, ethnically and linguistically such as Khwarazm and the Syr Darya provinces like Chāch, Īlāq, Ushrūsana and Farghāna.

Gardīzī's account of the history of the Mashriq, and especially that of the Samanids up to *ca.* AD 950, is particularly valuable in that it apparently enshrines material from the lost *Ta'rīkh Wulāt Khurāsān* of Abū ʿAlī al-Ḥusayn al-Sallāmī, a protégé of the Muḥtājids of Chaghāniyān (*flor.* in the middle decades of the fourth/tenth century), judging by the material common both to Gardīzī and the chronicle of Ibn al-Athīr;[5] though both these historians' sources for the last decades of the fourth/tenth century and the demise of Samanid rule towards its end remain unclear.[6] It is also conceivable that Gardīzī took some information from another lost work, a *Kitāb Kharāj Khurāsān* by Ḥafṣ b. Manṣūr al-Marwazī, a secretary of Hārūn al-Rashīd's governor in Khurasan ʿAlī b. ʿĪsā b. Māhān (in post there 180–91/796–807), although nothing whatever is known about this treatise on the tax system of Khurasan apart from Gardīzī's mention of its name.[7]

In recounting the earliest history of Islam, Gardīzī deals with the four Patriarchal Caliphs only cursorily, and gives a neutral and dispassionate treatment of ʿUthmān and ʿAlī (without even a mention of the controversial topic of ʿUthmān's murder by the rebel Egyptian troops), accounts of these two reigns being normally a touchstone of an Islamic author's personal religious and sectarian attitudes. ʿUthmān is accorded the *tarḍiya*, 'May God be pleased with him', after his name, the normal convention for caliphs (it is, however, true that Gardīzī gives a conventional imprecation after the name of the Umayyad Yazīd b. Muʿāwiya, in whose reign the Third Imam of the Shīʿa, al-Ḥusayn b. ʿAlī b. Abī Ṭālib, was killed). Gardīzī is in general respectful towards the ʿAlids, but not particularly enthusiastic about them, and his retelling of episodes in which they figure, such as the numerous revolts of ʿAlid pretenders, is set forth in a non-partisan tone. The reigns of the four Patriarchal Caliphs are described as *khilāfat*s, but those of the Umayyads as *wilāyat*s only, and the term *khalīfat* reappears only with the first ʿAbbāsid al-Saffāḥ; whether Gardīzī is echoing here the attitudes and practices of a post-ʿAbbasid period writer like al-Sallāmī is unknown but seems possible. The story of the ʿAbbasid caliphs is continued, in very summary fashion for the period of less-and-less effective caliphs between al-Maʾmūn and al-Muʿtaḍid, up to Gardīzī's own time, hence ending with the reign of al-Qāʾim (succeeded in 422/1031).

Julie Meisami has noted that a general thread running through Gardīzī's History is the transfer of power in the Islamic East.[8] This starts with the overthrow of the Sasanids, whose emperors had in general been arrogant and tyrannical, by the Arabs. It proceeds through the replacement of the Umayyads, whose rule is implicitly characterised as a mere *mulk* and not a divinely buttressed *khilāfat*, by the ʿAbbasids, with detail on the role of the Umayyad governors in Khurasan, in particular with that of the last governor, Naṣr b. Sayyār, and the tribal conflicts and animosities which heralded the downfall of Umayyad rule there. Gardīzī's thus far matter-of-fact narrative takes on an accelerated, livelier tone when he deals, at considerable length, with the role of Abū Muslim al-Khurāsānī in the planning and eventual success of the ʿAbbasid *daʿwa* in Khurasan, and then with his fall and execution at the hands of the jealous and suspicious second ʿAbbasid caliph al-Manṣūr; the narrative here includes many references to prophetic and apocalyptic lore prefiguring these events. The next cataclysmic event in the history of the Islamic East, the transfer of the caliphate from the hedonistic, lightweight al-Amīn to his serious and virtuous brother al-Maʾmūn, is dealt with in less detail, though there is an account of the attack on Baghdad by al-Maʾmūn's general Ṭāhir b. al-Ḥusayn and the subsequent killing of al-Amīn which casts the latter, founder of the subsequent line of Tahirid governors in Khurasan, in a neutral light.

Meisami has further noted that Gardīzī seems to have a special interest in recounting the messianic and heterodox movements which occur so frequently in the course of Persian history, beginning with brief mentions of the movements of Mani and Mazdak in Sasanid times and going into some detail with certain of the early Islamic outbreaks, such as those arising in the wake of Abū Muslim's meteoric career and violent death: those in Khurasan and Transoxania of Bihāfarīd, Ustadsīs, al-Muqannaʿ and various anti-ʿAbbasid 'Wearers of White'. As with other historians showing a similar concern, Gardīzī's motive was doubtless to emphasise the good Islamic ruler's duty to God in upholding the true faith and in suppressing false prophets and religious dissidence; it may also be, as Meisami suggests, that Gardīzī was consciously providing a background for the depiction of Maḥmūd of Ghazna as the suppressor of heresy within his own empire and as the great ghāzī and hammer of infidels in the Indian subcontinent.[9]

Apart from the fairly brief, atypical interlude of Saffarid domination in the East, whose short-lived control of Khurasan was ended by the more virtuous Samanid Ismāʿīl b. Aḥmad, Gardīzī's narrative moves on from the Tahirids to the penultimate stage of power transfers there, the century or so of the Samanids in Transoxania and Khurasan, before the culmination of the History is reached in the Ghaznavids. Gardīzī has little on the general history of the Samanid dynasty that is not found in other sources like the local historian of Bukhara, Narshakhī, and the later Ibn al-Athīr, but he is, with al-ʿUtbī (see below), the main contemporary or near-contemporary source on the mounting chaos in Khurasan and the rivalries of the various contenders for power there, as the Samanid amirate disintegrated under both internal and external pressures, with the Ghaznavids emerging as a new *dawla* or change in the succession of dynasties and as bringers of a new order in the lands south of the Oxus.

Gardīzī has no information on the Turkish ghulām predecessors of Sebüktegin in Ghazna after the Samanid commander Alptegin's withdrawal from Bukhara to the far eastern periphery of the empire in 351/962, and his material on the career of Sebüktegin is fragmentary and is interwoven with the story of the last Samanid amirs. His connected, chronological account of the Ghaznavids really begins with Maḥmūd b. Sebüktegin's victory in 388/998 over his brother Ismāʿīl after a succession struggle and his investiture with the governorship of Khurasan by the caliph al-Qādir in 389/999, the beginning of the *de facto* independent Ghaznavid state. In the preface to his account of Maḥmūd's reign, Gardīzī sets out his qualifications for his task as historian, prominent amongst which is the fact that he had been a first-hand observer of many of the events concerned. He avers that the greater part of his chronicle here is based on what he saw with his own eyes, including the Amir's campaigns in India, in Sistan, in Khurasan and in Western Persia, but that he has nevertheless been selective in what he has set down, aiming at concision and hoping to avoid longwindedness.[10]

Given this last aim, it is not surprising that Gardīzī's account of the early Ghaznavids, running from the rise to power of Maḥmūd to the opening of his grandson Mawdūd's reign, hence spanning less than five decades, is mostly a bare chronicle of events, although he does expatiate on a lavishly staged event like the meeting of Maḥmūd with his ally, the Qarakhanid Great Khān Yūsuf Qadïr Khān, with such corroborative detail that one surmises that the author was either himself present or had first-hand information from someone who was there (see below, pp. 91–2). It may thus be said that, in general, Gardīzī's historical narrative lacks the enlivening comments on events and the analyses of human motivation regarding the sultans, their Turkish commanders and their Persian bureaucrats, that we find in the extremely detailed, gossipy, often day-to-day account of Sultan Masʿūd's reign found in Bayhaqī, but Gardīzī shares with Bayhaqī an aversion from fantastic and legendary adornments to his narrative. Virtually nothing of Gardīzī's own personality or attitude to events comes through, beyond such occasional conventionalities and hypocrisies, unavoidable for a servant of the regime, as eulogies of the sultans (he praises Maḥmūd's ascent to power as an effortless rise, achieved without any deceitfulness, trampling on people or bloodshed!), and his referring to Masʿūd (whose being killed through an army coup could be taken as one of the normal hazards of rulership in medieval Islam) as the 'Martyr Sultan'.

Nevertheless, his account of Ghaznavid history is in certain places quite detailed, as when he describes, at considerable length and with much circumstantial detail, Maḥmūd's crossing in 415/1024 of the Oxus north of Balkh by means of a bridge of boats chained together and the Sultan's subsequent meeting to the south of Samarqand in 416/1025 with Yūsuf Qadïr Khān b. Bughrā Khān Hārūn or Ḥasan, and the subsequent exchange of luxurious presents (see below, pp. 91–2); it is likely that Gardīzī accompanied the Ghaznavid army and was a first-hand witness to these events. The *Zayn al-akhbār* is liberally provided with dates, often with month and day specified, most of which appear in fact to be accurate. For the first two-thirds of Maḥmūd's reign it supplements, in a much more judicious, straightforward and readable manner, the ornate and often opaque Arabic account of al-ʿUtbī in his *al-Kitāb al-yamīnī*, which was probably completed in its present form, Peacock has suggested, at some point between 413/1022 and 416/1025, certainly before the fall from office of Maḥmūd's vizier Aḥmad b. Ḥasan Maymandī in 416/1025.[11] Gardīzī's account of Masʿūd's reign deals with the new sultan's administrative and military changes, the replacement of men of the former regime, the Maḥmūdiyān or Pidariyān, with 'new men', the Naw-khāstagān or upstarts, Masʿūd's own creatures; and also with his Indian campaigns and the suppression of Aḥmad [b.] Ināltegin's rebellion there. These merge into the crisis of the latter part of his reign, the story of the growing ascendancy of the Seljuqs in Khurasan and their ultimate victory at Dandānqān. Naturally, his account of these happenings cannot compare with Bayhaqī's enormously detailed treatment of the events, yet there is a special value in Gardīzī's story of the two brief reigns of Muḥammad b. Maḥmūd (421/1030 and 432/1041), for the extant books of Bayhaqī's *Mujalladāt* only deal with the first reign as the curtain-raiser for Masʿūd's reign, and break off before the killing of Masʿūd by his mutinous troops and their raising to power Muḥammad for his momentary, second reign.

It is regrettable that Gardīzī's extant narrative ends with Mawdūd's accession and triumphal avenging of his father in 432/1041, so that we do not possess accounts from him of the reign of Mawdūd and of those of his two ephemeral, shadowy successors Masʿūd (II) b. Mawdūd and ʿAlī b. Masʿūd (II), or of his own patron ʿAbd al-Rashīd, especially as these reigns are not well documented in the other historical sources.[12] The narrative of the manuscripts ends abruptly with Mawdūd's execution of those involved in his father's death; it is possible that Gardīzī carried it on for another ten years or so up to ʿAbd al-Rashīd's reign, or he may have been prevented from achieving this by the usurpation of the slave commander Ṭoghrïl and the violent end of his sovereign in 443/1051–52;[13] all this, however, is speculation.[14]

Gardīzī's Persian style is simple and straightforward, even dry, though not without difficulties in a few places, whose resolution is probably rendered more hazardous by the absence of any early manuscripts. The two surviving ones of the *Zayn al-akhbār*, both probably copied in India, are not very satisfactory. The date of the first and better one, that of King's College, Cambridge, is uncertain but is very probably sixteenth or seventeenth century. The Bodleian, Oxford, one bears the incontestable late date of 1196/1781. It is inferior to the Cambridge one in accuracy, and it seems that either the Oxford ms. was copied from the Cambridge one or else both were copied from a now-lost common source.[15] In effect, we are dependent on a unique manuscript, which itself has lacunae in various places, the most serious ones being the loss of the preface or exordium and the historical section's ending (see above). We have in any case a gap of some four centuries or more between the time when Gardīzī wrote and the oldest extant manuscript was made (a gap comparable to that existing for the more numerous manuscripts of Bayhaqī). The extreme paucity of extant manuscripts of Gardīzī's work must be a reflection of the fact that, produced as it was on the far eastern fringes of the Islamic world, it seems to have been little known to subsequent generations of historians and *udabā'* in the Persian and Indo-Muslim lands of later times, hence it was not until E.H. Palmer in 1868 published a catalogue of the oriental manuscripts of King's College, Cambridge, that either Western or modern Persian scholars began to be aware of its existence.[16]

By the sixteenth and seventeenth centuries, Persian or, more likely, Indo-Muslim copyists had lost familiarity with the Persian vocabulary and style of half-a-millennium before, and inevitably could only guess at the correct forms of many Turkish and Indian names.[17] Gardīzī's style was described by Malik al-Shuʿarā' Bahār as 'very mature and flowing' (*bisyār pukhta wa rawān*), and he attached it to an earlier period of New Persian style than that discernible in Bayhaqī, one more closely resembling that of the Samanid vizier and translator Balʿamī in the previous century.[18] Gilbert Lazard has noted that the conditions under which the text was transmitted are not favourable to the analysis of the *Zayn al-akhbār* for its linguistic content, but that the text nevertheless does not seem to have been subjected systematically to what its scribes thought was a modernisation (as is clearly the case with the manuscripts of Bayhaqī's History, also only known from late manuscripts). There remain archaic features of vocabulary and rare expressions. Forms like *hamī* as the verbal prefix for continual or habitual action; the preposition *andar* for *dar*, and the use of *mar . . . rā* before complements of verbs, with a resultant meaning often much wider than that of simple direct and indirect object, are frequently to be found.[19] Gardīzī's vocabulary is largely Persian, with few Arabic words, and those mainly of an Islamic religious and cultural nature; it is indeed more strongly Persian than the vocabulary of Bayhaqī. God is always *Khudā* or *Īzad* and never *Allāh*; Muḥammad is almost always the *Payghambar*, and only occasionally the *Rasūl [Allāh]*. In the stylistic field, one notes touches like the frequent use of more euphemistic terms for death, e.g. *farmān yāft* 'he received the Divine Summons' and *wafāt* 'fulfilment of one's life span' for rulers and other exalted figures, whereas more ordinary persons just 'die' (*murdan*).[20] Gardīzī's use of the conventional pious phrases after person's names (the *taṣliya*, *taslīm*, the *tarḥīm*, the *tarḍiya*, etc.) is restrained.[21] Interesting is his occasional use of phrases which show the beginnings of the penetration of basically Arabic expressions into the vocabulary of standard Persian, such as *sana-yi hādhihi* for 'this present year'.[22] A further notable feature of Gardīzī's sober style is the absence from his narrative of poetical citations, in contrast to the more expansive and literary style of his contemporary Bayhaqī; the extant portion of Bayhaqī's History has no fewer than 473 lines of Arabic and Persian verse.[23]

The present translation has been made essentially on the basis of Ḥabībī's text, the first edition of Gardīzī approaching completeness (but see below). The first scholar to publish any part of the *Zayn al-akhbār* was Wilhelm Barthold/V.V. Bartol'd in his *Otchet o poyezdkye v Srednyuyu Aziyu* (St. Petersburg, 1897), pp. 78–103,[24] and in the volume of texts to accompany his *chef d'œuvre, Turkestan v epokhu mongolskago nashestviya* (St. Petersburg, 1900), Vol. 1, pp. 1–18 (these last texts are not included in Sir E. Denison Ross's English translation in the Gibb Memorial Series, *Turkestan down to the Mongol Invasion* [London, 1928]). A substantial section of the historical part of the work, covering the rulers in Khurasan from the Tahirids to the Ghaznavids, was edited by Muhammad Nazim (E.G. Browne Memorial Series, 1, Berlin-Steglitz, 1928). Nazim's work had a certain virtue in that it emanated from an Indo-Muslim editor who was able to interpret and make sense of many place and personal names in the accounts of the Indian campaigns of Maḥmūd and Mas'ūd, and he used Gardīzī's information here for his book of three years later, *The Life and Times of Sulṭān Maḥmūd of Ghazna*. His version of the text was, however, far from adequate from the philological point of view, and was the target of savage criticism by the Persian scholar Mīrzā Muḥammad Qazwīnī, who characterised its editor as stupid (*aḥmaq*), unlettered (*bīsawād*) and ignorant (*nādānā*). Qazwīnī himself produced his own edition of this same section of Gardīzī at Tehran in 1315/1937, and in 1333/1954 Sa'īd Nafīsī published at Tehran his text of the historical section of Gardīzī from the Sasanids up to the beginning of the Samanids; these two publications marked a significant advance in achieving a reliable text for this section.

But a critical edition of the greater part of the work was only secured by the Afghan scholar, the late 'Abd al-Ḥayy Ḥabībī, who produced a text, in elegant *ta'līq* calligraphy, at Tehran in 1347/1968, with various appendices, including the texts of the prefaces by Qazwīnī and Nafīsī to their editions. For the historical section of the book, Ḥabībī built on Nafīsī's work and often cites it in his apparatus criticus; in a few places, Nafīsī's reading has nevertheless seemed to the present writer to be the better of the two.[25] As both K. Czeglédy and A.P. Martinez have observed in their valuable studies concerning Gardīzī's information on the Turks of Inner Asia, Ḥabībī's text is a most meritorious work based on a careful, critical examination of the two manuscripts, although the editor was often defeated by non-Arabic or non-Persian geographical, ethnic and tribal names through his failure to consult Barthold's printed texts (see above) and subsequent translations of these sections by scholars like Count Géza Kuun, Josef Marquart/Markwart and C.A. Macartney.[26] Ḥabībī did with profit consult Minorsky's *Ḥudūd al-'ālam* translation and commentary, and he added materials from this to his knowledge of the historical geography and topography of his native Afghanistan, and also used Minorsky's article, 'Gardīzī on India', in *BSOAS* XII (1947–9), pp. 625–40. However, he did not apparently have access to *Sharaf al-Zamān Ṭāhir Marvazī on China, the Turks and India* (London, 1942), in which Minorsky edited and translated the sections on these Inner Eurasian peoples and regions from the *Ṭabā'i' al-ḥayawān* of the Seljuq period, late fifth/eleventh and early sixth/twelfth century author Sharaf al-Zamān Ṭāhir; this writer made considerable use of Gardīzī in these sections but also derived material from other, unspecified sources. Nor did Ḥabībī consult the geographical section which survives of Ibn Rusta's *al-A'lāq al-nafīsa* (probably written between 290/903 and 300/913) and which contains important sections on the Byzantines, the Slavs, the Rus, the Magyars, the Turkish lands, India, etc. These caveats apart, Ḥabībī's work (reprinted at Tehran in 1363/1984 but now with the calligraphic section set up in type) was a solid, scholarly achievement, and over the last forty or so years it has formed a firm basis for utilisation of the *Zayn al-akhbār* by Islamic historians and by researchers on the ethnogenesis of the Turks and other steppe peoples, the religions of India, questions of festivals, dating and chronology, etc.

However, in 1384/2005, a fresh edition of the whole work by Raḥīm Riḍāzāda Malik appeared at Tehran under the auspices of the Anjuman-i Āthār wa Mafākhir-i Farhangī (pp. 72 + 636).[27] This has a substantial Introduction which *inter alia* surveys previous work on Gardīzī's text. The editor then provides for the first time a complete edited text (Ḥabībī had omitted opening sections on the creation of the world and on the prophets and also a brief amount of matter at its end, and had inserted his own arbitrary renumbering of the work's sections and subsections),[28] with an attempted restoration of contemporary orthography, e.g. with intervocalic and post-vocalic *dh* for *d*. There are detailed and useful indices, with biographical details for prominent personages, and some *ta'līqāt* on certain specific topics or citing parallel passages, such as the account from Muḥammad b. al-Munawwar's *Asrār al-tawḥīd fī maqāmāt al-Shaykh Abī Sa'īd* on the coming of the Seljuqs to Bāvard and Mayhana. However, there is virtually no apparatus criticus (the essential work here having been admittedly done by Ḥabībī and not requiring repetition), and this means that many small discrepancies of Riḍāzāda Malik's text with Ḥabībī's – involving changes of words, different interpretations of consonant ductus and even additional or missing words and phrases – are unsupported and their rationale unexplained. Occasionally, Riḍāzāda Malik's interpretation has been adopted in the present translation (this being stated in the notes), but on the whole, and certainly for this historical section of the *Zayn al-akhbār*, his text does not replace that of Ḥabībī.

A rough English ms. translation by Major H.G. Raverty (who must have been the first Western scholar ever to utilise Gardīzī's work) of nearly the whole work, as preserved in the Cambridge ms., is mentioned by Storey, by his time deposited in what was the India Office Library (now incorporated within the British Library, London). Raverty presumably made this in connection with his *magnum opus*, his translation of and very discursive and idiosyncratic commentary on the History by an author from the period of the first Slave Kings of Delhi, Minhāj al-Dīn Jūzjānī's *Ṭabaqāt-i nāṣirī*.[29] A Russian translation of the section of Gardīzī's work concerning the history of Khurasan, from the first governorship of 'Abdallāh b. 'Āmir b. Kurayz to the demise of Sultan Mas'ūd of Ghazna, was made by A.K. Arends (already known as the translator into Russian of Bayhaqī's History). Arends, however, died in 1976 with the bare translation that he had made, essentially from Sa'īd Nafīsī's edition (see above) still unpublished and with only an incomplete introduction. The Uzbek Academy of Sciences gained possession of Arends's manuscript and commissioned a former student of his, L.M. Epifanova, to put this into publishable form. She checked his translation against Ḥabībī's text, completed the introduction and added some notes, so that the complete work was at last published as *Zain al-akhbar. Ukrashenie izvestiy. Razdel ob istorii Khorasana* (Uzbekistan Academy of Sciences, Tashkent, 1991).[30] However, the rarity of copies of this book in Western libraries, published as it was in the Uzbek Republic in a limited number of copies, and the inaccessibility of works written in the Russian language to many scholars and researchers anyway, have seemed to the present writer ample justification for the present work, one which has been made independently of its Russian predecessor.

In the historical section of his work whose translation is the subject of the present book, Gardīzī and his copyists were dealing with a section of eastern Iranian history whose personal and place names were largely familiar to them, except when they came up against the Turkish names of various military slave commanders and against Indian geographical names and personal names and titles, prominent in the recounting of Ghaznavid raids into the subcontinent. Nazim's efforts towards the elucidation of these last has already been noted, but of more recent importance have been the work of Minorsky mentioned above and that of S.H. Hodivala, even though the latter does not deal specifically with the *Zayn al-akhbār* (as implied above, not known to the scholarly world when Elliot and Dowson put together in the mid-nineteenth century their collection of English translations bearing on the history of the subcontinent). The usefulness of the work of Nazim and Hodivala may be supplemented by the more recent study, specifically of Masʿūd's campaigns into India, by Nazir Ahmad.[31]

The notes which accompany the present translation are not intended to provide a thoroughgoing commentary on the text and its historical background; such a commentary on four centuries of Eastern Islamic history could well be of an enormous size. The notes here are meant merely to render the period and its events intelligible in a summary fashion; and in general, studies and translations are given rather than the primary sources, which may be traced from the historical works mentioned below. Ḥabībī's edition has a detailed apparatus criticus, and variants are only noted here when they affect the meaning of the passage in question and when they concern the correct forms of personal or place names, for which Ḥabībī did not always have the best information. The studies of various scholars on the history of Khurasan and the East during the four centuries or so covered by this section of Gardīzī (Wellhausen, Marquart, Barthold, Gibb, Nāẓim, Shaban, Sharon, Daniel, Kaabi, Bosworth, etc.) are well known, and these works are all thoroughly documented; moreover, a more recent generation of scholars like Patricia Crone, Matthew Gordon, Étienne de la Vaissière, Luke Treadwell and Deborah Tor is adding new insights into particular, under-researched aspects of the period. Reference will be made to such studies, but without repetition of the primary sources on which they are based. For the end of the Samanids and the early Ghaznavid period, a very detailed commentary on the greater part of the relevant events – since Bayhaqī has many anecdotal flashbacks to what happened before Masʿūd assumed the throne from his brother Muḥammad, with stories on aspects of Samanid history, on the seizure of power in Khurasan by Sebüktegin and Maḥmūd during the last years of Samanid rule, on Maḥmūd's annexation of Khwarazm, etc. – is given in the translation by the present author of the *The History of Beyhaqi (The History of Sultan Mas'ud of Ghazna, 1030–1041) by Abu 'l-Fazl Beyhaqi,* 3 vols. (New York, 2009), and reference may be made to this, to the commentary that forms vol. 3 and to the extensive bibliography given at vol. 3, pp. 399–420.

TRANSLATION OF THE TEXT

PART ONE: THE ARAB GOVERNORS

[M 156]
[Chapter Ten]Concerning the Table of the Governors of Khurasan

In regard to the governors of Khurasan, in ancient times a different arrangement prevailed. From the time of Afrīdūn to that of Ardashīr Bābakān, there used to be one single military commander (*sipāhsālār*) for the whole [Persian] world. When Ardashīr came to power, he appointed four military commanders for the [Persian] world: one for Khurasan; one for the western lands (i.e. Fars and Khuzistan); one for Nīmrūz (i.e. Sistan); and one for Azerbaijan. He appointed four wardens of the marches (*marzbāns*) for Khurasan: one for Marw Shāyigān; one for Balkh and Tukhāristān; one for Transoxania; and one for Herat, Pūshang and Bādghīs.[1] When the Muslims seized control of the Persian realm and Khurasan passed into the Muslims' hands, all those customs and practices of the Magians (*mughān*) were swept away.

During the time of our Prophet, may God pray over him and grant him peace, the Muslims had not extended their domination over Khurasan, nor likewise in the caliphate of Abū Bakr Ṣiddīq, may God Most High be pleased with him. When 'Umar, may God Most High be pleased with him, succeeded to the caliphate, he sent Khālid b. al-Walīd to the Persian lands to subdue them. When Khālid reached the plain of Qādisiyya, the Persian army advanced towards him on the orders of Yazdajird b. Shahriyār, and the commander of the army was Rustam b. Farrukh. A battle took place there, and the adherents of Islam were victorious. They defeated the Magians and made large numbers of them captive, selling them as slaves. Yazdajird fled and was killed at Marw Shāhigān. The Muslim forces entered Iraq (i.e. 'Irāq-i 'Ajamī, western Persia) and continued onwards in the same fashion, continually conquering cities, till they reached Khurasan.

During 'Umar's caliphate, no-one penetrated as far as Khurasan. When 'Uthmān, may God be pleased with him, succeeded to the caliphate, he sent 'Abdallāh b. 'Āmir b. Kurayz to Khurasan. 'Abdallāh b. 'Āmir sent 'Abdallāh b. Khāzim as commander of his advance guard. They (i.e. the Muslim troops) went by the Fars, [M 157] Kirman (text, Gurgān) and Ṭabasayn road.[2] They subdued the Ṭabasayn, and the people of the

Ṭabasayn became the first ones of Khurasan to become Muslims. After him, other governors kept coming and made various conquests, up to the present time.

I have set down here the names of each governor and the cities of each administrative region; the names of the caliphs during the time of their tenure of power; the duration of each governorship; and the date of the beginning of each governorship. I have put them into tabular form here so that the information may be more speedily found and more easily come to hand. The table is as follows:

[Here Gardīzī inserts his table, at H 93–8, M 157–9, with a total of seventy-six entries, from ʿAbdallāh b. ʿĀmir b. Kurayz to his patron the Ghaznavid Sultan ʿAbd al-Rashīd.]

[H 101, M 160]
Chapter Eleven Concerning the Historical Accounts of the Governors of Khurasan

I shall now relate the historical accounts concerning the governors of Khurasan in the same order as I set them down in the table. Success comes from God!

ʿAbdallāh b. ʿĀmir b. Kurayz

He was ʿAbdallāh b. ʿĀmir b. Kurayz b. Rabīʿa b. Ḥabīb b. ʿAbd Shams.[3] ʿUthmān b. ʿAffān, may God be pleased with him, had made Abū Mūsā al-Ashʿarī governor of Basra, but he now took the charge away from him and gave it to ʿAbdallāh b. ʿĀmir, entrusting to him the governorship of Khurasan also. ʿAbdallāh b. ʿĀmir sent forward ʿAbdallāh b. Khāzim al-Sulamī as commander of his advance force. He set out for the Ṭabasayn via the route through Fars and Kirman and subdued the Ṭabasayn, their people becoming Muslims.

Other authorities relate that ʿAbdallāh b. ʿĀmir travelled to Qūmis and then to Gūyān (i.e. Juwayn) and halted there. Then [from] there he came to Āzādwār and made a peace agreement (i.e. with its people). He seized the daughter of Milḥān Gūyānī and presented her to ʿAbdallāh b. Khāzim as a wife. ʿAbdallāh had three sons by her, Muḥammad, Mūsā and Ṣāliḥ. ʿAbdallāh b. ʿĀmir came to Nishapur, accompanied by Aḥnaf b. Qays, Muhallab b. Abī Ṣufra and a group of the leading men of Basra. He subdued Quhistān, Abarshahr (i.e. Nishapur), Ṭūs and Sarakhs from amongst the towns of Khurasan in the year 29 [/649–50]. He sent Ḥātim b. al-Nuʿmān al-Bāhilī with a force of 4,000 Arabs and 1,000 Persians to attack the Hephthalites (*Hayṭalān*),[4] and in the course of the fighting Aḥnaf was wounded in the head, and from that wound fluid ran down into his eyes. [H 102]

He built the fortress (*dizh*) of Aḥnaf (i.e. Qaṣr Aḥnaf) near Marw al-Rūd,[5] and took the town of Marw al-Rūd on the basis of a peace agreement. ʿAbdallāh [M 161] b. ʿĀmir likewise made a peace agreement with the *dihqān* of Herat on the basis of a tribute of fifty purses of dirhams. When it was the year 31 [/651–2], he went off on the Pilgrimage and appointed Qays b. al-Haytham al-Sulamī as his deputy over Khurasan, but when ʿAbdallāh came to [the caliph] ʿUthmān, the latter kept him there in his own entourage.

Umayr b. Aḥmar al-Yashkurī

ʿUthmān then sent out Umayr b. Aḥmar as governor of Khurasan. Umayr sent Maʿmūr b. Sufyān al-Yashkurī to perform the Muslim worship in the citadel of Merv. He remained governor of Khurasan for some time. He established a policy of commandeering people's houses for his troops and made it a customary practice. The reason for this was that Umayr b. Aḥmar had established himself at the gate of Merv in an encampment of tents. The weather became very cold, and the *dihqān*s of Merv feared that Umayr and his troops would perish from the cold. So they gave them accommodation in their own houses. But after several days had passed, they regretted what they had done and formulated the plan of seizing those troops and Umayr. The market traders and the urban rowdies (*ʿayyārān*) undertook this hostile action. The military leader and *dihqān* of the town, Barāz b. Māhūya, got wind of this planned attack and immediately informed Umayr b. Aḥmar about it.

The Amir gave orders, and all the troops girded on their weapons and set about with their swords, and they killed a large number of the men of Merv and plundered many houses, until all the people of the town gathered together and sent some persons to negotiate a settlement, offering a sum of money and seeking Umayr's pardon. He curbed the troops' violence and that strife subsided. After that, the practice was adopted for the troops to be billeted (i.e. in the houses of the people of Merv).[6] [H 103] Umayr b. Aḥmar gave compensation for what Barāz had done. Thereafter he used to behave very properly and respected people's rights.[7]

ʿAbdallāh b. ʿĀmir b. Kurayz

ʿUthmān then appointed ʿAbdallāh b. ʿĀmir governor for a second time. [M 162] ʿAbdallāh sent Rabīʿ b. Ziyād to subdue Sistan, and he brought back from there 40,000 slave captives. These slaves included Mihrān, the *mawlā* of ʿUbayd[allāh] b. Ziyād; Ṣāliḥ b. ʿAbd al-Raḥmān; Pīrūz, the *mawlā* of Ḥuṣayn b. Mālik al-ʿAnbarī; Bassām,[8] the *mawlā* of the Banū Layth, who has numerous children and progeny at Merv; Muʿādh b. Muslim, the forebear of the Muʿādhī governors of Khurasan; and ʿIkrima, the *mawlā* of ʿAbdallāh b. al-ʿAbbās.[9]

This man Pīrūz, the *mawlā* of Ḥuṣayn, was with ʿAbd al-Raḥmān Ibn al-Ashʿath; Yazīd b. al-Muhallab took him prisoner and sent him to Ḥajjāj b. Yūsuf. Ḥuṣayn b. [Mālik] ʿAnbarī and Pīrūz had been in charge of the district of Maysān and the Euphrates and the collection of taxes there. They had collected a large sum of money. Ḥajjāj sought it from Pīrūz, but he refused to hand it over. For this reason, Ḥajjāj put him to death. When the conquest of Sistan was accomplished, Rabīʿ b. Ziyād returned to Basra. During that time, persons knowledgeable about irrigation works (*āb shināsān*) said to him, 'If we dig out for you a branch channel from the river, will you free us and our children?' He agreed to this condition for their enfranchisement. They then got to work and constructed a channel for the water. They constructed water channels at Nibāj, at Juḥfa, at Bustān Banī ʿĀmir and at Nukhayla one stage from Mecca,[10] and at ʿArafāt. They also dug out the irrigation channels of the Banū ʿĀmir, and these constructions have remained and are extant today.

Jaʿda b. Hubayra al-Makhzūmī

When ʿAlī b. Abī Ṭālib, may God be pleased with him, succeeded to the caliphate, he gave the governorship of Khurasan to Jaʿda b. Hubayra, who was the son of ʿAlī's maternal uncle and whose wife was ʿAlī's daughter Umm al-Ḥasan. ʿAlī wrote a letter to Barāz b. Māhūya, the *dihqān* of Merv, with instructions that he should hand over the land-tax (*kharāj*) to Jaʿda.[11] Jaʿda arrived in Merv. Barāz wrote a letter to all the *dihqān*s of Merv (i.e. of the Merv oasis) enjoining them to give Jaʿda their obedience [H 104] in handing over the land-tax. Jaʿda made many [M 163] conquests in Khurasan, as did likewise his son ʿAbdallāh. He was present at the Battle of the Camel at Basra in the year 36 [/656] and at the encounters at Ṣiffīn between ʿAlī, God's peace be upon him, and Muʿāwiya in the year 37 [/657]

ʿAbd al-Raḥmān b. Abzā al-Khuzāʿī

Then ʿAlī entrusted the governorship of Khurasan to ʿAbd al-Raḥmān b. Abzā. ʿAbd al-Raḥmān was a man of wisdom and of pure religious faith, who used patience and forbearance with people and who established beneficent practices. He was still in post in Khurasan when ʿAlī passed away (*farmān yāft*, lit. 'received the divine summons') Ḥasan b. ʿAlī, may the Exalted God be pleased with them both, succeeded his father in the caliphate. Muʿāwiya employed various stratagems, with the involvement of ʿAmr b. al-ʿĀṣ as an intermediary, and sowed confusion amongst them[12] with the result that Ḥasan abdicated the caliphate. ʿAmr b. al-ʿĀṣ said to Muʿāwiya that he would employ a ruse so that Ḥasan would publicly announce his abdication and make a formal declaration (*khuṭba*); he would not be able to withstand Muʿāwiya and would not be able to overcome his wiles.

Ḥasan rose to his feet and pronounced a *khuṭba*, whose Persian translation is as follows:

> O people! The Almighty God has prohibited the shedding of your blood, and I have made a compact and covenant with Muʿāwiya on your behalf, that he will behave justly with you and that he will pay out to you the income due to you from the captured lands (*fay'*).[13] He will not busy himself with questions of status and will not exact vengeance or tyrannise over you.

He turned towards Muʿāwiya and said, 'O Muʿāwiya, is this the state of affairs agreed upon?' Muʿāwiya replied, 'Yes, it is.' Ḥasan then set about reciting this verse of the Qur'ān, 'I do not know; perhaps it is a test for you and a period of enjoyment of life for a time.'[14] When Ḥasan fell silent, Muʿāwiya reproached ʿAmr b. al-ʿĀṣ, 'Why did you give me such counsel as this?'

ʿAbdallāh b. ʿĀmir b. Kurayz

When Muʿāwiya successfully achieved his aim, he gave the governorship of Khurasan to ʿAbdallāh b. ʿĀmir. The latter made ʿAbdallāh b. Khāzim his deputy and sent him to Khurasan. [M 164] He remained there until ʿAbdallāh b. Samura al-Umawī came. He conquered the frontier regions (*thaghr*) of Kabul and Balkh, and then went back to Iraq. In the year 43 [/663–4] ʿAbdallāh b. ʿĀmir sent Mujāshiʿ b. Masʿūd to Sistan. Mujāshiʿ conquered Bust and Zamīndāwar and then set out back to Iraq. When he reached Kirman at a place [H 105] which they used to call K.r.kān and is now called Qaṣr Mujāshiʿ, an intense cold set in. It began to rain, and snow and icy winds became continuous. As a result, neither animals nor men were able to do anything. They were all affected by the cold[15] and buried under the snow. No-one was left alive, but all died beneath the snow.[16]

Ziyād b. Abīhi

Muʿāwiya then appointed Ziyād b. Abīhi governor of Khurasan, and the latter sent out Ḥakam b. ʿAmr al-Ghifārī to Khurasan [as his deputy there].[17] Ḥakam reached Herat, and from there marched out into the mountains of Khurasan. Muhallab b. Abī Ṣufra was with him as commander of the army's rearguard. Muhallab behaved in a praiseworthy fashion and achieved a reputation for chivalrous conduct, dashing behaviour in battle and vigilance. When reports about Muhallab reached Saʿd b. Waqqāṣ, the latter invoked divine favour on him and said, 'O Lord, be Muhallab's counsellor and protector, and never expose him to any ignominy!'[18]

Saʿd's prayers and invocations to God were wont to be answered, and he sent a sword for Muhallab; Muhallab's progeny and descendants always retained that sword because of its charisma. It is related that Sulaymān b. Muḥammad al-Hāshimī tried to buy that sword from Durayd b. al-Ṣimma b. Ḥabīb b. Muhallab for 100,000 dirhams, but Durayd refused to let him have it. Whatever Muhallab achieved, people would say that it came from the efficaciousness of Saʿd's invocations to God.

Ḥakam b. ʿAmr died in the city of Merv, and they buried him in a tomb there. He was the first amir of the Muslims [who] died in Khurasan, and was the first amir who drank water from the river of Balkh.[19] Ziyād b. Abīhi sent to Khurasan as his successor ʿAbdallāh al-Laythī, [H 106] who was one of the Companions (*yārān*) [M 165] of the Prophet. After him, Ziyād sent Rabīʿ b. al-Ḥārithī in the year 50 [/670]. Rabīʿ came to Khurasan at Merv, and routed the Hephthalites. He also died there. In the year 51 [/671] the people of Bādghīs and Ganj Rūstā(q) apostasised from Islam. Shaddād b. Khālid al-Asadī led an attack on them; he killed a group of them and carried off a considerable number of them as slave captives. However, Muʿāwiya ordered that these slave captives should be sent back because of the covenant (*ʿahd*) with them. This was the first group of slave captives given back in Khurasan.

ʿUbaydallāh b. Ziyād

Muʿāwiya appointed to Khurasan Ziyād's son ʿUbaydallāh.[20] ʿUbaydallāh came to Khurasan and crossed the river (i.e. the Oxus) with 16,000 cavalrymen. He was the first of the Muslims ever to have crossed the Oxus. He sent Muhallab b. Abī Ṣufra to Bukhara with 4,000 troops to sack the city (and they did so). The ancestress of the Bukhār Khudāt, Khātūn, was in control of Bukhara; her sons were still children. All the Iranians (*ʿajam*)[21] had come together round Khātūn. ʿUbaydallāh put the whole lot of them to flight and seized as plunder their wealth and possessions. He took

4,000 slave captives from Bukhara and returned to Basra.[22] He held the governorship of Iraq [and the East] for seven years until Ibrāhīm b. al-Ashtar killed him.

Saʿīd b. ʿUthmān b. ʿAffān

Muʿāwiya then appointed Saʿīd b. ʿUthmān governor of Khurasan in the year 55 [/675] and he put Aslam b. Zurʿa al-Kilābī in charge of the land-tax of Khurasan.[23] He went off with Saʿīd to a certain place. Aslam increased the yield of the land-tax of Merv by 100,000 dirhams, and it is paid over at this rate today.

Saʿīd b. ʿUthmān conquered Bukhara and the region of Sogdia around Samarqand. He was struck in the eye by an arrow at the gate of Samarqand and lost the sight of one eye. He had a tent for the army, and there was room for the whole of his army within [M 166] that tent enclosure. During Saʿīd's governorship, in accordance with Muʿāwiya's command, the Arabs at Merv laid out and constructed agricultural estates, crop-producing lands and residences, and settled down there, so that the Turks should not be able to cross the Oxus (i.e. into Khurasan).[24] [H 107]

ʿAbd al-Raḥmān b. Ziyād

Muʿāwiya then appointed ʿAbd al-Raḥmān b. Ziyād governor of Khurasan. ʿAbd al-Raḥmān collected in taxation from Khurasan eighty million dirhams. Ḥajjāj b. Yūsuf appropriated the whole of that from him and reduced ʿAbd al-Raḥmān to penury. Mālik b. Dīnār related that ʿAbd al-Raḥmān had gathered together 1,000 dirhams each day during the many years[25] of his life, apart from landed estates and fine possessions. Ḥajjāj reduced him to such straits that, one day, he was mounted on an ass, and Mālik asked him, 'What became of all that wealth of yours?' He replied, 'It vanished, and even this ass is actually borrowed.' At this point, Muʿāwiya died.

Salm b. Ziyād

When Yazīd, God's curse be upon him, succeeded to power, he sent Salm b. Ziyād to Khurasan as governor.[26] The Iranians had banded together in Transoxania under the leadership of Khātūn.[27] Salm came to Khurasan, rallied his forces and went to Transoxania. The Iranians advanced towards him with the intention of giving battle and they fought with great ferocity, but in the end Salm put the Iranians to flight. In this battle no-one achieved such glorious deeds as Muhallab b. Abī Ṣufra; he fought with great élan and wrought many praiseworthy feats of arms on that field of battle. When Salm had finished with the affairs of Transoxania, he entrusted the governorship of Sistan to Ṭalḥat al-Ṭalaḥāt, whose proper name was Ṭalḥa b. ʿAbdallāh al-Khuzāʿī.[28]

Eventually, Salm became angry with Ṭalḥa. When Ṭalḥa learnt about this, he fled, together with the Ispahbad of Sistan, and they went to the court of Yazīd b. Muʿāwiya, remaining there until Yazīd's death. On Yazīd's death, they returned to Sistan and [M 167] established themselves firmly there. Ṭalḥa remained in Sistan till the time of the internecine strife (*fitna*) involving ʿAbdallāh b. al-Zubayr.[29] Salm b. Ziyād entrusted Khurasan to ʿArfaja b. ʿĀmir al-Saʿdī and himself went off to Mecca. [H 108]

ʿAbdallāh b. Khāzim

When Salm set out for Mecca, ʿAbdallāh b. Khāzim went with him. En route, the latter performed deeds of service for Salm. ʿAbdallāh became emboldened to ask Salm for a grant of the goverorship of Khurasan. Salm conferred the governorship of Khurasan on him.[30] ʿAbdallāh came to Merv, engaged ʿArfaja in battle, killed him and seized control of Khurasan. He wrote letters to ʿAbdallāh b. Zubayr offering his allegiance and summoned the troops obediently to follow him in giving this allegiance. Conflicts broke out between ʿAbdallāh b. Khāzim and the tribesmen of Muḍar at Merv. The conflicts became prolonged, and revolts broke out in the towns of Merv, Marw al-Rūd, Ṭālaqān and Herat. A group of tribesmen from Tamīm killed ʿAbdallāh b. Khāzim's son Muḥammad, who was the amir in Herat. As an act of vengeance for his son's death, ʿAbdallāh slew a group of Tamīmīs.

ʿAbdallāh b. al-Zubayr's cause flourished, and ʿAbdallāh b. Khāzim[31] remained in Khurasan for eight years, five months and twenty-five days until the time of the internecine strife between Muṣʿab b. al-Zubayr and ʿAbd al-Malik b. Marwān. Muṣʿab was killed, and ʿAbd al-Malik summoned ʿAbdallāh b. Khāzim to his obedience, but ʿAbdallāh refused to give it. Muṣʿab's head was sent to Ibn Khāzim. The Khurasanians rose in rebellion against him.[32] Both of them converged on Ṭūs, and there was a battle between the two sides. Wakīʿ b. al-Dawraqiyya and Bukayr b. Wishāḥ went off with a body of troops. When Ibn Khāzim[33] had killed Wakīʿ's brother, Wakīʿ and ʿAbdallāh came into confrontation with each other and clashed in battle. Wakīʿ felled ʿAbdallāh to the ground, sat down on his chest and cut off his head. He brought it to Baḥīr, and Baḥīr heaped praises on him. He sent ʿAbdallāh's head to Khālid b. ʿAbdallāh al-Qasrī, who forwarded it to ʿAbd al-Malik b. Marwān.[34] [M 168]

Baḥīr b. Warqā'

ʿAbd al-Malik b. Marwān then appointed Baḥīr b. Warqā'[35] as governor of Khurasan in the year 71 [/690–1]. When he was settled into his post, ʿAbd al-Malik ordered that Baḥīr should cancel all appointments to offices, issues of stipends for the troops, additional payments and grants of land for the upkeep of state servants (*waẓā'if wa ʿaṭā'-hā wa ziyādat-hā wa iqṭāʿ-hā*) that had been made in the time of ʿAbdallāh b. al-Zubayr. He (sc. ʿAbd al-Malik) treated the people of Khurasan in a benevolent manner. Baḥīr was a feeble and ineffective figure and entirely under the thumb of the troops. [H 109] As a result of this, Khurasan was in a permanently disturbed state. Baḥīr then sent a letter to ʿAbd al-Malik to the effect that Khurasan could not be held except by a man of Quraysh.[36] So ʿAbd al-Malik deprived Baḥīr of his office and appointed Umayya in his stead.

Umayya b. ʿAbdallāh

This was Umayya b. ʿAbdallāh b. Abi 'l-ʿĀṣ [Umayya b.] ʿAbd Shams.[37] ʿAbd al-Malik entrusted Khurasan to Umayya in the year 72 [/691–2]. Umayya arrived in Khurasan, but Baḥīr rebelled and shut himself up in the citadel of Merv. He held out for some time in the citadel, but in the end Umayya got him out and killed him. Baḥīr had two brothers, one called Budayl and the other Shamardal, and Umayya killed them both with Baḥīr. Umayya b. ʿAbdallāh remained governor in Khurasan for seven years. Umayya's position as governor was a perpetual source of irritation to Ḥajjāj b. Yūsuf, and he employed various stratagems till ʿAbd al-Malik dismissed Umayya and gave Khurasan and Sistan to Ḥajjāj b. Yūsuf.

Ḥajjāj b. Yūsuf

ʿAbd al-Malik gave Khurasan to Ḥajjāj b. Yūsuf.[38] Ḥajjāj sent Muhallab b. Abī Ṣufra to Khurasan in the year 79 [/698–9]. Muhallab proceeded to the town of Kish and made a peace agreement with the people of Sogdia. The king of Sogdia at that time was the Ṭarkhūn, and Muhallab took hostages from him. Muhallab died in the vicinity of Marw al-Rūd at a village called Zāghūl, having made his son Yazīd his successor. His son was four years in Khurasan [M 169] as deputy for Ḥajjāj, and then after him Ḥajjāj appointed to Khurasan Yazīd's brother Mufaḍḍal b. Muhallab. Mufaḍḍal was a well-known figure, possessing gravitas, and was a shrewd judge of people.[39] [H 110]

Ḥajjāj had entrusted Sistan to ʿAbd al-Raḥmān b. Muḥammad [b.] al-Ashʿath. When the latter came to Sistan, he rebelled against Ḥajjāj and marched out against him. Eighty engagements took place between the two of them. ʿAbd al-Raḥmān was defeated at Dayr al-Jamājim, and he fled from there to Kabul, seeking refuge with Ratbīl, the ruler there.[40] Ḥajjāj sent an envoy to Ratbīl, seeking ʿAbd al-Raḥmān's extradition. Ratbīl handed him over to the envoy, who put him in bonds. He put one leg iron on ʿAbd al-Raḥmān's ankle, linked to an iron placed on another man's leg. Whilst on the journey back, they halted at a rest house and went up on the roof. ʿAbd al-Raḥmān hurled himself down from that roof, together with the man fettered to him, and both died.[41]

When Walīd b. ʿAbd al-Malik succeeded to power, Ḥajjāj dismissed Mufaḍḍal b. Muhallab from Khurasan, and subjected the sons of Muhallab to violent financial mulcting. He divorced Muhallab's daughter Hind, who was his wife, and sent 100,000 dirhams to her as her returned marriage portion. Hind, however, sent the money back and refused to accept it. Ḥajjāj kept Muhallab's sons imprisoned at Basra for three years until Yazīd b. Abī Muslim interceded for them and they gave sureties for six million dirhams. They were released into the custody of a keeper (*muwakkil*), but all four of them devised stratagems: swift-running camels[42] were got ready, and they escaped on them. They made their way to Syria, and sent Rajāʾ b. Ḥaywa al-Kindī, having sought his help regarding their predicament, to relate their story to Sulaymān b. ʿAbd al-Malik, and Sulaymān agreed to help.

Sulaymān b. ʿAbd al-Malik and ʿAbd al-ʿAzīz b. Walīd took charge of the matter, and interceded forcefully with Walīd b. ʿAbd al-Malik, and the latter responded to their pleas. He instructed Sulaymān to send Muhallab's sons to him. [M 170] Sulaymān sent his son Ayyūb together with Yazīd b. Walīd, and told Ayyūb, 'Don't leave Yazīd b. al-Muhallab for one moment! If he (sc. Walīd b. ʿAbd al-Malik) intends to do any harm to him, they'll have to kill you first!'

Yazīd b. al-Muhallab then came before Walīd. Walīd accepted Sulaymān's intercession and sent Yazīd back to Sulaymān, but laid down that he was to be mulcted of three million dirhams, giving Ḥajjāj the order, 'Give a grant of protection to all of those of the sons of Muhallab and their kindred who have been left with you and despatch them to Syria.' They all came to Damascus and Sulaymān's entourage, remaining there for six years till the end of Walīd b. ʿAbd al-Malik's reign. He ordered Qutayba b. Muslim, who was governor of Ray, to go to Khurasan (i.e. as governor). [H 111]

[Qutayba b. Muslim]

Qutayba came to Khurasan in the year 87 [/706] by the Qūmish road; previously, people used to travel to there by the road through Fars and Kirman.[43] When Qutayba reached Qūmish, he looked for his investiture document (*ʿahd*) but could not find it, since it had been forgotten and left behind at Ray. He sent someone to Ray, and it was brought back from there. Yazīd [b.] al-Muhallab had a very pleasant garden in Khurasan. Qutayba destroyed it and built a camel stable on the site. A *marzbān* asked him, 'Why did you do a thing like this?' Qutayba replied, 'My father was a camel-driver and Yazīd's father a gardener!'

In the year 87 he got ready his army. During his time, the greater part of the towns of the Bukhara region were conquered, together with Kish, Nakhshab and Samarqand. It is said that Khwarazm, Kabul and Nasā were also subdued during his time as governor. After that time, in the year 95 [/713–14], he conquered Farghāna. In that same year, Ḥajjāj died. In his treasury were found 219 million dirhams. Ḥajjāj's governorship (i.e. of Iraq and the East) lasted twenty years. [M 171]

When Qutayba heard the news of Ḥajjāj's death, he became apprehensive and returned to Marw. Walīd b. ʿAbd al-Malik sent letters of encouragement to Qutayba and gave him promises of favour. So Qutayba returned to Farghāna and was involved in much fighting. He took large numbers of slave captives, and then made a peace agreement with the local people, taking hostages for good behaviour, and then returned to Merv. When he reached Kushmayhan,[44] he heard the news of Walīd's death and the succession of Sulaymān b, ʿAbd al-Malik. Qutayba was fearful regarding Sulaymān, who sent to him a missive containing menaces and admonitions.

Sulaymān had appointed Yazīd b. al-Muhallab as governor of Khurasan. When Qutayba's response reached him, he suspended his intended action and wrote a fresh investiture document for him in Arabic,[45] forwarding it to him by hand of an envoy. Qutayba's mind nevertheless remained troubled, and he was all the time fearful that Sulaymān was going to dismiss him. There was bad blood between Sulaymān and Qutayba, since Qutayba was a proponent of recognition of ʿAbd al-ʿAzīz b. al-Walīd as designated successor in the caliphate and had been involved in the attempt to get the succession arrangements changed. For this reason, Qutayba was fearful of Sulaymān.

Qutayba, together with the greater part of his leading commanders (*sarhangān*) and his retainers, now rose in revolt aganst Sulaymān. Before he broke out in rebellion, Qutayba had dismissed Wakīʿ b. Abī Sūd al-Ghudānī from headship of the Tamīmīs but had given him no other official position in place of the headship, and he had given this last office to Ḍirār b. Ḥuṣayn al-Ḍabbī. For that reason, Wakīʿ had sought his revenge on Qutayba and he was inciting the army [against him]. Wakīʿ had given out that he was ill and had remained in his house for some time. When he emerged from it, he joined up with those dissidents of the army. They seized an opportunity in Farghāna to kill Qutayba. They killed eleven of the progeny of Muslim, including seven of his sons, comprising Qutayba, ʿAbd al-Raḥmān, ʿAbdallāh, ʿUbaydallāh, Ṣāliḥ, Yasār and Muḥammad, and four of Muslim's grandsons. Out of Muslim's sons, there only remained alive ʿAmr, who was away in Gūzgānān. Wakīʿ ordered that the heads of all of them should be cut off, and he sent them on to Sulaymān b. ʿAbd al-Malik.[46] [H 112, M 172]

Wakīʿ b. Abī Sūd al-Ghudānī

Sulaymān then sent an investiture document for the governorship of Khurasan to Wakīʿ b. Abī Sūd al-Ghudānī.[47] Wakīʿ embarked on a policy of instilling fear and terror. Anyone who went beyond the limits laid down by Wakīʿ or who showed the slightest trace of treacherous behaviour, he would immediately be put to death. His policy went to such lengths that, one day, someone drunk was brought before him and he ordered his head to be cut off. People protested to him that death was not the obligatory penalty for someone drunk, but rather that the *ḥadd* penalty[48] was a flogging. Wakīʿ replied, 'My punishment isn't the whip or rod, but the sword alone!' When people heard that, they all felt terrified of him; moreover, no-one dared commit any offence since correction, punishment and death would ineluctably follow. Things continued like this till the end of his period of governorship. His governorship began in the year 97 [/715–16].

Yazīd b. al-Muhallab

Sulaymān b. ʿAbd al-Malik then entrusted Khurasan to Yazīd b. Muhallab for a second term of office.[49] Yazīd sent his son Mukhallad to Khurasan to act as his deputy, and Yazīd himself followed after him to Khurasan, this in the year 97. He arrested Wakīʿ b. Abī Sūd and inflicted much torture on Qutayba b. Muslim's officials and seized their possessions, thereby amassing a great amount of wealth. He set off from Merv to Gurgān in the year 98 [/716–17], travelling along the Nasā road and passing through the region of the Iron Gate.[50] He subdued Gurgān, but when he left, the people of Gurgān apostasised for a second time.

Yazīd b. al-Muhallab accordingly once more prepared a military expedition and proceeded to Gurgān. The Gurgānīs fled for refuge to the mountains, and Yazīd pursued them into the mountains and killed 12,000 of them. He took an oath that he would not leave that place until he had made a watermill go round with the Gurgānīs' blood and had ground flour in that mill, had baked bread from the flour and had eaten his morning meal from it.

When the men were being killed, their blood kept on congealing and would not flow. Yazīd was told, 'Give orders [M 173] for a flow of water to be brought to the mill.' The mill went round and flour was milled. Bread was baked from that flour and he was able to eat it. He was thus able properly to fulfil his oath. He took captive 6,000 Gurgānīs and the whole lot were sold into slavery. He sent a proclamation of victory (*fatḥ-nāma*) regarding the conquest of Gurgān to Sulaymān b. ʿAbd al-Malik, in which he said,

> No-one has conquered this province since the time of Shāpūr Dhu 'l-Aktāf. Kisrā [Aparwīz] the son of Hurmuz, ʿUmar b. al-Khaṭṭāb and everyone else have tried to conquer it, but for all of them it proved impossible and no-one could subdue this province. Now it has been conquered for the Commander of the Faithful.

The prince of Gurgān was Ṣūl,[51] and Yazīd took him prisoner; at this present time there are numerous descendants of this Ṣūl in Gurgān. Ṣūl then said to Yazīd b. al-Muhallab, 'Is there any person within Islam nobler than you, for me to become a Muslim at his hand?' Yazīd answered, 'The Commander of the Faithful is nobler than I!' Ṣūl said, 'Send me to him!' Yazīd sent him to Sulaymān. Ṣūl said to Sulaymān, 'Is there no-one within Islam greater than you?' Sulaymān replied, 'At the present time, there is no-one within Islam more noble than myself, except at the tomb of the Prophet, peace be upon him!' Ṣūl said, 'Send me to that place so that I may become a Muslim [there]!'[52]

Sulaymān sent him to Medina, and he became a Muslim at the Prophet's tomb. He returned, and came into Yazīd's entourage [H 113] and remained with him permanently, fulfilling many offices and duties until he was killed in the time of Maslama b. ʿAbd al-Malik. Muḥammad b. Ṣūl became one of the leading propagandists (*dāʿiyān*) for the house of ʿAbbās, and was killed in Syria by ʿAbdallāh b. ʿAlī.

Yazīd b. al-Muhallab made his son Mukhallad his deputy over Khurasan, and he himself turned back and headed for Sulaymān. When he reached Fars, he heard the news of Sulaymān's death. During the reign of ʿUmar b. ʿAbd al-ʿAzīz he formed the intention of going to Basra. When he reached there, the local governor, ʿAdī b. Arṭāt al-Fazārī, came to him with a letter from ʿUmar b. ʿAbd al-ʿAzīz ordering him to relinquish his office forthwith. Yazīd b. al-Muhallab was despatched to ʿUmar, and when he reached ʿUmar, [M 174] the latter consigned him to prison. Whenever anyone tried to make intercession with ʿUmar on Yazīd's behalf, his reply was, 'Yazīd has done much killing; there's no better place for him than prison!' He then ordered that Yazīd should be subjected to violence and torture in order to extract from him the wealth and possessions listed in the letter written to Sulaymān, and all the possessions and wealth confiscated from him were included in a reckoning raised up against him.

Jarrāḥ b. ʿAbdallāh al-Ḥakamī

ʿUmar b. ʿAbd al-ʿAzīz appointed Jarrāḥ b. ʿAbdallāh al-Ḥakamī to Khurasan.[53] He went to Khurasan with instructions from ʿUmar that Mukhallad b. Yazīd was to be sent back to him. When Jarrāḥ reached Khurasan in the year 99 [/717–18], he immediately arrested and imprisoned Mukhallad. He put him in chains and sent him to ʿUmar. On the road to Kufa, Mukhallad dispensed 800,000 dirhams in charity, and all the people expressed good wishes and spoke favourable words regarding him. During this time when Jarrāḥ was governor in Khurasan, Muḥammad b. ʿAlī al-Imām[54] sent Maysara to Iraq and Khurasan. He sent out other propagandists, and they secured pledges of allegiance (i.e to the ʿAbbasid cause) from large numbers of people and then came back.

ʿAbd al-Raḥmān [b.] Nuʿaym al-Ghāmidī

Then ʿUmar b. ʿAbd al-ʿAzīz appointed ʿAbd al-Raḥmān b. Nuʿaym to Khurasan in the year 100 [/718–19], and ʿAbd al-Raḥmān came to Khurasan in this same year. When Mukhallad b. Yazīd b. al-Muhallab came before ʿUmar b. ʿAbd al-ʿAzīz, the latter regarded Mukhallad with favour and spoke kindly words about him. He gave out that Mukhallad was a better man than his father and ordered that he should not be harmed or harassed. [H 114]

Saʿīd b. ʿAbd al-ʿAzīz

Yazīd b. ʿAbd al-Malik conferred the governorship of Khurasan on Saʿīd b. ʿAbd al-ʿAzīz.[55] Saʿīd acted in a beneficent fashion and did not give rein to excesses and tyranny. When [M 175] he arrived in Khurasan, he behaved towards the people with kindness[56] and did not demand additional taxation from anyone. He remained in office in Khurasan for a year, but was then after one year recalled and ʿUmar b. Hubayra was sent out.

ʿUmar b. Hubayra

Yazīd b. ʿAbd al-Malik then gave the governorship of Khurasan [and the East] to ʿUmar b. Hubayra.[57] ʿUmar dismissed Saʿīd b. ʿAbd al-ʿAzīz from Khurasan, sending out Saʿīd b. ʿAmr al-Ḥarashī as his replacement, and Saʿīd arrived in Khurasan in the year 104 [/722–3]. He did not remain long in office before ʿUmar b. Hubayra deprived him of it and sent out in his stead Muslim b. Saʿīd b. Aslam. Muslim remained in office during the year [10]4, the whole of the year [10]5 and several months of the year 106 [/722–4].

Khālid b. ʿAbdallāh al-Qasrī

When Hishām b. ʿAbd al-Malik was firmly ensconced in power within the realm, he appointed Khālid b. ʿAbdallāh as governor of Khurasan and sent him thither, also awarding him the governorship of Iraq. Khālid stayed in Iraq and sent his brother Asad b. ʿAbdallāh to Khurasan [as his deputy].[58] Asad remained there for three years. He stirred up factional strife (*taʿaṣṣub-hā*) amongst the people. He arrested Naṣr b. Sayyār, and also ʿAbd al-Raḥmān b. Nuʿaym, who was in charge of collecting the land-tax; Baḥr b. Dirham, who was in charge of pay arrangements for the army; and Sūra b. al-Ḥurr al-Dārimī. He made accusations against them that they had been spreading disturbing, alarmist stories.[59] Using this as a pretext, he had them flogged, their heads shaved and their beards plucked out, and he put fetters on their hands. He then despatched the lot of them to his brother (sc. to Khālid). These persons informed Hishām about all that they had suffered. Hishām wrote a letter to Khālid ordering him to release them, and they all came back to reside in Iraq and Syria. No person went out to Khurasan [as governor] whilst Khālid was alive. [H 115, M 176]

Ashras b. ʿAbdallāh

Hishām appointed Ashras b. ʿAbdallāh to Khurasan. Because of his excellent qualities, Ashras used to be called 'The Perfect One' (*al-Kāmil*).[60] He arrived in Khurasan in the year 110 [/728–9], but now altered his behaviour and committed many inadmissible acts. He perpetrated numerous acts of oppression and unjust behaviour against the subjects. The people of Khurasan were driven to rebellion, and they went to Hishām complaining of tyranny and injustice; he accordingly dismissed Ashras.

Junayd b. ʿAbd al-Raḥmān

Hishām then appointed Junayd b. ʿAbd al-Raḥmān as governor of Khurasan, and the latter came to Khurasan in the year 112 [730–1]. When he reached there, the Khāqān of the Turks led an invasion.[61] Junayd engaged him in battle and put him to flight, and he killed a great number of his troops. The next year, the Khāqān came back to the attack. Junayd marched out to engage him. He wrote to Sūra b. al-Ḥurr al-Dārimī, who was the amir of Samarqand, seeking his help, and Sūra marched forth and engaged the Turks in battle. The Turks were defeated, but Sūra was himself killed in the fight. Junayd arrived, and he at once routed the Turks, and the Khāqān fled. When Junayd returned from that campaign, he seized [Ḥārith b.] Surayj the rebel,[62] who had led an uprising in Khurasan, together with a large number of his partisans, and put the whole lot of these followers to death. In the year 116 [/734] he died.

ʿĀṣim b. ʿAbdallāh al-Hilālī

Hishām then appointed ʿĀṣim to Khurasan in the year 116.[63] When ʿĀṣim reached Khurasan, affairs of state had not returned to the required state of good order, since Ḥārith b. Surayj rebelled and seized control of Gūzgānān, Ṭālaqān, Fāryāb and Marw al-Rūd. He led his movement on the basis of the Qur'ān and the traditions of the Prophet and [M 177] displayed opposition to the Marwānids. He gave out that the 'Protected Peoples' should observe the conditions of their Dhimmī status, that he would not take land-tax from the Muslims and that he would not act unjustly towards anyone. A great number of people flocked to join him. He set out for Merv with the intention of attacking ʿĀṣim. A battle between Ḥārith and ʿĀṣim took place at Merv. Intermediaries came forward and arranged a peace agreement between the two sides on the basis that an envoy should be sent to Hishām and that he should be informed about this state of affairs. If he should give a favourable response to Ḥārith's propositions, well and good; but if not, then they would continue fighting. Both sides agreed upon this course of action. [H 116]

Khālid b. ʿAbdallāh al-Qasrī

Information about Ḥārith's activities reached Hishām. He entrusted the governorship of Khurasan to Khālid b. ʿAbdallāh al-Qasrī, and the latter sent his brother Asad b. ʿAbdallāh (sc. as his deputy in Khurasan) in the year 116.[64] The envoys of Ḥārith and ʿĀṣim came into Asad's presence. He sent them back and himself came to Merv with a force of 20,000 men and mounted an attack on Ḥārith. The two sides confronted each other at the gates of Tirmidh. Battle was joined, and in the end, Ḥārith was defeated and fled into Turkestan. Asad seized a group of persons who were summoning people to the cause of the house of ʿAbbās and killed them. When he sought further directions from his brother Khālid, Khālid wrote back, 'Don't shed blood!'

Asad remained in Khurasan for four years. He died in the year 120 [/738], having appointed Jaʿfar [b.] Ḥanẓala as his deputy, and Jaʿfar remained in Khurasan for five months. Asad b. ʿAbdallāh founded the settlement of Asadābād in the rural district of Nishapur,[65] and his descendants retained possession of it till the time of ʿAbdallāh b. Ṭāhir. Then ʿAbdallāh b. Ṭāhir purchased it and made it into a perpetual endowment (*waqf*) for travellers and wayfarers (*abnāʾ al-sabīl*).[66]

Naṣr b. Sayyār

Hishām appointed Naṣr b. Sayyār governor of Khurasan in the month of Rajab in the year 120 [/June–July 738] and sent him an investiture charter for it, which reached him at Balkh.[67] Naṣr spoke with ʿAbd al-Salām b. Muzāḥim, and the two of them went to Jaʿfar and delivered to him the letter requiring Jaʿfar to hand over his office. [M 178] Jaʿfar set up Naṣr in his own former place and personally hailed and congratulated him, and the people likewise came to congratulate him. Naṣr treated the people of Khurasan with kindness and consideration and lightened the burden of taxation on them. [68]

Naṣr arrested and imprisoned Yaḥyā b. Zayd b. ʿAlī b. al-Ḥusayn b. ʿAlī b. Abī Ṭālib, may God be pleased with them all, who had gone into hiding at Balkh after Hishām had killed his father.[69] Hishām died at this juncture, as did also Muḥammad b. ʿAlī al-Imām at this time. In accordance with his command, the leading men of the Shīʿa appointed twelve agents (*naqībs*).[70] The first was Sulaymān b. Kathīr; the second, Qaḥṭaba b. Shabīb; the third, Mūsā b. Kaʿb; the fourth, Mālik b. al-Haytham; the fifth, Abū Dāwūd [Khālid b. Ibrāhīm]; the sixth, Khālid b. Ibrāhīm;[71] [H 117] the seventh, Bakr b. al-ʿAbbās; the eighth, Lāḥiz b. Qurayẓ; the ninth, Shibl b. Ṭahmān; the tenth, Abu 'l-Najm b. ʿImrān b. Ismāʿīl; the eleventh, ʿAlāʾ b. Ḥurayth; and the twelfth, ʿAmr and ʿĪsā the two sons of Aʿyan.

ʿAlāʾ went to Khwarazm to spread propaganda (i.e. in the ʿAbbasid cause) and Ṭalḥa b. Ruzayq[72] took ʿAlāʾ's place. When Hishām died, Walīd b. Yazīd succeeded to power. He sent an investiture charter for Khurasan to Naṣr b. Sayyār and commanded him to capture Yaḥyā b. Zayd. When Yaḥyā came to a rural district of the administrative region of Nishapur, he threw off allegiance to Walīd and summoned people to his own cause. He went back with 120 men and encamped at a village by the gate of Nishapur. ʿAmr b. Zurāra al-Qasrī, the amir of Nishapur, sent an envoy to Yaḥyā with the message, 'Get out of this district!' Yaḥyā replied, '[I'll stay here] until I have rested and the beasts have rested!'

When he drew near to ʿAmr, the latter immediately mounted and rode forth. They clashed in battle, ʿAmr was defeated and in the course of his flight was killed. Yaḥyā b. Zayd headed for Balkh. When Naṣr got news of these events, he sent his police commander (*ṣāḥib-shurat*) Salm b. Aḥwaz in pursuit of Yaḥyā. Yaḥyā went to Bādghīs and from there to Marw al-Rūd, Ṭālaqān and Fāryāb. Salm [M 179] pursued him continuously until he came upon him at Arghūy[73] in Gūzgānān. A battle was fought and Yaḥyā b. Zayd was killed. His head was cut off, mounted on a pole and borne to Merv.

Walīd was killed in Syria in Jumādā II of the year 126 [/March–April 744], and Yazīd b. al-Walīd was set up as ruler in this same year 126. When Yazīd was secure in his power, he sent an investiture charter for Khurasan to Naṣr b. Sayyār and sent him a letter instructing him to offer a grant of protection to Ḥārith b. Surayj. Ḥārith came back to Merv, but [at that point] Yazīd died and Ibrāhīm b. al-Walīd succeeded to power on 1 Dhu 'l-Ḥijja of the year 126 [/14 September 744]. His authority was not, however, firmly established, since Marwān b. Muḥammad came along and deprived him of power. Marwān himself assumed the throne in Ṣafar of the year 127 [/November–December 744] and deposed Ibrāhīm. Marwān used to be called 'Marwān al-Ḥimār' because, in Arabic, when each hundred years of the life of a dynasty elapsed, that year used to be called Ḥimār (lit. 'wild ass'), and the dynasty of the Banū Umayya had lasted for almost a hundred years.[74]

Marwān Ḥimār [H 118] sent an investiture charter for Khurasan to Naṣr b. Sayyār. The Yamanīs and Rabī'a opposed Naṣr. They went to Juday' b. 'Alī al-Kirmānī, Juday' being an adherent of the party (*shī'a*, sc. of the 'Abbasids). Ḥārith b. Surayj allied with them, and they engaged in warfare with Naṣr b. Sayyār. Jahm b. Ṣafwān, the head of the Jahmī sectaries, was with Ḥārith but was killed.[75] His son 'Alī stepped into his place. He sought help from Shaybān the Khārijite (*ḥarūrī*),[76] and with a guarantee of protection from him went to Merv. The Yamanīs, the Muḍarīs and the Ḥarūrīs came together as allies and joined battle with Naṣr The warfare went on for nine months, and in this space of time there were seventy engagements between the two sides. Naṣr was invariably victorious on every occasion except for the fighting he was engaged in with Abū Muslim, who had come out in revolt in the month of Ramaḍān of the year 129 [/May–June 747]. He proclaimed his adherence [M 180] to the House of Muḥammad, and dug a protective ditch.[77]

Abū Muslim was a native of Isfahan, and his name was 'Abd al-Raḥmān b. Muslim. Ibrāhīm al-Imām had sent Abū Muslim to Khurasan.[78] When Ibrāhīm al-Imām received information about these dissensions (i.e. in Khurasan), he wrote a letter to Sulaymān b. Kathīr, saying, 'Unsheathe your sword against Naṣr b. Sayyār!' When the disturbances in Khurasan became acute, Naṣr b. Sayyār made an appeal for help to Marwān but got no response. Every time that Naṣr b. Sayyār despatched a letter from Nishapur, Yazīd b. 'Umar b. Hubayra would detain Naṣr's messengers and keep them back from Marwān, and would himself send secret messages to Marwān complaining of Naṣr b. Sayyār's oppressive behaviour. Marwān was, moreover, completely taken up with combatting the Khārijite Ḍaḥḥāk and could not reach Naṣr. Abū Muslim recruited to his side the Yamanīs and the Rabī'a who were with Ibn Kirmānī, and Shaybān the Khārijite, and brought them, with himself, within the defensive trench, and the combined forces marched against Naṣr. He fled before them, and moved from Merv to Nishapur. When Naṣr fell back, Abū Muslim sent his experienced agents to the towns and districts of Khurasan, and he sent Qaḥṭaba b. Shabīb al-Ṭā'ī in pursuit of Naṣr b. Sayyār. Qaḥṭaba came upon Tamīm b. Naḍr at Ṭūs, a battle took place and Tamīm was killed.[79] Naṣr retreated towards Iraq, but when he reached Sāwa he died there. [H 119]

Abū Muslim ʿAbd al-Raḥmān b. Muslim

Abū Muslim, the leader of the ʿAbbasid movement, marched out of Merv. His home was in the village of Mākhān.[80] When he had disposed of the matter of Naṣr, he wrote a letter to Qaḥṭaba. Qaḥṭaba went to Gurgān and attacked Nubāta b. Ḥanẓala, who was the governor of Gurgān and had with him 40,000 Syrian troops, and killed Nubāta together with several of his sons, and a large number of troops were killed. Marwān sent an army against Qaḥṭaba by the Shahrazūr route, and ʿUmar b. Hubayra b. Yazīd joined up with him from Kufa. Abū Muslim came to Nishapur in Ṣafar of the year 131 [/October 748].

ʿUthmān, the son of Kirmānī, was in Ṭukhāristān together with Abū Dāwūd. Abū Muslim sent a letter to Dāwūd [M 181] instructing him to kill ʿUthmān, and Abū Dāwūd did this. Before this, Abū Muslim had killed ʿAlī b. Judayʿ al-Kirmānī in Shawwāl of the year 131 [/May–June 749]. ʿAlī had been hailed as Amir before Abū Muslim took charge. He sent an army to Qaḥṭaba so that the latter had a force of 70,000 men round him, thus confirming the authenticity of that saying, transmitted from ʿAlī b. ʿAbdallāh b. al-ʿAbbās, that '70,000 swords will come from the east in aid of the Prophet's House'.[81]

Qaḥṭaba went to Isfahan. He engaged in a battle with ʿĀmir b. Ḍubāra, killing him and a large number of his troops in Rajab of the year 131 [/February–March 749]. He then took Nihāwand and from there went to Ḥulwān. Abū Muslim built the congregational mosque at Merv and also reconstructed the one at Nishapur which Fādūspān had presented to Abū Muslim. This person Fādūspān was one of the *dihqān*s of Nishapur. He had been very helpful and kind to Abū Muslim when the latter was secretly conducting his propagandist activities, and when things turned out well for Abū Muslim, he repaid the favours which he had received from Fādūspān.

Bihāfarīd the Magian led a movement in the rural districts of Khwāf and Busht near Nishapur. This Bihāfarīd came from the rural district of Zawzan. Amongst [H 120] the Zoroastrian community he claimed to be a prophet, and he raised up a dissident group amongst them involving a large number of people. He laid down an obligatory seven acts of worship (*namāz*)[82] to be performed (i.e. each day) facing the sun wherever one might be. Of these acts of the worship, the first was proclaiming the unity of God, He is Exalted and Magnified (*tawḥid*). The second was [acknowledgement of] the creation of the heavens and the earth. The third was [acknowledgement of] the creation of all living things and their sustenance. The fourth was [acknowledgement of] death. The fifth was [acknowledgement of] the resurrection of the body and the last reckoning. The sixth was [acknowledgement of] heaven and hell. The seventh was giving thanks and praise for the people of paradise. He forbade them to eat the flesh of anything that had died naturally. Marriage with one's mother, sister and the child of one's sister or brother was prohibited. He prohibited the marriage portion for a woman being more than 400 dirhams. He required one-seventh from people's wealth and possessions and likewise from what was gained by the labour of their hands (i.e. for charitable purposes). He introduced corruption into that religion of the Magians. [M 182]

The Zoroastrian priests (*mūbadān*) came before Abū Muslim and raised a complaint about Bihāfarīd, saying, 'He has introduced corruption into your faith and ours.' Hence Abū Muslim arrested Bihāfarīd and hanged and gibbeted him, and he killed a group of his adherents.[83]

Abū Muslim had sent Abū ʿAwn to attack Marwān al-Ḥimār. When Qaḥṭaba reached the bank of the Euphrates, Yazīd b. Hubayra came out to give battle with him. An overnight battle took place between the two sides. Qaḥṭaba's army was victorious, but Qaḥṭaba fell into the river and was drowned. After the passage of some days, Qaḥṭaba's troops made his son Ḥasan their commander, and they entered Kufa. ʿAbdallāh b. Muḥammad b. ʿAlī b. ʿAbdallāh b. ʿAbbās, who had the honorific title of *[al-]Saffāḥ* ('The Blood-thirsty One' or 'The Generous One') and who had been hidden, with his brothers, in the house of Abū Salama Khallāl, was brought forth, and allegiance given to him as caliph.

Saffāḥ then sent his paternal uncles ʿAbdallāh and ʿAbd al-Ṣamad, together with Abū ʿAwn, to attack Marwān. When Marwān got news about them, he advanced to give battle, but was speedily defeated. He withdrew towards Egypt, but Abū ʿAwn kept on pursuing him until he came upon Marwān at Būṣīr in Egypt at ʿAyn al-Shams.[84] ʿĀmir b. Ismāʿīl confronted Marwān, killed him, cut off his head and laid it before Abū ʿAwn. The latter sent it on to Abu ʾl-ʿAbbās Saffāḥ. The killing of Marwān was in Dhu ʾl-Qaʿda of the year 132 [/June–July 750].

When Abu ʾl-ʿAbbās succeeded to the caliphate, he sent his brother Manṣūr to Khurasan in order to get an oath of allegiance from Abū Muslim and oaths from all the people of Khurasan. When Ibrāhīm al-Imām had been killed, Abū Salama al-Khallāl, who was the amir in Kufa, acquired an inclination to the cause of the ʿAlids. Abu ʾl-ʿAbbās got to know about this and informed Abū Muslim of the situation. Abū Muslim then sent Murār b. Anas and he killed Abū Salama.

Sharīk was in Farghāna. He rebelled against Abū Muslim and rallied people to the cause of the House of Abū Ṭālib, [M 183] gathering a numerous body of people around him. Abū Muslim sent Ziyād b. Ṣāliḥ to attack Sharīk. When Ziyād b. Ṣāliḥ reached the Oxus, the Bukhār-Khudāh came to him seeking a grant of protection, [H 121] and joined Ziyād for the fight against Sharīk. A battle ensued, large numbers of people were killed and Sharīk was captured. His head was cut off and sent to Abū Muslim, who forwarded it to Abu ʾl-ʿAbbās, this in the month of Dhu ʾl-Ḥijja of the year 132 [/July–August 750].[85]

When order was restored in Khurasan, and there was nowhere giving him cause for concern, Abū Muslim set out for the Pilgrimage with 8,000 men. When he came to Nishapur and then Ray, he disbanded all these followers and set off with a force of just 1,000 men.[86] His aides and advisers told him, 'Don't go, for you'll never come back!', but he refused to renounce his intention. Abū Muslim killed Sulaymān b. Kathīr, who had inaugurated the movement for the claims of the House of the Messenger [of God], peace be upon him and may God pray over him and his house and grant them peace. When he set off on the Pilgrimage, and came to the court of Abu 'l-ʿAbbās al-Saffāḥ, the latter fulfilled for Abū Muslim the due rewards for service and gave orders that he should be lodged in a handsome fashion. When Abū Muslim came into Saffāḥ's presence, the latter questioned him in an encouraging fashion. When Abū Muslim departed on the Pilgrimage, Abu 'l-ʿAbbās al-Saffāḥ died in Dhu 'l-Ḥijja of the year 136 [/May–June 745] and his brother Manṣūr succeeded to the caliphate. When Abū Muslim came back from the Pilgrimage, Manṣūr sent him to attack his paternal uncle ʿAbdallāh b. ʿAlī. Abū Muslim defeated him, and he seized his wealth and possessions as plunder. Jumhūr b. Murār captured ʿAbdallāh b. ʿAlī in the course of that battle and brought him before Abū Muslim, who sent him on to Manṣūr. Manṣūr kept him in captivity till the end of [ʿAbdallāh b.] ʿAlī's life.[87]

Abū Muslim had had the deciding voice in all affairs, and all that had come back to Manṣūr's ear, hence he continually sought an opportunity for killing Abū Muslim. When Abū Muslim returned from the Pilgrimage, he was told, 'There's a Christian at Ḥīra[88] who is 200 years old and who knows about everything.' Abū Muslim summoned him into his presence. When that aged man saw Abū Muslim, he exclaimed, 'You've achieved enough, [M 184] you've brought your efforts to perfection and you've reached the ultimate point! You've consumed yourself (i.e. in strenuous action) and spread wide your efforts! Now you have come face to face with your own killing!' Abū Muslim was overcome by melancholy. The old man went on to say to him, 'Defects do not arise from perfect, resolute behaviour, nor from good judgement or advantageous planning arrangements, nor from the sharp-edged sword; on the contrary, no-one ever attains all his desires, for Fate catches up with him when only a part of his aims has been achieved'.

Abū Muslim replied, 'What's your prognosis for the outcome! Where will this affair end?' The old man replied, 'When two caliphs are agreed upon a course of action, it will reach completion. The divinely ordained decree rests with that One before Whom all human plans are in vain. If you go back to Khurasan, you'll remain safe and secure.' Abū Muslim had the intention of returning, but Manṣūr sent envoys to him with the message, 'Come speedily!' The divine decree had come down, and Abū Muslim had lost his powers of perception and foresight. He asked someone, 'What do you think they're going to do with me?' That person replied, 'Good treatment, and the reward for all that you've done for them (sc. the ʿAbbasids) can only be good!' Abū Muslim said, 'I suspect otherwise!'

The opening phase of the killing of Abū Muslim by Abū Jaʿfar Manṣūr was on this wise. Manṣūr sent Yaqṭīn to Abū Muslim, and Yaqṭīn [H 122] said to Abū Muslim, 'He's sent me with this charge, that I should investigate whether this amount of wealth is sufficient for the body of troops or not.'[89] Abū Muslim realised that the real intention did not lie in his words. He started out along the road to Khurasan, disobeying Manṣūr's instructions until he reached Ḥulwān and encamped there. Manṣūr despatched Jarīr b. Yazīd b. Jarīr b. ʿAbdallāh al-Bajalī. This man Jarīr was an extremely wily and crafty person, and was shrewd, to an unequalled degree. He invoked many incantations and magical spells on Abū Muslim, and as a result got him to return to Manṣūr.

It is related that when Abū Muslim came back from Ḥulwān with Jarīr al-Bajalī to Abū Jaʿfar's court, he asked for a horse that was the finest in the stables and mounted that horse with the intention of going into Manṣūr's presence. The horse bolted beneath Abū Muslim three times. One of [M 185] his retainers told him, 'Turn back!', but Abū Muslim replied, 'What the Most Exalted God wills, will be.' When he came into Manṣūr's presence, the latter bade him sit down and asked after him in a friendly way. Then he asked him, 'Which sword did you wield in all those victories and battles of yours?' Abū Muslim responded, 'With this one,' and he indicated the sword that was girded at his waist. Manṣūr said, 'Give it to me,' and he handed it to him. Manṣūr then said, 'Do you know what you did against me? You did so-and-so,' and he enumerated the charges one by one. Abū Muslim gave a reply to each accusation until Manṣūr made a sour face and shouted at him.

Abū Muslim said, 'O Commander of the Faithful, this is not a fair requital of all those beneficial deeds I did!' Manṣūr replied,

> O Father of Criminal Deeds![90] Remember when you came into Abu 'l-ʿAbbās's presence and rendered service to him, when I was sitting there and you paid no attention to me! Remember that you said to my nephew ʿĪsā b. Mūsā, 'Are you agreeable that I should deprive Abū Jaʿfar of his succession rights and set you up in his place?' Remember how, in Syria, in the presence of Yaqṭīn b. Mūsā, you vilified me and called me 'Son of Salama',[91] and [you said that] Salama was of lower status than your own mother!

Abū Muslim gave an answer to each one of these charges.[92]

Manṣūr then said, 'You didn't do these things out of friendship for us! On the contrary, the successful establishment of our power was due to a heavenly decree and divine favour!' He made a sign to the person who was standing over Abū Muslim, and the latter struck Abū Muslim with the sword. Abū Muslim fell to the ground, crying out 'Oh! Oh!' Manṣūr expostulated, 'O you who wrought the deeds of mighty warriors, you're crying now like a small child!' ʿUthmān b. Nahīk, who had previously been Abū Muslim's personal bodyguard,[93] was the first person to strike Abū Muslim, and then the Ḥājib Abu 'l-Khaṣīb struck him with his sword and finished him off. Abū Muslim's troops rioted at the palace gate. Abu 'l-Khaṣīb went out and gave out a message from Manṣūr to the Khurasanian troops which stated, 'The Commander of the Faithful announces that the Amir Abū Muslim was our servant, and we ordained punishment for his disobedience. You are not behaving in this manner', and he ordered that a year's pay allotment should be taken from the treasury [and distributed to them]. They all became quiescent. Manṣūr then sent Abū Muslim's head to Abū Dāwūd [H 123] so that [M 186] it could be paraded round throughout all Khurasan.[94]

Abū Dāwūd Khālid b. Ibrāhīm al-Dhuhlī

Manṣūr appointed Abū Dāwūd governor of Khurasan in the month of Ramaḍān of the year 137 [/February–March 755], and Abū Dāwūd remained there as governor till his death.[95] The 'Wearers of White' (*sapīd-jāmagān*) killed him in the month of

Rabīʿ I of the year 140 [/July–August 757].[96] This group which killed Abū Dāwūd were from the community of Saʿīd Jawlāh. In the end, Abū Dāwūd's retainers captured all that group and killed them. Their chief, Saʿīd Jawlāh, was also captured and put to death with the rest of them.[97]

ʿAbd al-Jabbār b. ʿAbd al-Raḥmān

This man ʿAbd al-Raḥmān was Manṣūr's commander of the police guard. When Abū Dāwūd Dhuhlī was killed, Manṣūr gave ʿAbd al-Jabbār b. ʿAbd al-Raḥmān an investiture patent for the governorship of Khurasan.[98] He came to Merv with forty riding beasts of the postal and intelligence service (*barīd*), and was accompanied by his secretary, a man called Muʿāwiya [b. ʿUbaydallāh], who was directing his affairs. ʿAbd al-Jabbār then became puffed up with self-pride, and he wrote a letter to Manṣūr asking for his family and children to be sent to Khurasan. Manṣūr duly despatched them. ʿAbd al-Jabbār now embarked on a policy of rebelliousness. He imposed extra impositions, in addition to the land-tax, on Merv, Balkh and many other towns of Khurasan. He gave the governorship of Nishapur to his sister's son Khaṭṭāb b. Yazīd. However, Khaṭṭāb adopted evil ways and treated the people in an oppressive manner. The subjects laid complaints against him before Manṣūr. Manṣūr wrote a letter to ʿAbd al-Jabbār instructing him to send Khaṭṭāb to the caliphal court. ʿAbd al-Jabbār did not do this, and merely sent excuses and assumed a rebellious attitude.

ʿAbd al-Jabbār's attention was then drawn to a man named Barāz-banda b. B.m.rūn. This man claimed to be Ibrāhīm b. ʿAbdallāh al-Hāshimī,[99] and he summoned people to support his claim. ʿAbd al-Jabbār sent an envoy to him communicating his secret intentions and pledging allegiance to him. He raised the white banner [M 187] and summoned people to give their allegiance to Barāz-banda.[100] He killed several of the leading commanders of the Khuzāʿa, who had all refused to respond to his summons: ʿIṣām, Abū Dāwūd's commander of the police guard; Abu 'l-Qāsim Tājī and his brother; ʿUmar b. Aʿyan; Murār b. Anas; [H 124] Abu 'l-Qāsim Khuzāʿī; Shurayḥ b. ʿAbdallāh; Qudāma al-Ḥarashī, Manṣūr's envoy; Abū Wahb; Bārmānī (?); Abū Hilāl Ṭālaqānī; and Muḥtāj.

Manṣūr now entrusted Khurasan to his son Mahdī. Mahdī despatched Ḥarb b. Ziyād to attack ʿAbd al-Jabbār. When news of this reached ʿAbd al-Jabbār, he sent Sawwār with 5,000 men against Ḥarb, but Ḥarb defeated Sawwār and headed towards Merv. When he drew near [to the city], ʿAbd al-Jabbār marched out to fight. In the course of that fight, the person who had styled himself Ibrāhīm Hāshimī was killed by Ḥarb personally, and ʿAbd al-Jabbār was put to flight. A great number of his troops were killed. ʿAbd al-Jabbār fled along the road to Zam,[101] but lost his way and found himself in a cotton-growing tract of land in the vicinity of the dwellings of the Azd. ʿAbd al-Ghaffār b. Ṣāliḥ Ṭālaqānī was in pursuit of him with a detachment of troops. They came upon him there, and seized him and his secretary Muʿāwiya, tied up their hands and set them on a stout mount. ʿAbd al-Jabbār was brought before Ḥarb b. Ziyad, who had taken up his quarters in the government headquarters (i.e at Merv). He consigned them both to prison and wrote a letter to Mahdī announcing that victory. The letter came into the hands of Khāzim b. Khuzayma, Mahdī's deputy, who attributed the victory to his own doing. This routing [of the enemy] was on Saturday, 6 Rabīʿ I of the year 142 [/7 July 759]. Khāzim remained at Merv. He sent Ḥarb to Herat and Ṭālaqān, and Ḥasan b. Ḥumrān to Balkh, Zam and the banks of the Oxus. Khāzim then sought to be relieved of his post. Mahdī agreed to this, and he relinquished his office.[102]

Abū ʿAwn ʿAbd al-Malik b. Yazīd

Manṣūr gave the governorship of Khurasan to Abū ʿAwn ʿAbd al-Malik b. [M 188] Yazīd. Abū ʿAwn came to Merv in the year 143 [/760–61] and remained in Khurasan for seven years. During his time, a group of mutinous troops, who were demanding an increase in their pay allowances, killed Ḥasan b. Ḥumrān and his brother. In the year 146 [/763–4], Manṣūr completed the building of Baghdad and moved there from Wāsiṭ. He dismissed Abū ʿAwn from his post in the year 149 [/766] and summoned him back from Khurasan.

Usayd b. ʿAbdallāh

Manṣūr gave the governorship of Khurasan to Usayd b. ʿAbdallāh. Usayd came to Khurasan in the month of Ramaḍān [/October–November 766]. This man Usayd was Manṣūr's commander of the guard. During his tenure of the governorship in Khurasan, the rising of Ustādsīs of Bādghīs took place. [H 125] He claimed to be a prophet, and followed the path of Bihāfarīd.[103] The reason for this was that Bihāfarīd's adherents in Bādghīs sent a letter to Mahdī in these terms: 'We have become Muslims through you, so treat us with consideration!'[104]

Mahdī sent Muḥammad [b.] Saʿīd to lead a raid on Kabul. He sent along with him these men of Bādghīs and made them sharers in the captured plunder (*fayʾ*). Muḥammad set off, and carried on warfare for several days, and he allotted them a share in that captured plunder.[105] They then returned to their homes and apostasised from Islam. Ustādsīs came out in revolt. Mahdī sent Abū ʿAwn and Khāzim to attack him. When Ustādsīs got news of this, he came with a group of his followers to seek a guarantee of protection from Abū ʿAwn. Abū ʿAwn accepted the submission of them all, kept faithfully to his promised terms and refrained from harming Ustādsīs and the judge (?) and his son. He seized the fortress that they held together with all its contents. Some people assert that Marājil, the mother of Ma'mūn, was Ustādsīs's daughter, and [M 189] that Ghālib, Ma'mūn's maternal uncle, was Ustādsīs's son; it was Ghālib who assassinated Faḍl b. Sahl in the baths at Sarakhs on Ma'mūn's orders.[106] Usayd b. ʿAbdallāh died in the year 150 [/767].

ʿAbda b. Qadīd

The governorship of Khurasan was then given to ʿAbda b. Qadīd. He came to Merv in Muḥarram of the year 151 [/January–February 768]. He was governor of Khurasan for seven months and was then dismissed.[107]

Ḥumayd b. Qaḥṭaba

Manṣūr gave the governorship of Khurasan to Ḥumayd b. Qaḥṭaba at the beginning of Shaʿbān of the year 151 [/20 August 768]. Ḥumayd was one of the principal propagandists (*dā'iyān*, i.e. for the ʿAbbasid movement).[108] During his tenure of office Manṣūr died, and Mahdī succeeded to the caliphate. He sent Ḥumayd an investiture patent for Khurasan. During Ḥumayd's governorship, Muqannaʿ ('The Veiled One') came out in rebellion and raised a white banner.[109] This Muqannaʿ was one-eyed. He was a fuller at Merv, with the name of Ḥakīm. When he first rebelled, he made a claim to prophethood and then, ultimately, he claimed to be divine. He summoned people to become his devotees, having covered his face with a golden mask. He used to have this over his face so that no-one should see his face, since it was hideous to behold. He used to say,

> God, He is Exalted and Magnified, created Adam and became immanent in him, and when Adam died, He became immanent in the form of Noah, then of Abraham, of Moses, of Jesus and then of Muḥammad, peace be upon them all, and this continued until He was immanent in the form of Abū Muslim. After Abū Muslim, He became immanent in the form of Hāshim [i.e. Muqannaʿ].

This Muqannaʿ had adopted the name of Hāshim for himself.[110]

Large numbers of misled and errant people followed him and would prostrate themselves before him. On the battlefield they would raise the cry of 'O Hāshim, give aid!' just as a person will seek aid from God, He is Exalted and Magnified, [H 126, M 190] and a great throng of people flocked round him. The fortress of Sanām, which is in the rural district of Kish, had been got ready and had been provided with defences against a siege. The 'Wearers of White' in Bukhara and Sogdia came out into the open and provided reinforcements for Muqannaʿ, and he also summoned help from the infidel Turks.[111] They were busy plundering the Muslims' wealth and possessions. Most of their activities manifested themselves in Sogdia.

Abū Nuʿmān attacked them, but was unable to achieve anything [against them]. They came to the district and town of Kish and erected barricades in its streets and alleys,[112] and they likewise seized control of the citadel of Nuwākath near Sanām and S.n.k.r. Abu 'l-Nuʿmān, Junayd, Layth b. Naṣr, Ḥassān b. Tamīm b. Naṣr b. Sayyār and Muḥammad b. Naṣr made war on them, but none of these was able to get the upper hand over them and all turned back defeated. Mahdī then sent Jibrā'īl b. Yaḥyā and his brother Yazīd. They became busy dealing with the 'Wearers of White' of Bukhara, who had manifested themselves in the year 157 [/774] during the time of Ḥusayn b. Muʿādh. Jibrā'īl attacked them in the town of Nuwajkath (? Numijkath)[113] and killed 700 of them, and he also killed Ḥakīm Bukhārī, their leader. The rest of them took to flight and went to Muqannaʿ.

Jibrā'īl then went on to Samarqand and led an attack on the Sogdians,[114] killing one of their leaders. Ḥumayd b. Qaḥṭaba died, and his son ʿAbdallāh b. Ḥumayd held the governorship of Khurasan after him till the end of the year 159 [/October 776].

Abū ʿAwn ʿAbd al-Malik b. Yazīd

Mahdī conferred the governorship of Khurasan on Abū ʿAwn, and the latter sent on ahead his son as commander of the advance guard, this on Monday, 15 Ṣafar of

160 [/2 December 776]. He held office in Khurasan for one year and one month, and he led military actions against Muqannaʿ. Yūsuf Thaqafī the Khārijite (Ḥarūrī) had rebelled in the time of Ḥumayd, and he was joined by Ḥakam Ṭālaqānī and Bū Muʿādh Fāryābī.[115] They had captured Pūshang from Muṣʿab b. Ruzayq, and Yūsuf had conquered Marw al-Rūd, Ṭālaqān and Gūzgānān, until [M 191] the Hāshimites of Balkh engaged him in battle [H 127] and put him to flight. Bū Muʿādh Fāryābī was captured and was sent to Mahdī. The latter gave orders and Bū Muʿadh was gibbeted at Baghdad. Mahdī then dismissed Abū ʿAwn from Khurasan.

Muʿādh b. Muslim

Mahdī conferred the governorship of Khurasan on Muʿādh b. Muslim, and Muʿādh sent his brother Salama to Khurasan as his deputy, whilst he himself followed after him in the month of Rabīʿ II of the year 161 [/January 778].[116] During his time there, his son Ḥusayn was appointed governor of Nishapur. During Ḥusayn's time there was a famine, and a large number of people gathered round Ḥusayn's gate and lamented about the famine and the high level of prices. They made supplication to him, 'Release grain for sale, so that others may see what you've done and sell it too!' Ḥusayn replied, 'I'd have very much liked a grain of wheat to cost a dinar!' The people went back in despair and sent up invocations to God. Before a week was out, Ḥusayn died.

When Muʿādh went to Merv and the affairs of Khurasan were on an even course, he then marched against Muqannaʿ. He appointed Saʿīd Ḥarashī as commander of his vanguard, and ʿUqba b. Salm also brought reinforcements for him at Ṭawāwīs.[117] They went on to Samarqand. Khārija,[118] one of Muqannaʿ's partisans, with 15,000 men from the 'Wearers of White', was involved in fighting with Jibrāʾīl b. Yaḥyā, and Jibrāʾīl killed 3,000 of them. When the reinforcements (i.e. those of ʿUqba b. Salm) arrived, the Muslims grew more confident and the 'Wearers of White' became weaker. Large numbers of them were killed, and the remainder fell back towards Muqannaʿ. Muqannaʿ dug a defensive trench in front of the fortress of Sanām and gave battle to the Muslims. The position of the 'Wearers of White' became parlous. They nevertheless held out, until the point was reached when they were reduced to eating each other. They sought to come to a peace agreement with Ḥarashī, unbeknown to Muqannaʿ. Ḥarashī agreed to this, and 30,000 men came up out of the defensive trench and went off, [M 192] leaving behind Muqannaʿ with 2,000 persons, his retainers, his fellow-sectaries and his followers.

There were bad relations between Saʿīd Ḥarashī and Muʿādh b. Muslim. Muʿādh sought from Mahdī permission to lay down his office of collecting the taxes of Khurasan. He got the caliph's agreement and returned to Iraq.

Musayyab b. Zuhayr

Mahdī then appointed Musayyab b. Zuhayr as governor of Khurasan and sent him there. Musayyab reached Khurasan in Jumādā I of the year 166 [/December 782–January 783].[119] As soon as he arrived there, he set about levying the land-tax. He formed the plan of marching against Bukhara and attacking Muqannaʿ. Then he received news of Saʿīd Ḥarashī's victory and how he had tightened up the besieging of Muqannaʿ. [H 128] When Muqannaʿ gave up all hope of preserving his life, he gathered around him all his womenfolk. He prepared a poison and gave his personal assurance that they would all enter Paradise, and then all of them drank the poison and died immediately. Muqannaʿ also drank the poison and died some time later. He had given orders that one of his partisans should cut off his head, and he stipulated in a last charge that his body should be burnt so that it should never be found.[120]

Some lost and deluded people who had adopted Muqannaʿ's cause said that he had gone to Paradise. For this very reason, a group of persons raised up disturbance and strife on his behalf, and there are supporters of his cause (*mutaqannaʿiyān*) to this day.[121] The [Muslim] troops poured into that fortress. They found it deserted, and they carried off as plunder whatever they could find. Musayyab b. Zuhayr remained in Khurasan for eight months. He raised the land-tax above the customary amount fixed. The subjects raised complaints about him, until Mahdī dismissed him [from the governorship]. The Musayyabī dirhams which are current in Transoxania are named after him, just as the Ghiṭrīfī ones are named after Ghiṭrīf b. ʿAṭā' al-Kindī and the Muḥammadī ones after Muḥammad b. Zubayda[122] (i.e. the caliph al-Amīn). These dirhams are made of an alloy of copper and lead.[123]

Abu 'l-ʿAbbās al-Faḍl b. Sulaymān

Mahdī then appointed Abu 'l-ʿAbbās al-Faḍl b. [M 193] Sulaymān al-Ṭūsī to the governorship of Khurasan.[124] Abu 'l-ʿAbbās sent out Saʿīd b. Bashīr as commander of the advance guard, and Saʿīd came to Merv in Muḥarram of the year 167 [/August–September 783]. He went into Musayyab's presence (Musayyab having received no information about the change), greeted him ceremoniously and gave him a letter instructing him to hand over his charge to Saʿīd. When Musayyab had read it, he rose from his place and said, 'The seat of authority is now yours.'

Abu 'l-ʿAbbās then arrived also in the month of Rabīʿ I of this same year [/October 783], and embarked on a course of [praiseworthy] conduct. He gave back to the people of Merv the 5,000 boards for measuring the quantities of water allowed to the cultivators (*bast-āb*)[125] which the military commanders and prominent persons had arbitrarily appropriated. He enlarged the mosque of Merv. He purchased tracts of land, comprising enclosures and gardens (i.e. for public use). He enlarged the burial grounds at Merv. He increased the pay allotments of the military leaders. He divided up the land-tax amongst the people in a just manner. In our places Quhistān, the Ṭabasayn, Āmul, Nasā, Bāward, Herat and Pūshang, the situation now prevailed that only the customary rate of taxation fixed by him should be approved, and he removed from the people all the extra taxes on top of the land-tax that Musayyab had imposed. He founded the settlement of Faḍlābād in the desert of Āmūy.[126] A stout wall was constructed between Sogdia and Bukhara to protect the people from the Turks. He lightened the burden of the land-tax on the leading figures of the Arabs.

During his time, Hādī succeeded to the caliphate, and for the whole of his reign, Abu 'l-ʿAbbās remained amir of Khurasan. But when Hārūn al-Rashīd succeeded to the caliphate,[127] he appointed Ja'far b. Muḥammad b. al-Ash'ath to the governorhip of Khurasan. [H 129]

Ja'far b. Muḥammad b. al-Ash'ath

Hārūn al-Rashīd then appointed Ja'far b. Muḥammad b. al-Ash'ath to the governorship of Khurasan and sent him there. In Dhu 'l-Ḥijja of the year 176 [/March–April 793],[128] Ja'far sent his son 'Abbās against Kabul. He subdued Shābahār, and seized as plunder all the wealth and possessions in that place. Ja'far was recalled. It is related that, one day, Ja'far came into Hārūn's presence at a moment when Hārūn had become angered against a certain person. [M 194] Ja'far said, 'O Commander of the Faithful, one should only be gripped by anger on God's behalf. Whenever you become angered on God's behalf, don't be carried away by it to a greater degree than God Himself, He is Exalted and Magnified, would be!' Hārūn was pleased at these words, and he showed benevolence towards the man with whom he had originally been angry.

'Abbās b. Ja'far

When Hārūn recalled Ja'far, he bestowed Khurasan on the latter's son 'Abbās b. Ja'far.[129] The latter came to Khurasan and followed the same policies as his father. He remained governor of Khurasan for three years, and in the year 175 [/791–2] he was recalled.

Ghiṭrīf b. 'Aṭā' al-Kindī

Hārūn then appointed Ghiṭrīf b. 'Aṭā' al-Kindī to the goverorship of Khurasan.[130] Ghiṭrīf sent out as his deputy Dāwūd b. Yazīd b. Ḥātim, and then himself followed after Dāwūd in the months of the year 175. He despatched 'Umar b. Jamīl, who ejected the Jabūya[131] from Farghāna and remained there for some time. He ordered the Ghiṭrīfī dirhams to be struck, and these are used at Bukhara for commercial and financial transactions.[132]

During Ghiṭrīf's governorship, Ḥuḍayn the Khārijite, who was from Ūq, came out in rebellion. The amir of Sistan at that time was 'Uthmān b. 'Umāra b. Khuzayma. Ḥuḍayn defeated 'Uthmān's army and then invaded Khurasan, coming to Pūshang and Herat. Hārūn ordered that forces should be sent against him. [H 130] Ghiṭrīf sent his deputy (i.e. Dāwūd b. Yazīd) and the latter's brother Jarīr b. Yazīd with 12,000 troops. It is related that Ḥuḍayn had 300 men. Ḥuḍayn killed a substantial number of his opponents. When he went to Isfizār, he was killed there, together with his wife, this in the year 177 [793–4].[133]

al-Faḍl b. Yaḥyā al-Barmakī

Rashīd then appointed as governor of Khurasan Faḍl b. Yaḥyā al-Barmakī.[134] [M 195] Faḍl b. Yaḥyā sent on ahead Yaḥyā b. Mu'ādh as his deputy over Khurasan, and Yaḥyā came there in Ramaḍān of the year 177 [/December 793–January 794]. Faḍl b. Yaḥyā himself reached Khurasan in Muḥarram of the year 178 [/April–May 794]. and went off to lead a raid (*ghazw*) into Transoxania.[135]

Khārākhuruh, the ruler (*malik*) of Ushrūsana,[136] submitted to Faḍl, never having before submitted to anyone and never having given obedience to anyone. In Faḍl's time, the Khārijite Khurāsha b. Sinān had come out in rebellion and had seized Dīnawar. Faḍl b. Yaḥyā sent against him Ibrāhīm b. Jibrā'īl. Ibrāhīm defeated Khurāsha, and in three days the latter retreated ninety parasangs to Shahrazūr. He came to Chāh-i Asad (?), was captured there and put to death.[137]

Hārūn had entrusted Muḥammad al-Amīn to Faḍl-i Yaḥyā's care for his upbringing, and Ma'mūn to the care of Ja'far b. Yaḥyā. Hārūn used to call Yaḥyā b. Khālid 'Father'. He gave the vizierate to Yaḥyā b. Khālid. Faḍl and all the Barmakis were noted for their generosity and liberality, to the extent that, one day, it was said to Faḍl b. Yaḥyā, ''Umar b. Jamīl is a generous and liberal person, hospitable to guests'. Faḍl ordered that 'Umar should be given 200,000 dirhams and made him his deputy over Khurasan on the basis of this story which had been related about him. When Faḍl was dismissed from the governorship, 'Umar b. Jamīl got together resources in Chaghāniyān and settled there; there remain in Chaghāniyān many of his progeny, and to this very day there are numerous descendants of his there.[138] It is related that, one day, 'Umar saw a fox which went down a hole. He had the hole dug out, and saw there a great treasure. He built a residence (*kūshk*) over that spot and brought away that treasure. All his kindred and close retainers built places round that house. Rashīd dismissed Faḍl b. Yaḥyā [from the governorship of Khurasan].[139] [H 131]

Manṣūr b. Yazīd

Rashīd then appointed Manṣūr b. Yazīd, who was the maternal uncle [M 196] of Mahdī, as governor of Khurasan.[140] Manṣūr made his son Sa'īd his deputy, and Sa'īd reached Khurasan in Dhu 'l-Qa'da of the year 179 [/January–February 796]. Manṣūr himself arrived in Dhu 'l-Ḥijja of that year [/February–March 796]. During his governorship, the Khārijite Ḥamza b. Ādharak came out in revolt. He went to Quhistān, and whatever Ḥamza demanded, the people of Quhistān gave it to him. He then returned.[141]

'Alī b. 'Īsā b. Māhān

Hārūn then appointed 'Alī b. 'Īsā b. Māhān governor of Khurasan. 'Alī sent his son Yaḥyā as commander of his advance guard, and Yaḥyā b. 'Alī reached Khurasan at the opening of the year 180 [/16 March 796]. 'Alī remained governor of Khurasan for ten years.[142] His secretary was Ḥafṣ b. Manṣūr Marwazī. Ḥafṣ died, leaving behind him sixty children, twenty of them grown up and forty still small. Ḥafṣ has composed the book *Kharāj Khurāsān* ('The Land-tax of Khurasan').[143]

During 'Alī b. 'Īsā's governorate, the Khārijite Ḥamza rebelled. 'Amr b. Yazīd al-Azdī was in charge of the region of Herat as far [south] as Pūshang. 'Amr marched against Ḥamza with 6,000 troops and defeated him, killing a large part of Ḥamza's army. A substantial number of men died from the excessive heat of the time, including also 'Amr; they brought him back and buried him. Ḥamza went to Astarābād. 'Alī b. 'Īsā b. Māhān sent forward his son Ḥusayn with a force of 10,000 men. Ḥusayn came to Bādghīs and wrote a letter to Ḥamza, made over the poor-tax (*zakāt*) to him and did not engage in warfare with him. In the end, his father dismissed him for this reason.

He then sent another of his sons, ʿĪsā, who engaged Ḥamza in battle. Ḥamza smashed ʿĪsā's army,[144] and ʿĪsā retreated to Balkh. His father provided him with another army and he went out to engage Ḥamza. He killed large numbers of Ḥamza's troops, and Ḥamza fled in retreat with 40,000 of his followers to Quhistān. [M 197] ʿAlī b. ʿĪsā sent several of his senior officers to Ūq and Juwayn, and any of the quietist Khārijites (*khārijī qaʿadī*) they came across they killed without exception. They also killed the menfolk of the villages that had given aid and support to Ḥamza [H 132] and burnt down the villages themselves, and then returned to Zarang. It is related that they killed 30,000 people in this fashion. ʿAbdallāh b. ʿAbbās was left in Zarang (sc. as governor and tax-collector) with a force of 4,000 men, and he levied a tax precept of three million dirhams.

Ḥamza advanced towards him as far as Sabzawār, and a battle took place there. The troops from Sogdia and Nakhshab fought on doggedly until Ḥamza became weakened and fatigued, and then they launched an attack. They killed his close retainers and wounded Ḥamza in the face. ʿAbdallāh b. al-ʿAbbās seized the plunder there and marched away. Ḥamza fell upon the villages and killed everyone he could find there. He came to a school and thirty children and their teacher were killed. When Ṭāhir[145] heard about this, they were in a village of the quietist Khārijites (*qaʿadiyān*) who do not have the custom of waging war and and who had stayed in their houses. After 300 men and women were killed, and he had carried off their wealth and possessions as plunder, he had them (sc. the survivors of the Khārijites) brought in. Two stout branches of a tree were tied together with strong ropes connecting the two of them, and the two legs of a quietist Khārijite were each tied to one of the two branches. Then the rope was released, and the strength of those two branches thus released would split the man in two. Several battles took place between the troops of ʿĪsā and those of Ḥamza. ʿĪsā's affairs now went well, and he constructed ten mills at Balkh.[146]

Harthama b. Aʿyan

Rashīd gave the governorship of Khurasan to Harthama b. Aʿyan, and he came to Khurasan in the year 191 [/207].[147] Rāfiʿ b. al-Layth b. Naṣr b. Sayyār had rebelled at Samarqand, and on several occasions Harthama was involved with him.[148] Then Harthama wrote out a guarantee of protection for Rāfiʿ and sent it to him, but Rāfiʿ took no notice of it. When Rashīd heard about this, he said, 'Anyone who rejects a document offering protection becomes a contemptible wretch.' Harthama b. Aʿyan summoned Ṭāhir b. al-Ḥusayn [M 198] to join forces with him, and Khurasan became empty of troops. When Hārūn heard the news about Rāfiʿ and Harthama, he became worried and perturbed. He set out from Baghdad with the intention of proceeding to Samarqand, but when he reached Ṭūs he died, in the year 193 [/809].[149] Ḥamza came out in revolt [again], and began to kill and plunder, and craftsmen and artisans (*kārdārān*) from Herat and Sistan were flocking to his side.

ʿAbd al-Raḥmān Nishābūrī led a movement at Zarang, and 20,000 ghāzīs whose names were registered[150] on the army's strength rallied round him, and in the year

194 [/809–10] he marched out to attack Ḥamza. Ḥamza had 6,000 men. Most of Ḥamza's troops were killed, [H 133] and Ḥamza was [eventually] killed. He went to Herat, pursued by the ghāzīs. Finally, they killed him at some point in the months of 213 [/828–9]. The judge Abū Isḥāq took his place.[151] Harthama besieged Rāfi' b. al-Layth in Samarqand, and much fighting took place till he took Samarqand and killed Rāfi'.[152]

In the year 195 [/810–11], [the governorship of] Transoxania was given to Yaḥyā b. Mu'ādh. Subsequently, he was dismissed from the post, and it was given[153] to Bānījūr[154] in Sha'bān of the year 199 [/March–April 815].

al-Ma'mūn 'Abdallāh b. Rashīd

When Rashīd passed away, Ma'mūn was at Merv. Rashīd had left behind his testament (*waṣiyyat*) that 'All the wealth and treasure I have with me is to be conveyed to Ma'mūn.' But Faḍl b. al-Rabī' betrayed these instructions, and all the wealth and treasure was conveyed to Muḥammad b. Zubayda at Baghdad, contrary to what Rashīd had stipulated in his testament. Ma'mūn was the next covenanted heir (*walī 'ahd*) after Amīn.

Since Ma'mūn was in Khurasan at the time of his father's demise, he remained there permanently and kept the government of Khurasan firmly under his own control. Amīn summoned Mu'taman back from the western lands (*maghrib*) and ordered him to renounce his succession rights. Amīn had allegiance made to his own son as his successor, and the son was given the honorific title (*laqab*) of *al-Nāṭiq bi 'l-Ḥaqq* 'He Who Enunciates the Divine Truth'. He wrote a letter to Ma'mūn summoning him back from Khurasan. Ma'mūn, however, was very shrewd and sagacious, and realised what Muḥammad al-Amīn was up to. He made excuses and did not go to Baghdad. [M 199] Muḥammad al-Amīn then despatched 'Alī b. 'Īsā to attack Ma'mūn. When Ma'mūn got news of this, he consulted with Faḍl b. Sahl about what he should do, and with his concurrence and advice, and that of Dhūbān the astrologer,[155] he sent Ṭāhir b. al-Ḥusayn b. Muṣ'ab against 'Alī b. 'Īsā. The two commanders met up with each other one stage away from Ray, and the armies made contact and engaged in battle. It was not long before Ṭāhir gained the victory and 'Alī b. 'Īsā was killed. Ṭāhir cut off his head and sent it to Ma'mūn, and from there he headed towards Iraq.

Muḥammad Amīn sent 'Abd al-Raḥmān b. Jabala with an army of 30,000 troops to combat Ṭāhir. A mighty battle took place between the two sides near Hamadān. 'Abd al-Raḥmān was defeated and withdrew into Hamadān. Ṭāhir laid siege to the town. At that point, 'Abd al-Raḥmān came forth seeking a guarantee of protection (*zīnhār*), but after a certain period of time had elapsed, he then adopted a stratagem. With a contingent of troops that had arrived from Baghdad as reinforcements for him, 'Abd al-Rahmān fell upon Ṭāhir's army at midday. Ṭāhir had marched out, and they joined together in battle. All that body of troops (i.e the reinforcements from Baghdad) were killed. 'Abd al-Raḥmān was taken prisoner, his head was cut off and Ṭāhir sent it to Ma'mūn. He then advanced against Baghdad. Harthama b. A'yan arrived from Khurasan to reinforce Ṭāhir. The united forces proceeded to Baghdad. The troops encamped in the vicinity of Baghdad, and battle was joined, Baghdad was besieged and Muḥammad b. Zubayda's position became desperate.

When he was reduced to extremities and the treasury was empty, and all the court troops (*ḥasham*), soldiers, subjects and clients (*mawlāyān*) abandoned Muḥammad al-Amīn, and he was left isolated with no possible way out, he sent a note to Harthama saying, 'I'm coming to you this night.' Harthama [H 134] took a river boat (*zawraq*) and sailed along the Tigris to Baghdad. Muḥammad came up to him, and they were both in the boat. Ṭāhir was informed of this situation. He blocked Muḥammad's way of escape and ordered stones to be hurled till Muḥammad's boat was eventually shattered. The skipper of the boat got hold of Harthama and hauled him out. Muḥammad knew how to swim [M 200] and tried to get out of the Tigris waters. One of Ṭāhir's slave guards (*ghulām*) seized him, brought him to his own tent and informed Ṭāhir. Ṭāhir ordered that same ghulām to cut off Muḥammad's head. Then he sent Muḥammad, son of Zubayda's, head, and the cloak, staff[156] and prayer-mat of the Prophet, God's prayers and peace be upon him and his house, to Ma'mūn by the hand of his own paternal cousin Muḥammad b. al-Ḥusayn (text, *al-Ḥasan*) b. Muṣ'ab. Ma'mūn rewarded the latter with a present of a million dirhams.[157]

When Ma'mūn was installed in Khurasan, he dispensed justice and equity copiously. He used to come every day to the congregational mosque in Merv and there would hear complaints of tyranny and injustice. He would listen to what people had to say and give them appropriate redress.[158]

Ghassān b. 'Abbād

When the deposed caliph's head was brought to Khurasan and Ma'mūn was firmly established in the caliphate, he conferred the governorship of Khurasan on Ghassān b. 'Abbād in Rajab of the year 204 [/December 819–January 820].[159] Ghassān dismissed Layth b. Sa'd from Samarqand and gave the governorship there to Nūḥ b. Asad. During Ghassān's time of office, Ma'mūn left Merv and went to Baghdad. ['Alī b.] Mūsā al-Riḍā, may God Most High be pleased with him, died at Ṭūs, and Faḍl b. Sahl was killed in the bathhouse at Sarakhs. When what he had left behind was investigated, they found fastened round his waist a women's jewel box secured with a seal and lock. They opened the lock and found there a golden box which was fastened up. They opened it and found there a piece of silk on which was written, 'In the name of God, the Merciful, the Compassionate. This is the horoscope (*ḥukm*) for Faḍl b. Sahl which has been prepared on his behalf. He will enjoy forty-eight years of life and then he will be killed between water and fire.' He did indeed have this term of life, and then Ma'mūn's maternal relative, Ghālib b. Ustadsīs,[160] killed him in the bathhouse in the town of Sarakhs.[161]

PART TWO: THE TAHIRIDS AND SAFFARIDS

[N 5, M 201]

Ṭāhir (I) b. al-Ḥusayn

Then Ma'mūn gave Khurasan to Ṭāhir b. al-Ḥusayn b. Muṣʿab in Shawwāl of the year 205 [/March–April 821]. Ṭāhir sent his deputy [to Khurasan] [H 135] and himself went to combat Naṣr b. Shabath.[1] He engaged him in battle at Raqqa. Then Ma'mūn sent ʿAbdallāh b. Ṭāhir to Raqqa in place of his father, and Ṭāhir came to Khurasan in the month of Rabīʿ II of the year 206 [/September 821], and governed it for a year and a half. Subsequently, he omitted Ma'mūn's name in the bidding prayer (*khuṭba*) in one of the Friday worships, but died on that very same night, in Jumādā II of the year 207 [/October–November 822], having made his son Ṭalḥa b. Ṭāhir his deputy (*khalīfat*).[2]

Ṭalḥa b. Ṭāhir (I)

When Ṭāhir died, his son Ṭalḥā succeeded to the governorship of Khurasan. There was much warfare between Ṭalḥa and Ḥamza the Khārijite, until in the year 213 [/828–9] Ḥamza was killed.[3] Ma'mūn had given Ṭāhir b. al-Ḥusayn the honorific title of *Dhu 'l-Yamīnayn* ('The Man with Two Right Hands'). The reason for this was that, when Ma'mūn was despatching Ṭāhir against ʿAlī b. ʿIsā, at that moment [N 6] when Ṭāhir set out, Faḍl b. Sahl sought a prognostication and cast a horoscope, and found two favourable stars, one of them Canopus and the other the Great Dog Star, positioned in the centre of the firmament. For this reason, Ma'mūn gave Ṭāhir the name Dhu 'l-Yamīnayn. Because of that propitious prognostication which had been made, Ma'mūn took a great liking to the science of astrology. At the moment when he awarded a banner for Ṭāhir b. al-Ḥusayn (i.e. at his official departure to take up his new post), Faḍl said, 'O Ṭāhir, I have placed a banner in your hands which no-one will strike down for sixty-five years.' From the time when Ṭāhir marched out of Merv to confront ʿAlī b. ʿĪsā to the time of the downfall of the Tahirid house and Yaʿqūb b. al-Layth's seizure of Muḥammad b. Ṭāhir, was sixty-five years.

When Ṭalḥa b. Ṭāhir had disposed of the threat from Ḥamza the Khārijite and the latter had been killed, he himself died in that same year, having made Muḥammad b. Ḥamīd/Ḥumayd al-Ṭāhirī his deputy over Khurasan.[4] [M 202]

ʿAbdallāh b. Ṭāhir (I)

When Ma'mūn heard the news of Ṭalḥa's death, he conferred the governorship of Khurasan on ʿAbdallāh b. Ṭāhir, who sent ʿAlī b. Ṭāhir to Khurasan as his deputy whilst he himself remained at Dīnawar, from where he was sending armies to combat Bābak the Khurram-dīn.[5] The Khārijites launched an attack on one of the villages of Nishapur and slaughtered a large number of people. When news of that reached Ma'mūn, he ordered ʿAbdallāh b. [H 136] Ṭāhir to proceed to Nishapur and deal with that situation, sending ʿAlī b. Hishām to take ʿAbdallāh b. Ṭāhir's place at Dīnawar. ʿAbdallāh reached Nishapur in Rajab of the year 215 [/August–September 830] at a time when Khurasan was racked by Khārijite strife. He sent on ʿAzīz b. Nūḥ with the vanguard of the army together with 10,000 men, and he eventually cleared Khurasan of the Khārijites and killed large numbers of them.

Muḥammad b. Ḥamīd/Ḥumayd al-Ṭāhirī acted as ʿAbdallāh's deputy at Nishapur [N 7] and committed many oppressive acts, appropriating part of the main thoroughfare [through the town] and incorporating it within his own residential quarters. When ʿAbdallāh b. Ṭāhir came to Nishapur, he made enquiries. The Ḥājj Aḥmad, who was a professional witness (*muʿaddil*), told him that Muḥammad b. Ḥamīd/Ḥumayd had appropriated part of the main thoroughfare and incorporated it within his own residential quarters. ʿAbdallāh dismissed him from office and ordered that the wall blocking off the Muslims' road should be removed.[6]

During ʿAbdallāh's time, Ma'mūn passed away and Muʿtaṣim succeeded to the caliphate. Muʿtaṣim was hostile towards ʿAbdallāh. The reason for this was that, when ʿAbdallāh was Ma'mūn's chamberlain and palace doorkeeper (*ḥājib*), Muʿtaṣim had come one day to Ma'mūn's gate, with a retinue of his personal ghulāms, at an inappropriate time. ʿAbdallāh had said, 'This is not the right time to pay your respects with so many ghulāms.' Muʿtaṣim replied, 'You find it appropriate to ride out with 400 ghulāms, so why shouldn't I ride forth with this number of men?' ʿAbdallāh said, 'Even though I may ride out with 4,000 ghulāms, I won't agree to your coming with just four!' Muʿtaṣim went back filled with anger. When Ma'mūn heard about the incident, he summoned the two of them and brought about a reconciliation. [M 203]

When Muʿtaṣim succeeded to the throne, he sent to ʿAbdallāh an investiture diploma for the governorship of Khurasan. He also sent him an extremely beautiful slave girl, and he gave her a towel, telling her, 'When ʿAbdallāh has intimate relations with you, give him this towel so that he may clean himself up.'[7] But when the slave girl reached ʿAbdallāh's house, she became enamoured of him and told him about that secret plot. ʿAbdallāh maintained an attitude of prudence and took care always to keep himself out of Muʿtaṣim's clutches, openly displaying a feeling of mistrust and suspiciousness. One day, ʿAbdallāh said to his secretary Ismāʿīl [b. Ḥammād], 'I intend to go on the Pilgrimage.' Ismāʿīl replied, 'O Amir, you are too sensible to undertake such a senseless business!' ʿAbdallāh said, 'You've spoken truly; in saying this, I was only testing you!'[8]

In the year 224 [/839] there was an earthquake in Farghāna, with many dwellings destroyed.[9]

During ʿAbdallāh's time, [N 8] Māzyār b. Qārin rebelled in Ṭabaristān, adopted the religion of Bābak the Khurram-dīn and put on red garments. [H 137] ʿAbdallāh marched thither, engaged him in battle and captured Māzyār in the year 227 [/841–2]. He sent him on to Muʿtaṣim, who ordered Māzyār to be lashed with 500 strokes, from the effects of which he died that same day.[10]

The people of Nishapur and Khurasan used continually to come to ʿAbdallāh and there were continuous disputes over the subterranean irrigation channels (*kārīz-hā*). There was nothing to be found in the law books or the traditions of the Messenger [of God], God's prayers and peace be upon him, concerning the constituting of such channels and their regulation. Hence ʿAbdallāh assembled all the legal scholars of Khurasan and some of those from Iraq, and he commissioned them to compose a book on the legal aspects and regulation of such channels. This book was called the *Kitāb-i Qunī* 'Book Concerning Irrigation Channels', with the aim that the regulatory practices laid down there should now form the basis of [future] practice. That book remains in existence till this present time, and the legal and regulatory practices regarding underground irrigation channels and other watercourses[11] followed in our own time are conducted according to what is laid down in that book.

Many admirable practices and customs are attributed to ʿAbdallāh b. Ṭāhir. One of them was that he sent a letter to all his officials, saying,

> We have laid upon you the obligation to be alert and [M 204] not sunk in neglectfulness. You should avoid evil behaviour and seek to maintain an attitude of personal uprightness. You should treat with consideration the cultivators in your area of administrative responsibility, and should give support and strengthening to agriculture when it becomes depressed. Now return to your charges, for God, He is Exalted and Magnified, has provided our sustenance through the work of their hands, has brought about a state of peace and security through their utterances and has prohibited acts of oppression against them!

ʿAbdallāh b. Ṭāhir used to say, 'One should bestow knowledge on the worthy and the unworthy alike, since knowledge is too circumspect to find a permanent home with the unworthy [anyway].'

When Muʿtaṣim passed away, Wāthiq succeeded to the caliphate, and he sent an investiture diploma for the governorship of Khurasan [N 9] to ʿAbdallāh. ʿAbdallāh himself died during Wāthiq's caliphate, in the year 230 [/844–5].

Ṭāhir (II) b. ʿAbdallāh

Wāthiq then bestowed Khurasan on Ṭāhir b. ʿAbdallāh, whose patronymic was Abu 'l-Ṭayyib. The latter was at this time in Ṭabaristān but returned to Nishapur and appointed Musʿab b. ʿAbdallāh as his deputy (i.e. in Ṭabaristān). Wāthiq died in Dhu 'l-Ḥijja of the year 232 [/July–August 847].

Mutawakkil succeeded to the caliphate, and he sent an investiture diploma for Khurasan to Ṭāhir. After a certain period of time elapsed, Mutawakkil was killed. Muntaṣir succeeded to the caliphate, and he sent an investiture diploma for Khurasan to Ṭāhir.

Abu 'l-Ḥasan Shaʿrānī[12] related that Ṭāhir had a slave boy (*khādim*) who had a fair skin and handsome face. He handed him over to me, saying, 'Sell this lad!' The slave boy made much lamentation and burst out weeping. I delayed doing anything, for he was a remarkably handsome slave boy, and I went back to the Amir, asking him, 'Why are you selling this slave boy?' He replied, 'One night he was asleep within the palace, and a draught blew back his garment (i.e. from his body). [H 138] I looked at him and saw how delectable he was, and I was afraid lest an evil spirit put lascivious thoughts into my mind.' Then he gave orders for presents to be got ready and the slave boy was sent, accompanied by other presents, to Mutawakkil.

One day a document was written out and presented to him. In it was written, 'If the judgement of the rightly guided one (*ra'y-i rashīd*) thinks fit . . .' [M 205] He issued an ordinance under his signature and seal (*tawqīʿ*), saying, 'I don't want to be called "rightly guided", since this name should only be given to someone whom God, He is Exalted and Magnified, has made deserving of it.'

When Muntaṣir died, Mustaʿīn succeeded to the caliphate, and he retained Ṭāhir as governor of Khurasan. Ṭāhir passed away in the year 248 [/862].[13] [N 10]

Muḥammad b. Ṭāhir (II)

Mustaʿīn bestowed Khurasan on Muḥammad b. Ṭāhir. The latter was negligent and lacking in foresight. He plunged himself into wine drinking, and became occupied with music and singing and with merrymaking to the pitch that, through his neglectfulness, Ṭabaristān became disturbed and the ʿAlid Ḥasan b. Zayd rebelled in the year 251 [/865], at the time when Sulaymān b. ʿAbdallāh b. Ṭāhir was governor in Ṭabaristān. Ḥasan, son of Zayd, clashed with him in battle, Sulaymān was defeated and Ḥasan seized control of Ṭabaristān. Mustaʿīn was deposed.[14] Then Muhtadī succeeded to the caliphate, and ruled as caliph for fifteen months and sixteen days until he was deposed. Then Muʿtamid succeeded to the caliphate in Rajab of the year 256 [/June 870]. Muḥammad b. Ṭāhir remained governor in Khurasan, whilst Ṭabaristān and Gurgān had become stirred up in rebellion. The paternal nephews of Muḥammad b. Ṭāhir were jealous of him, and they gave support to Yaʿqūb, son of Layth, and emboldened him until he attacked Khurasan. He marched forth, took Muḥammad captive and himself assumed power in Khurasan.[15]

The Outbreak of Yaʿqūb b. al-Layth

Yaʿqūb b. al-Layth b. Muʿaddal was a man of obscure origins from the village of Qarnīn in the rural hinterland (*rūstā*) of Sistan. When he came to the city [of Sistan, i.e. Zarang], he chose to take up the profession of coppersmith and set about learning it. He worked as an artisan for fifteen dirhams a month. [H 139] The reason for his obtaining a position of maturity and leadership was that he was a bold youth (*jawān mard*) in all that he undertook and practised. [N 11] He used to eat and keep company with people, [M 206] and, in addition to that, he was sharp-witted and manly, and all his close companions held him in high respect.[16] In every undertaking that came up, amongst his co-participants he would assume the leadership.

From working as a coppersmith, he became an *ʿayyār*, and from that, took up robbery and brigandage.[17] He rose to become a senior commander (*sarhang*) and assembled around himself a troop of cavalry. In this way he gradually rose to become an amir. First of all, he achieved military command at Bust under Naṣr b. Ṣāliḥ, and [eventually] the position of amir of Sistan. When Sistan passed into his hands, he did not remain content to stay there but said, 'If I rest here on my laurels, people will not give me support again.' Then he came from Sistan to Bust and seized it, and from there marched against Panjwāy and Tegīnābād and attacked the Ratbīl/Zunbīl. He employed a ruse and killed the Ratbīl/Zunbīl, and seized Panjwāy in Rukhwad/Rukhūd.[18] From there he proceeded to Ghaznin, occupied Zābulistān and razed the inner city (*shahristān*) of Ghaznin to the ground. He came to Gardīz and made war on its amir, Abū Manṣūr Aflaḥ b. Muḥammad b. Khāqān. He wrought much slaughter until negotiations between the two sides took place, and Abū Manṣūr pledged and undertook to send to Sistan each year a tribute (*kharāj*) of 10,000 dirhams.[19]

From there, Ya'qūb went back, and [then] led an expedition to Balkh. He captured Bāmiyān in the year 256 [/870], destroyed Nawshād at Balkh and razed to the ground all the buildings that Dāwūd b. al-'Abbās b. Hāshim b. Bānījūr had erected.[20] From there he turned back and went to Kabul, and subdued the Kābul Shāh. Then he captured Pīrūz,[21] and went to Bust and laid on its people [H 140] financial impositions of all kinds. [N 12] He was angry with the people of Bust because they had previously inflicted a defeat on him. From there he returned to Sistan.

In the year 257[/871] he went to Herat. He besieged 'Abd al-Raḥmān the Khārijite in Karūkh.[22] When 'Abd al-Raḥmān faced defeat in that fortress, he came forth seeking a guarantee of protection, together with a group of his commanders, including Mahdī son of Muḥsin, Muḥammad b. N.w.la, Aḥmad b. Mūjib and Ṭāhir b. Ḥafṣ. From there Ya'qūb went on to Pūshang, [M 207] and took captive Ṭāhir b. al-Ḥusayn b. Ṭāhir, and from there returned to Sistan.

A conflict broke out between 'Abdallāh b. [Muḥammad b.] Ṣāliḥ Sagzī and his two brothers, Faḍl . . ., and Ya'qūb, son of Layth, in which 'Abdallāh struck Ya'qūb with his sword and wounded him. Because of this, all three brothers fled from Sistan and came to Nishapur seeking the protection of Muḥammad b. Ṭāhir. Ya'qūb wrote a letter demanding their extradition, but Muḥammad b. Ṭāhir refused. Ya'qūb came to Khurasan in pursuit of them and sent an envoy to Muḥammad b. Ṭāhir. When Ya'qūb's envoy arrived there (i.e. at Nishapur) and sought admission to the court, Muḥ ammad's doorkeeper replied, 'There's no court session, the Amir's gone to sleep'. The envoy said, 'Someone has come who will wake him from his slumbers!' and the envoy went back. Ya'qūb marched on Nishapur, and 'Abdallāh Sagzī fled to Gurgān with his brothers. When Ya'qūb reached Farhādhān,[23] three stages from Nishapur, the *sarhangs* and Muḥammad's paternal cousins all came out to meet Ya'qūb and offered their service, with the exception of Ibrāhīm b. Aḥmad. Ya'qūb entered Nishapur with them. Muḥammad b. Ṭāhir sent Ibrāhīm b. Ṣāliḥ al-Marwazi to Ya'qūb with a message, saying, 'If you have come on the Commander of the Faithful's instructions, show me your investiture diploma and patent and I'll hand over the governorship to you; if not, go back home!' When the envoy got back to Ya'qūb and delivered the message, Ya'qūb drew out his sword from beneath his prayer rug [N 13] and said, 'This is my document of appointment and standard!' Ya'qūb reached Nishapur and encamped at

Shādyākh. He seized Muḥammad and had him brought before him, heaped copious reproaches on him and seized all his treasuries. This arrest of Muḥammad took place on 2 Shawwāl of the year 259 [/1 August 873]. [H 141]

Yaʿqūb summoned Ibrāhīm b. Aḥmad and said, 'All the troops and retainers (*ḥasham*) have come over to my side; why didn't you come?' Ibrāhīm replied, 'May God vouchsafe strength to the Amir! I had no knowledge of or connection with you such that I should come to you, nor had I any correspondence with you. I had no grounds for complaint against Amir Muḥammad that [M 208] I should abandon him. I did not consider it lawful to betray my lord, and there was no question of repaying him or his father with treachery.' Yaʿqūb received these words with approbation, treated him as a close intimate and made him one of his court circle, saying, 'An unassuming person like you should be cherished!' All those persons who had come out to meet him and escort him to the town he mulcted of their possessions and stripped them of their wealth.[24]

He sent a letter to Ḥasan b. Zayd in Gurgān demanding of him the surrender of ʿAbdallāh Sagzī and his brothers. Ḥasan b. Zayd sent back a reply but did not forward them. Yaʿqūb launched an attack on Gurgān. Ḥasan b. Zayd was defeated and fled before him to Āmul. From there he went out by the road to Rūyān via the Kandasān pass.[25] When Yaʿqūb reached Ḥasan's encampment he found it empty. He gave orders to his troops to carry off everything they could and to burn the rest, and everything was consumed. This happened in the year 260 [/873–74].[26] ʿAbdallāh and his brothers went to Ray and sought refuge with Ṣallābī.[27] Yaʿqūb wrote a letter to Ṣallābī demanding that he should hand them over; if he should refuse, he would deal with him exactly how he had dealt with Muḥammad [b. Ṭāhir] and Ḥasan [b. Zayd]. The people in Ray were terrified by that letter, and Ṣallābī despatched both brothers[28] on to Yaʿqūb. Yaʿqūb brought them to Nishapur, and at Shādyākh had them crucified against the town wall with iron nails. He carried off the Tahirids' wealth and possessions and returned to Sistan. He had Muḥammad b. Ṭāhir, [N 14] together with seventy others, brought in bonds, and Muḥammad remained thus fettered up to the time when Muwaffaq defeated Yaʿqūb at Dayr al-ʿĀqūl and Muḥammad b. Ṭāhir managed to escape, this being in Rajab of the year 263 [/April 877].

Yaʿqūb then (i.e. after the Nishapur and Gurgān expeditions) led a campaign into Fars and occupied Fars and Ahwāz. He mounted an expedition against Baghdad with the aim of marching on it, deposing Muʿtamid from the caliphate and placing Muwaffaq on the throne. Muwaffaq revealed this intention to Muʿtamid. Yaʿqūb kept on secretly writing letters to Muwaffaq, and the latter would be showing these letters to Muʿtamid, until Yaʿqūb reached Dayr al-ʿĀqūl in the vicinity of [M 209] Baghdad, at the place where a connecting canal from the Euphrates joins the Tigris,[29] and his army encamped there. Muwaffaq gave orders for the waters of the Tigris to be released against him, the greater part of Yaʿqūb's army perished, and he himself was put to flight and retreated. Because of that ignominy he contracted dysentery, and when he reached Jundīshāpūr he died of it. He had never [previously] suffered defeat at the hands of his opponents, and no-one had ever been able to dupe him. [H 142] His death was on Saturday, 14 Shawwāl of the year 265 [/9 June 879].[30]

ʿAmr b. al-Layth

Muʿtamid and Muwaffaq then bestowed the provinces of Khurasan, Sistan and Fars on ʿAmr b. al-Layth. ʿAmr came back from Jundīshāpūr to [Fars], and from there set out towards Herat. Khujistānī established himself in Nishapur. Ḥ.y.kān (? Jaykān) the Qur'ān-reader, Yaḥyā b. Muḥammad b. Yaḥyā al-Dhuhlī,[31] and all the volunteer fighters for the faith (*muṭṭawwiʿa*) and religious lawyers of Nishapur inclined towards ʿAmr's side because he [N 15] was sent by the Commander of the Faithful and had an investiture diploma and standard from him. Khujistānī was spoken of opprobriously because he was a rebel against the ruling authority (*sulṭān*). When Khujistānī got news of this, he appointed Aḥmad b. Manna as his deputy in Nishapur and himself proceeded to Herat in order to engage ʿAmr b. al-Layth in battle. ʿAmr shut himself up in Herat in Ṣafar of the year 267 [/September–October 880], and Khujistānī was unable to make any headway. From there he (i.e. Khujistānī) led an expedition against Sistan. When he reached Ramal Samm (?), he besieged that stronghold, which was held by Shādān, son of Masrūr, and Aṣram. Then Khujistānī became frustrated and disappointed and went back to Nishapur, killing a number of people there. The pressure was thus lifted from ʿAmr's mind.[32]

It is related that ʿAmr b. al-Layth exercised governorship over Khurasan in the best possible and most complete fashion and established a governmental system according to the established norms, in such a way that no-one was seized or imprisoned in the course of that. It is further related that ʿAmr b. al-Layth had four treasuries, one treasury for weapons and three for money, and these used to accompany him at all times. One of these last three was a treasury for money collected as legal alms (*ṣadaqāt*), as poll tax (*gazīd-hā*[33]) and suchlike, [M 210] and that used to be expended on the quarterly-paid salaries (*bīstagānī*) of the troops. The second was the privy treasury (*māl-i khāṣṣ*), which used to be gathered in from levies on crop yields and estates (i.e. from crown lands), and that was expended on living expenses of the court and upkeep of the kitchen and suchlike. [H 143] The third was a treasury for monies derived from extraordinary taxes (*aḥdāth*) and confiscations from members of the court troops and retainers (*ḥasham*) who were in collusion with enemies, and these monies used to be expended on payments for the court troops and retainers, for spies and intelligence agents (*munhiyān*), diplomatic envoys and suchlike.

ʿAmr b. al-Layth was very active and energetic regarding the affairs of the court troops and retainers and the army at large, and every three months he would reward them with salary payments and gifts. He was also extremely acute and aware of what was going on. When he made confiscations he would make them at the opportune moment and adduce plausible excuses for mulcting a person of his wealth. It is related that, one day, Muḥammad b. Bishr came into ʿAmr's presence at a time when the treasury for salary payments (i.e. the third of the treasuries for money) was empty and the appointed time for handing out salary payments to the court troops and retainers had drawn near. ʿAmr was always in need of money. [N 16] He turned towards Muḥammad b. Bishr and began to heap reproaches on him, saying, 'You know what you would have done in my place? You'd have done such-and-such,' and he went on saying all sorts of things. Muḥammad realised what ʿAmr meant and said, 'May God strengthen the Amir! All the wealth that I possess, whether in the form of fine horses,[34] slaves or landed property, amounts to more than fifty purses full of dirhams. Accept this from me directly, and relieve me of those reproaches and menaces.' ʿAmr commented, 'I've never seen a more perspicacious fellow than this one!' and he told Muḥammad, 'Go and lodge this money in the treasury, and no fault shall be imputed to you.' Muḥammad b. Bishr then deposited that money in the treasury and thereby became safe from the many troubles, injuries and reproaches that his friends suffered.[35]

It was ʿAmr's customary practice that, when the beginning of the year came round (i.e. Nawrūz), he would have two drums, one called 'the blessed one' and the other 'the auspicious one'. He would order both drums to be beaten so that all the troops would be aware that it was pay day. Then the head of the army department (*ʿāriḍ*) Sahl b. Ḥamdān would sit down and pour out purses filled with dirhams before him and the *ʿāriḍ*'s assistant would bring forward the pay register. The name of ʿAmr b. [M 211] al-Layth would come up first. He would step forth from amongst the throng of troops. The *ʿāriḍ* would scrutinise him and authenticate him as the person described in the register, pass his mount and weapons as being in good order, examine thoroughly his whole equipment, and express approval and praise. He would weigh out 300 dirhams, place them in a purse and hand them over to him. ʿAmr would take them and place them down the leg of his boot, exclaiming, 'Praise be to God! God Most High has bestowed on me the privilege of showing my obedience to the Commander of the Faithful and has made me worthy of receiving His favours!' and then he would go back to his place. He would go up onto an eminence, sit down and watch the *ʿāriḍ* intently until the latter had in exactly the same way scrutinised every single soldier, would look searchingly at the horse, saddle, footwear and equipment of the cavalrymen and infantrymen, and would hand out pay to each [N 17] one of them according to their ranks. He used to have spies over every commander, field officer and leader so that he was aware of everything about that person.[36] ʿAmr was extremely intelligent, crafty and clearsighted.

The circumstance of the reversal of his power and fortunes were as follows. When ʿAmr [H 144] sent Rāfiʿ's head to Muʿtaḍid in the year [2]84 [/897], he sought from the caliph an investiture diploma for Transoxania such as Ṭāhir b. ʿAbdallāh had had. Muʿtaḍid sent the general (*ḥājib*) Jaʿfar b. Baghlāghuz (?) to ʿAmr, and Jaʿfar brought a document detailing presents to ʿAmr. When ʿAmr b. al-Layth read that document, it was the conferment of the governorship over Transoxania that pleased him more than all those presents. Jaʿfar then [went back] to the caliph's son ʿAlī b. al-Muʿtaḍid Muktafī. ʿUbaydallāh b. Sulaymān and Badr al-Kabīr, who were both at Ray, wrote to the seat of the caliphate. The investiture diploma for Transoxania was written out immediately and conveyed to ʿAmr by hand of Naṣr al-Mukhtārī, the ghulām of Abū Sāj.

Jaʿfar came into ʿAmr's presence with the investiture diploma and presents. The presents comprised seven sets of robes of honour, a coat (*badana*) woven with unpierced pearls (*durr*) and set with jewels and pearls (*marwārīd*); a crown set with rubies and other jewels; eleven horses, ten of which had saddles and accoutrements decorated with gold, and one of them [M 212] with a saddle, bridle and accoutrements decorated with gold and set with emeralds and pearls, and a horse with its saddle-felt and outer covering all set with jewels and the horse's four legs shoed with golden horseshoes; and many chests [of precious objects]. All these presents were successively laid out before ʿAmr and the chests placed within his palace. Jaʿfar clothed ʿAmr in those robes of honour one by one. Whenever he donned one of the robes, he performed two *rakʿat*s of the ritual worship and [N 18] offered up thanks for it. Then he laid the investiture diploma for Transoxania before him. ʿAmr said, 'What am I to do with this, since this province can't be wrested from Ismāʿīl b. Aḥmad except by a hundred thousand drawn swords?' Jaʿfar replied, 'You requested this; you will now know best how to achieve it.' ʿAmr took that investiture diploma, kissed it, placed it on his head and then set it down before himself. Jaʿfar went out.[37]

Against Ismāʿīl b. Aḥmad, ʿAmr b. al-Layth sent Muḥammad b. Bishr, ʿAlī b. Sharwīn and Aḥmad Darāz along the road to Āmūy with the vanguard of the army. Ismāʿīl b. Aḥmad crossed over the [Oxus] river by way of Zam, advanced towards them (sc. ʿAmr's commanders and their troops) and engaged them in battle. Aḥmad Darāz deserted to Ismāʿīl b. Aḥmad's side under a promise of safe conduct. Muḥammad b. Bishr was put to flight and the [Samanid] army went in pursuit after him. In the course of that flight he was killed together with 7,000 of his troops. ʿAlī b. Sharwīn was taken prisoner. This was on Monday, 18 Shawwāl of the year 286 [/27 October 899]. [H 145] When ʿAlī b. Sharwīn was captured, Aḥmad Darāz interceded for his life, but he was held in imprisonment at Bukhara till he died. Ismāʿīl b. Aḥmad went to Bukhara. The army of Sistan came back to ʿAmr in a defeated state and reached Nishapur. When ʿAmr saw them he became distressed and very cast down. He was told, 'O Amir, a large meal much finer than this has been cooked, and we have so far drunk only one goblet; whoever is a real man, say, "Come, drink down the rest".' ʿAmr, however, remained silent.

ʿAmr b. al-Layth then prepared an army and distributed weapons, and set out from Nishapur towards Transoxania with a well-armed, fully-equipped host. [M 213] When he reached Balkh he came directly up against Ismāʿīl b. Aḥmad and a battle ensued. It did not take long before ʿAmr b. al-Layth was defeated. His army was routed, and in the course of this, ʿAmr was taken prisoner and made captive, and was brought before Ismāʿīl b. Aḥmad. This defeat of ʿAmr was on Tuesday, 14–15 Rabīʿ [N 19] I of the year 287 [/19–20 March 900]. Ismāʿīl straightway sent ʿAmr to Samarqand. When the news reached Muʿtaḍid he was filled with joy, and sent ʿAbdallāh b. al-Fatḥ to Khurasan. In the year 288 [/901] he despatched to Ismāʿīl at Samarqand an investiture diploma for Khurasan, a standard, a crown and numerous robes of honour. Muʿtaḍid sent Ashnās to bring back ʿAmr with him. When ʿAmr was brought to Baghdad and he came before Muʿtaḍid, the latter exclaimed, 'Praise be to God that an end has been put to your evil and people's minds have been relieved of concern with you,' and he ordered him to be held in prison where he remained till he died. His death was in the year 289 [/902].[38] [M 214]

PART THREE: THE SAMANIDS

[Chapter Twelve Concerning] the Rule and the Lineage of the Samanids

The occasion of the Samanids' rise to power was as follows. Sāmān Khudā b. Ḥām.tān, after whom all this family is named, was a Magian (*mugh*) and followed the religion of Zoroaster. His genealogy was Sāmān Khudāh b. Khām.tā b. Nūsh b. Ṭamghāsb b. Shād.l b. Bahrām Chūbīn b. Bahrām [H 146] Ḥ.sīs b. Kūz.k b. Athfiyān b. Kirdār b. Dīrkār b. Jam b. J.y.r b. B.stār b. Kh.dād b. R.n.jhān b. F.y.r b. F.rāw.l b. Sīm b. Bahrām b. Shās.b b. Kūz.k b. J.r.dād b. S.f.r.s.b b. K.r.k.y.n b. M.y.lād b. M.r.s (?Narsī) b. Marzwān b. Mihrān b. Fādhān b. K.sh.rād b. Sād.sād b. Bishdād (Pishdād) b. Akhshīn (? Afshīn) b. Fardīn b. W.mām b. Ar.sāṭīn b. D.w.s.r Manūchihr b. Kūz.k b. Īraj b. Afrīdūn b. Athfiyān S.k. M.n S.k b. S.w.rkāw b. Ikhshīd Kāwā b. R.s.d.kāw b. Dīr.kāw b. R.y.m.n.kāw b. B.y.furūsh b. Jamshīd b. Dīw.n.k.hān b. '.s.k.h.d b. Hūshang b. F.rāwak b. M.n.shī b. Kayūmarth, the first ruler on earth.[1]

During that period when Muḥammad al-Amīn was caliph at Baghdad and [N 20] Ma'mūn was at Merv, the latter was governor of Khurasan. This Sāmān Khudāh came and joined Ma'mūn's entourage and became a Muslim at his instigation. He had a son called Asad. Ma'mūn used to look very favourably on this Asad, who had four sons, Nūḥ, Aḥmad, Yaḥyā and Ilyās. Ma'mūn showed favour to them all and they formed part of his entourage because they were men of ancient, noble lineage.

When Ma'mūn went to Baghdad, assumed the caliphate and appointed Ghassān b. ʿAbbād governor of Khurasan, Ma'mūn commended them to him. Hence Ghassān appointed Nūḥ b. Asad governor of Samarqand, Aḥmad b. Asad over Farghāna, Yaḥyā b. Asad over Chāch and Usrūshana, [M 215] and Ilyās b. Asad over Herat.[2]

When Ṭāhir b. al-Ḥusayn came to Khurasan on Ghassān's dismissal, he retained them in these same offices. Out of all these sons, [H 147] Aḥmad was the most useful and experienced. When he died, he left behind two sons, Naṣr and Ismāʿīl. During the time of the Tahirids, they held Samarqand and Bukhara: Naṣr held Samarqand and Ismāʿīl Bukhara. There used to be good relations between the two of them until backbiters incited them against each other and brought about a breach in relations between them. They kept on fanning the flames of that breach until it took firm shape and became permanently established. In the end, they became embroiled in warfare; they marshalled their armies and went out to give battle with each other. In the year 275 [/888–9] they came to blows: Ismāʿīl was victorious over Naṣr, the latter was taken prisoner and he was brought before Ismāʿīl. When he beheld Ismāʿīl, he went before him on foot, kissed his hand and sought his pardon. Ismāʿīl sent him back to Samarqand in a handsome fashion, accompanied by all his court troops and retainers (*ḥasham wa ḥāshiyat*). After that episode, Ismāʿīl made Naṣr his deputy over the whole of Transoxania, and things went smoothly and amicably.[3]

When ʿAmr b. al-Layth sought a grant of Transoxania from Muʿtaḍid and received a favourable answer, he led an expedition against Ismāʿīl. [N 21] Ismāʿīl deployed his army, advanced on ʿAmr and disposed of him once and for all, and he sent ʿAmr to Baghdad, as has been related.

Ismāʿīl b. Aḥmad (I) b. Asad b. Sāmān

When the governorship of Khurasan passed into Ismāʿīl's hands and Muʿtaḍid's investiture diploma and standard arrived, Ismāʿīl b. Aḥmad sent Muḥammad b. Hārūn to take over Gurgān and Ṭabaristān. The latter captured Muḥammad b. Zayd b. Muḥammad and sent him to Ismāʿīl, and the latter bestowed on Muḥammad b. Hārūn the governorship of Gurgān and Ṭabaristān. After a certain period of time had elapsed, Muḥammad b. Hārūn rebelled. Ismāʿīl led an expedition against him and marched to Ray. Ögretmish[4] was killed and Muḥammad b. Hārūn, with his two sons, was captured. This victory [M 216] was on 17 Rajab of the year 289 [/27 June 902]. Ismāʿīl returned and came to Nishapur, and he left Aḥmad b. Sahl in charge of those regions.

At this point, Muʿtaḍid died and Muktafī succeeded to the caliphate. He sent for Ismāʿīl, and after him, for his son Aḥmad, an investiture diploma for Khurasan by the hand of Muḥammad b. ʿAbd al-Ṣamad, together with a diploma for the governorship of Ray, Qazwīn and Zanjān, which he had joined to that of Khurasan. When Muḥammad b. ʿAbd al-Ṣamad reached Nishapur, Ismāʿīl treated him with great honour and presented him with a gift of 300,000 dirhams, sending him back with numerous presents. Then Ismāʿīl bestowed the governorship of Ray on Abū Ṣāliḥ Manṣūr b. Isḥāq, and Manṣūr gave command of the army there (*sarhangī*) to Aḥmad b. Sahl and made him responsible for his, Manṣūr's, personal guard (*ḥaras*). Ismāʿīl gave orders that he himself would be responsible for paying the living allowances of the entire body of troops so that Manṣūr should not have the worry of this.

Ismāʿīl entrusted Gurgān to his son Aḥmad [N 22] and Ṭabaristān to Abu 'l-ʿAbbās ʿAbdallāh b. Muḥammad [b. Nūḥ b. Asad]. He ordered his son to work harmoniously with ʿAbdallāh [H 148] in all affairs and never to oppose him in anything. But subsequently he dismissed his son from the governorship of Gurgān because he had not led a military expedition against Justān.[5] However, Nūḥ's son (i.e. Abu 'l-ʿAbbās ʿAbdallāh) defeated Justān, and he entrusted Gurgān to Bārs,[6] his Commander-in-Chief. Ismāʿīl b. Aḥmad died during the night of Tuesday–Wednesday, 14 Ṣafar of the year 295 [/24 November 907] and received the [posthumous] honorific title of 'The Incisive [Amir]' (*māḍī*).[7]

The Martyred One (*al-shahīd*), Abū Naṣr Aḥmad (II) b. Ismāʿīl

When Ismāʿīl was dying, he made his son Aḥmad his covenanted successor (*walī ʿahd*) over Khurasan.[8] Muktafī sent an investiture diploma for Aḥmad to succeed in Khurasan by the hand of Ṭāhir b. ʿAlī, and the latter raised the standard sent by the caliph with his own hand. When he reached Bukhara, Aḥmad b. Ismāʿīl lodged him handsomely, received him cordially and bestowed on him great sums of money.

In Dhu ʾl-Qaʿda of the year 295 [/August 908], Muktafī died and Muqtadir succeeded in the caliphate. [M 217] Aḥmad b. Ismāʿīl continued to hold the governorship of Khurasan. When he had got the situation at Bukhara fully under control, he formed the intention of going to Ray and of bringing that province likewise under control and putting its affairs in order. Ibrāhīm b. Zaydūya advised him, 'First of all, proceed to Samarqand and seize your paternal uncle Isḥāq b. Aḥmad lest he stir up trouble for you in Khurasan, since he has got delusions of power into his head.' Aḥmad b. Ismāʿīl proceeded to Samarqand, clapped Isḥāq in bonds and sent him to Bukhara. Then in the year 296 [/908–9] he went to Ray, where the investiture diploma sent by Muqtadir reached him.[9] Aḥmad then appointed Abū Jaʿfar Ṣuʿlūk as his deputy at Ray, and [N 23] himself went back homewards in the year 297 [/909–10].

He came to Herat, and from there sent against Sistan Ḥusayn b, ʿAlī al-Marwazī, together with Aḥmad b. Sahl, Muḥammad b. al-Muẓaffar, Ibrāhīm and Yāhyā the sons of Zaydūya, and Aḥmad b. ʿAbdallāh. They besieged Muʿaddal b. [ʿAlī b.] al-Layth in the citadel (i.e. of the capital Zarang).[10] Muʿaddal despatched Abū ʿAlī b. ʿAlī b. al-Layth to Bust and Rukhwad/Rukhūd in order to collect taxation from there and send it back to Muʿaddal. But ʿAlī assembled an army and brought along the wealth and the materials of war, and set out for Sistan. Aḥmad b. Ismāʿīl got news of this, led an expedition from Herat and defeated that army, capturing Abū ʿAlī and seizing all his wealth and materials of war, and despatching him to Baghdad. Ḥusayn b. ʿAlī was meanwhile continuously engaged in warfare with Muʿaddal. [H 149] When Muʿaddal received news of his brother Abū ʿAlī's capture, he made peace, handed over Sistan to Manṣūr b. Isḥāq and himself went back with Ḥusayn b. ʿAlī to Bukhara.

There was a certain man from Aḥmad b. Ismāʿīl's body of troops called Muḥammad b. Hurmuz, known as Mawlā Ṣandalī, who held the tenets of the Khārijites. He was an old and much-experienced man. One day he came to the review ground (*ʿarḍ-gāh*) for his regular pay allotment (*waẓīfat*) and got into an argument with the Head of the Army Department Abu ʾl-Ḥasan ʿAlī b. Muḥammad. The latter told him, 'It would be better if you retired to a *ribāṭ* since you've grown old [M 218] and become useless'. Muḥammad b. Hurmuz became filled with anger. He sought from the Amir permission to depart and went to Sistan. He established himself there and gathered together from the highways all the common people and riff-raff of Sistan. He led a rebellion against Manṣūr b. Isḥāq and secretly gave allegiance to ʿAmr b. Yaʿqūb b. Muḥammad b. ʿAmr b. al-Layth.[11] The commander of the rebels was Muḥammad b. al-ʿAbbās, known as 'Son of the Grave-Digger' (*pisar-i ḥaffār*). They captured Manṣūr b. Isḥāq, placed him in bonds, [N 24] held him in jail and made the *khuṭba* for ʿAmr b. Yaʿqūb.

When Aḥmad b. Ismāʿīl got news of this, he sent Ḥusayn b. ʿAlī to Sistan a second time and fighting between the two sides ensued. The warfare went on continuously for nine months. Subsequently, this old man known as Mawlā Ṣandalī came out onto one of the angles of the citadel (i.e. of the capital Zarang) and called down, 'Tell the *'āriḍ* Abu 'l-Ḥasan that I've fulfilled his command and taken a stronghold (*ribāṭ*) – what else does he ordain?' 'Amr b. Ya'qūb and the Son of the Grave-Digger then sought a guarantee of safe conduct from Ḥusayn [b. 'Alī]. He granted them this and they released Manṣūr b. Isḥāq. Ḥusayn made the Son of the Grave-Digger one of his close circle and used to treat him in a handsome fashion. But then, one day, 'Amr b. Ya'qūb and the Son of the Grave-Digger came into his presence, and he arrested them and placed them in bonds. Ḥusayn understood that Aḥmad [b. Ismā'īl] was going to entrust the governorship of Sistan to him. But Aḥmad then gave it to the Keeper of the Inkstand (*dawīt-dār*) Sīmjūr[12] and ordered Ḥusayn to return with those persons who had been granted safe conduct. Ḥusayn brought 'Amr b. Ya'qūb and the Son of the Grave-Digger to Bukhara in the year 300 [/912–13].[13]

It is related that Aḥmad b. Ismā'īl was extremely fond of hunting. He had gone for a while to Firabr[14] for hunting. When he returned to Bukhara, he gave orders that the army encampment should be set on fire. Whilst he was on the road, a letter from Abu 'l-'Abbās [Muḥammad] Ṣu'lūk, the governor of Ṭabaristān, arrived with the news that Ḥasan b. 'Alī b. Ḥasan b. 'Umar b. 'Alī b. al-Ḥusayn b. 'Alī b. Abī Ṭālib, may God be pleased with them all, who was known as Ḥasan Uṭrūsh, had rebelled.[15] [H 150] When he read the letter, he became perturbed and very downcast. He raised his head towards the heavens and cried, 'O Lord! If Your pre-ordained judgement and the fixed decree of the heavens have so prescribed that this kingly power should pass from me, [M 219] take my soul unto Yourself!' From there he went to the army encampment but found that it had been set on fire, [N 25] and he took that as an unfavourable omen.

There used to be a lion on guard every night at Aḥmad b. Ismā'īl's door so that no-one should be able to make an attempt on his life. That night they did not bring that lion and there were, moreover, none of his retainers sleeping at his door. During the course of the night, a band of his personal ghulāms burst in and cut his throat. This took place on Thursday, 21 Jumādā II of the year 301 [/22 January 914]. He was brought back from there to Bukhara and buried, and a detachment of troops was sent after those ghulāms, some of whom were captured and killed. The secretary Abu 'l-Ḥasan Naṣr b. Isḥāq was suspected of having colluded with the ghulāms in killing the Martyred Amir, and he was seized and executed. Aḥmad b. Ismā'īl was given the honorific title of 'The Martyred Amir'.[16]

The Fortunate One (*al-sa'īd*), Naṣr (II) b. Aḥmad (II)

The Fortunate One Naṣr b. Aḥmad then succeeded to the governorship of Khurasan on 21 Jumādā II of the year 301 [/22 January 914], being eight years old at the time, and he was Amir of Khurasan for thirty years and three months. When the Martyred Amir was killed, the senior religious leaders and court troops came together in Bukhara and agreed upon the succession of his son Naṣr b. Aḥmad. The eunuch (*khādim*) Sa'd placed him on his shoulders and brought him forth so that formal allegiance could be given to him.[17]

The official exercising administrative authority on his behalf was Abū ʿAbdallāh Muḥammad b. Aḥmad al-Jayhānī, who took up the reins of government in a laudable fashion and was running affairs. Abū ʿAbdallāh Jayhānī was a knowledgeable person, very intelligent, strong-willed and virtuous, and he showed percipience and foresight in all matters. He was the author of many compositions in every genre and branch of learning. When he assumed the vizierate, he wrote letters to all the lands of the world and asked for accounts to be written concerning the customs and practices of every court and every government office. [N 26] These accounts were written out and brought to him, including those from such lands as those of Byzantium, Turkestan, [M 220] India, China, Iraq, Syria, Egypt, the land of the Zanj, Zābul, Kabul, Sind and the land of the Arabs. All these customs and practices of the world were brought to him and all those written accounts set down before him. He examined them very closely, and he selected every custom and practice that was specially good and commendable but set aside the less praiseworthy ones. He adopted those good customs and practices, and gave orders that all the personnel of the court and central Dīwān at Bukhara should employ them. Thanks to Jayhānī's good judgement and statesmanship, all affairs of the realm now ran on orderly lines.[18]

Various rebels (*khawārijiyān*) reared their heads. He sent an army against each of them, and all the armies came back victorious and triumphant. He never embarked on any affair without accomplishing his aim. When Naṣr b. Aḥmad assumed office as Amir, the first person to show himself as a rebel was his father's paternal uncle Isḥāq b. Aḥmad at Samarqand. [H 151] His son Ilyās b. Isḥāq assumed command of the army, and the army marched against Bukhara. Naṣr sent Ḥamụya b. ʿAlī against him. The two armies met at Khartang[19] and clashed in battle in the month of Ramaḍān of the year 301 [/April 914]. It was not long before Isḥāq was defeated and fell back on Samarqand. Ḥamūya b. ʿAlī followed him in pursuit. Isḥāq's situation became constricted such that daily existence became disturbed and uncertain for him. When he was reduced to really desperate straits, he sent a message asking for a guarantee of personal safety, and this was accorded him. He came to Bukhara, was well treated during that time and remained there till his death.

When Ḥusayn b. ʿAlī had conquered Sistan, he was anxious for the governorship of Sistan to be given to him, but this was refused. Because of this he became discontented and was watching out for an opportunity to wreak mischief in Aḥmad's rule. When Aḥmad died, Ḥusayn rebelled at Herat, and he kept up his rebellion for some considerable time. One day [N 27] he mustered his army and led an attack on Nishapur. Aḥmad b. Sahl was sent out from Bukhara to engage him in battle. He came to Herat and conquered it, and Manṣūr b. ʿAlī, Ḥusayn's brother, [M 221] sought a guarantee of safety, and they (i.e. Manṣūr and his entourage?) came to Aḥmad, son of Sahl. Aḥmad then came to Nishapur in the month of Rabīʿ I of the year 306 [/August–September 918]. He launched an attack on Ḥusayn b. ʿAlī, in which he took Ḥusayn prisoner, and he established his base at Nishapur. Muḥammad b. Ajhad,[20] commander of the police guard (*ṣāḥib-i shuraṭ*) at Bukhara, was at Merv. He came to Aḥmad b. Sahl, together with Muḥammad b. al-Muhallab b. Zurāra[21] al-Marwazī, and from there they turned back and went to Bukhara.

This Aḥmad b. Sahl stemmed from one of the noble families of the Persians. He was a descendant of Yazdajird, son of Shahriyār,[22] and came from one of the landholding families (*dihqān*) of Jīranj,[23] one of the large villages of Merv. Aḥmad's forefather was called Kāmgār, and there is at Merv a rose which they still call the 'Kāmgārī rose', said to be a deep red colour. This Kāmgārī family was in the service of the Tahirids. Aḥmad's brothers, Faḍl, Ḥusayn and Muḥammad, were all secretaries and experts in astrology, their father Sahl b. Hāshim having been very knowledgeable about the science of astrology. One day, Sahl was asked, 'How is it that you don't look at the horoscopes (lit. 'rising stars') of your sons to see what their future fates will be?' He replied, 'What does it matter if I look, since all three of them are going to be killed on the same day in the course of the factional fighting (*ta'aṣṣub*) of the Arabs,' and it happened exactly thus.

When Aḥmad grew to manhood, he sought to avenge his brothers' blood. A thousand men rallied round him. ʿAmr b. al-Layth sent a body of troops against him, and Aḥmad grew fearful. The person who went in pursuit of him was continually engaging him in fighting but without success. ʿAmr b. al-Layth at that point offered him a guarantee of protection and summoned him to his presence. [N 28] When Aḥmad appeared before ʿAmr, the latter had him seized and consigned him to prison in Sistan (i.e. at the capital Zarang). Aḥmad's sister Ḥafṣa continued to be with Aḥmad during this time. ʿAmr commanded Aḥmad, son of Sahl, to give his sister [in marriage] to his ghulām Sebük-eri[24] and ordered that Aḥmad should be sent to Merv. [H 152] Aḥmad refused to give up his sister but was afraid that ʿAmr would take vengeance on him. So he then had recourse to a stratagem. He told his sister to be assiduous in attendance on ʿAmr's daughter. Aḥmad's sister then interceded with ʿAmr's daughter that Aḥmad should be given permission to go to the bathhouse [M 222] since his hair had grown long. When he received this permission he went along to the bathhouse and kicked up a great deal of fuss regarding his head and his beard. He came out looking like a youth with ringlets and forelocks, put on unfamiliar clothes and went out without any of the keepers of the bathhouse recognising him, and came out into the city of Sistan thus disguised.

Abū Jaʿfar Ṣuʿlūk then sought pardon for him from ʿAmr; the latter granted this and Aḥmad came out into the open in his own guise. ʿAmr laid upon him the condition that he should not don a cap and wear boots (i.e. assume the uniform of a military commander) and Aḥmad promised to adhere to these conditions. Aḥmad secretly fitted out swift riding-camels, left Sistan and came to Merv. He gathered together a force of troops and seized and bound Abū Jaʿfar Ghūrī, ʿAmr's representative there. He sought a guarantee of protection from Ismāʿīl b. Aḥmad and went to Bukhara. Ismāʿīl received him in a hospitable fashion, and mighty deeds were done by Aḥmad and fine victories achieved by him. Aḥmad, son of Sahl, was a man with sound judgement, wily, knowledgeable and shrewd. Since he found a good reception at Ismāʿīl b. Aḥmad's court, he took up residence there. He performed various manly deeds so that he rose higher in the Amir's favour each day. He remained in this favoured position all through the Martyred Amir's reign and [N 29] in the time of the Fortunate Amir was governor of Nishapur.

Then, however, he rebelled at Nishapur and dropped the Fortunate Amir's name from the *khuṭba*. Qarategin, who was governor in Gurgān,[25] led an expedition against him. Aḥmad abandoned Nishapur and went to Merv, constructed there a secure fortress and shut himself within it. When the news reached Bukhara, the Amir despatched Ḥamụya b. ʿAlī to combat him. When the latter's troops entered [the town of] Merv, Ḥamūya ordered the senior officers of his army to enter into an exchange of correspondence with Aḥmad and give themselves out as inclining to his side. When the letters reached Aḥmad, he was taken in by them and dropped his guard. He marched out of Merv (i.e. out of the security of his fortress there) to attack Ḥamūya. The two opposing forces met together at Ḥawzān on the banks of the river.[26] After a time Ḥamūya's forces put Aḥmad's army to flight, and only Aḥmad himself remained. The fighting continued for as long as [M 223] his mount had strength. When his horse collapsed to the ground, he dismounted and fought the opposing troops on foot. In the end, they captured him, bound him and sent him to Bukhara. The Fortunate Amir ordered him to be imprisoned, and he died in jail in Dhu 'l-Ḥijja of the year 307 [/April–May 920].[27]

In the year 317 [/929] the Fortunate Amir went from Bukhara to Nishapur. He kept his brothers Ibrāhīm, Yaḥyā and Manṣūr captive in the citadel of Bukhara, and ordered that their daily sustenance should continue to be supplied there. There was a cook called Abū Bakr b. ʿ.m.y (ʿAmr, ʿUmar?) al-Khabbāz ('The Baker') who used to supply them with this sustenance. He was somewhat stupid and used always to say that the Fortunate Amir was going to experience something unpleasant from him, but people used to laugh at his slow wits. This Abū Bakr acted as an intermediary between the Fortunate Amir's brothers on one side and disruptive elements (*fuḍūliyān*) in Bukhara and the army on the other. One day, they made an agreement amongst themselves and issued forth. They seized the custodian of the citadel, [N 30] released Aḥmad's brothers and everyone who was incarcerated in the citadel and took control of Bukhara. Yaḥyā gave this Abū Bakr the Baker the military command and made him part of his close entourage. [H 153]

When the Fortunate [Amir] got news of this, he came back from Nishapur and led an expedition against Bukhara. Yaḥyā sent Abū Bakr the Baker with his cavalry force to the Oxus bank in order to secure the way and prevent anyone from crossing. He sent with him Ḥusayn b. ʿAlī al-Marwazī's son. When they reached the bank of the Oxus, Muḥammad b. ʿUbaydallāh al-Balʿami[28] sent a message to Ḥusayn's son, and the latter seized Abū Bakr the Baker and placed him in bonds. The Fortunate Amir was able to cross the river; he came to Bukhara and ordered that Abū Bakr should be flogged to death. Then his body was placed in an oven to be roasted. He was roasted in it overnight. The next day his body was pulled out, but none of his limbs had been burnt at all; everyone marvelled at this.[29]

The Fortunate Amir's brothers scattered in various directions. Yaḥyā went to Samarqand and from there to Balkh, thence to Nishapur and finally to Baghdad, where he died. His coffin [M 224] was brought back to Isfijāb.[30]

In the year 320 [/932] al-Qāhir bi'llāh succeeded to the caliphate. The Fortunate Amir came to Nishapur, and he put the affairs of Gurgān in order. When he had finished restoring order there, he gave command of the army in Khurasan to Abū Bakr Muḥammad b. al-Muẓaffar [b. Muḥtāj Chaghānī].[31] When he came back to Bukhara . . .[32] Then al-Rāḍī bi 'llāh succeeded to the caliphate. He sent to Naṣr b. Aḥmad an investiture diploma for Khurasan by the hands of ʿAbbās b. Shaqīq (Shafīq?).

At this moment, Muḥammad b. al-Muẓaffar was at Nishapur and Mardāwīz at Ray. Mardāwīz planned to go from Ray to Isfahan. En route he went into a bathhouse, and there in the year 323 [/935] the ghulāms killed him, Bajkam Mākānī [N 31] being the commander of those ghulāms.[33] Muḥammad b. al-Muẓaffar returned to Nishapur ill and suffering, and his sickness became serious. The Fortunate Amir then sent Abū ʿAlī Aḥmad b. Muḥammad b. al-Muẓaffar [Chaghānī] to Nishapur and recalled Muḥammad [b. al-Muẓaffar]. In Muḥarram of the year 328 [/October–November 939] [Abū ʿAlī] Aḥmad proceeded to Gurgān and besieged Mākān in the town. Mākān's position became constricted, and all his followers sought guarantees of protection from Abū ʿAlī, since supplies of food and fodder had run low. Mākān himself fled to Ṭabaristān, and Abū ʿAlī moved to Qūmis in the year 329 [/940–1] and from there marched against Ray. Wushmgīr b. Ziyār was there, and sought help from Mākān. Mākān came from Ṭabaristān, and a battle took place at the gates of Ray. Abū ʿAlī put them to flight and killed large numbers of their troops. Mākān was killed in the battle. [H 154] Abū ʿAlī sent his head to Bukhara, and the Amir sent it on to Baghdad in the charge of ʿAbbās b. Shaqīq.[34]

Abū ʿAlī freed Mākān's son and 900 Daylamī soldiers of note who had been taken captive in the campaign, set them on camels and sent them to Bukhara. They were kept detained in the Bukhara prison until Wushmgīr came to Bukhara offering his submission; he asked for their release, and he (sc. the Amir) granted the captives to him. [M 225]

Then al-Muttaqī succeeded to the caliphate in the year 329 [/940–1], and he sent an investiture diploma for Khurasan to the Fortunate Amir. Ahmad b. Muḥammad, son of Muẓaffar, was at Ray and Wushmgīr was in Ṭabaristān. The latter had taken refuge in the citadel of Sārī. When Aḥmad attacked him, his position became parlous. Aḥmad overran all his province. Winter drew on and the rains became continuous. They entered into negotiations for peace and made an agreement by the terms of which Wushmgīr was to stick to his promised obedience. Abū ʿAlī Aḥmad b. Muḥammad returned to [N 32] Gurgān in Jumādā II of the year [3]31 [/February–March 943], the same month in which the Fortunate Amir passed away.[35]

On his death, none of those executive officials (*mudabbirān*) and secretaries who had worked at his court remained, and a sharp division and two parties emerged within his army.[36] The direction of affairs passed from [Abu 'l-Faḍl] Muḥammad b. ʿUbaydallāh al-Balʿamī to Abū ʿAlī Muḥammad b. Muḥammad al-Jayhānī.[37] Muḥammad b. Ḥātim al-Muṣʿabī showed opposition and affairs were in chaos.

The Praiseworthy One (*al-ḥamīd*)
Abū Muḥammad Nūḥ (I) b. Naṣr (II)

The Praiseworthy Amir succeeded to the governorship of Khurasan in Shaʿbān of the year 331 [/April–May 943]. He reigned for twelve years and three months and then died in the month of Rabīʿ I of the year 343 [/July–August 954]. When he assumed power, he entrusted the vizierate and the conduct of government to Abu ʾl-Faḍl Muḥammad b. Muḥammad [b. Aḥmad] al-Ḥākim, who was known as 'The Exalted Administrator' (*ḥākim-i jalīl*).[38] The Amir made him responsible for paying out the army's salaries and allowances, and Abu ʾl-Faḍl put in place laudable procedures. Abu ʾl-ʿAbbās Aḥmad b. Ḥamūya was fearful of the Praiseworthy Amir, since the Fortunate Amir had, during his own lifetime, appointed as his covenanted successor Ismāʿīl b. Naṣr, and Aḥmad b. Ḥamūya was the latter's adviser and executive. Hostile elements had stirred up trouble between Ismāʿīl and Nūḥ, the sons of Naṣr. Ismāʿīl died before Naṣr (i.e. before Naṣr's accession to the throne), but that feeling of anger had remained in the Praiseworthy Amir's heart. Aḥmad b. Ḥamūya continued to be apprehensive; the Fortunate Amir had told him, 'If anything should happen to me, [M 226] Nūḥ won't treat you well'. When the Praiseworthy Amir succeeded in the amirate, [N 33] Aḥmad b. Ḥamūya crossed over the Oxus and came to Āmūy, keeping all the time in concealment. [H 155]

After a year had passed, a general accounting was made. [The Vizier] Ḥākim had paid out six million odd dirhams to the army, but everyone was dissatisfied, the treasuries were empty and the troops full of complaints. The Vizier was revealed as feeble and lacking in judgement.

The region of Nasā suffered an earthquake in Dhu ʾl-Ḥijja of the year 331 [/August 943]; it destroyed many villages and over 5,000 people were crushed beneath the rubble.

Treasonable words uttered by the Ḥājib Muḥammad b. Ṭoghān[39] were brought to the Praiseworthy Amir's attention, and he gave orders that he and his son should be killed. When Amir Nūḥ reached Merv in the year 332 [/943–4], Aḥmad b. Ḥamūya was taken unawares. He went out of his house on the spur of the moment, but was seized and brought before Nūḥ. When the latter saw Aḥmad, he did not ill-treat him but, on the contrary, spoke kindly words and encouraged him to look for favourable treatment in the future. He questioned him in an amicable fashion, and gave orders for a monthly salary to be allotted him on the grounds that he had been of service to the state.

Amir Aḥmad then proceeded from Merv to Nishapur in Rajab of the year 333 [/February–March 945] and stayed there for fifty days. A deputation from the subjects there came along and complained about Abū ʿAlī [Aḥmad Chaghānī]'s evil behaviour and the tyrannical measures of his subordinates. Hence the Praiseworthy Amir dismissed him and appointed in his place Ibrāhīm b. Sīmjūr, himself returning to Bukhara.

In the year 334 [/945–6] Mustakfī succeeded to the caliphate.

The army at Ray rose up against Amir Nūḥ and broke out in rebellion. When news of this reached Amir Nūḥ, he left there (i.e. Bukhara) for Merv. [The Vizier] Ḥākim made slanderous accusations and told the Amir, 'All this is Aḥmad b. Ḥamūya's doing, with the aim of causing trouble for you.' He went on speaking in this vein until Nūḥ became roused against Aḥmad b. Ḥamūya; he issued orders and Aḥmad was beaten to death in Ḥākim's presence in the year 335 [/946–7]. [N 34, M 227] The troops came into Merv[40] and raised complaints about Muḥammad b. Muḥammad al-Ḥākim, alleging that 'He doesn't attend to the army's concerns, he doesn't show any solicitude for them and doesn't pay their salaries. He has stirred up disaffection towards you, he has driven Abū 'Alī to rebellion and he has rendered the troops disaffected.' (Abū 'Alī had exercised his wiles,[41] and had won over to his own side large sections of the troops.) The soldiers demanded that the Amir should put an end to the Vizier's tyrannical practices against them; if not, they would abandon his service. The Praiseworthy Amir commanded that Ḥākim should be dragged from where he was on his face. He was brought to the gate of the palace and there he was killed on the Amir's orders. This was in the year 335, two months after the execution of the Son of Ḥamūya.

Then Abū 'Alī Chaghānī came to Nishapur with Ibrāhīm, the Praiseworthy Amir's paternal uncle, and with an army. Ibrāhīm b. Sīmjūr, together with Manṣūr b. Qarategin and his cavalry force, withdrew and went to join Nūḥ at Merv. Abū 'Alī sallied forth from Nishapur at the end of the month of Rabī' I of the year 335 [/29 October 946] and came to Sarakhs, and from there decided to march against Merv. When he reached the village of Ayqān,[42] there arrived letters from a considerable number of persons, these being adherents and senior officers of Nūḥ, having shown an inclination to Abū 'Alī's side. Abū 'Alī encamped at the village of Sing[43] a parasang away from Merv, whilst Nūḥ fell back on Bukhara. Abū 'Alī entered Merv and stayed there for some time, and then set out for Bukhara, crossing the Oxus. [H 156]

Nūḥ withdrew to Samarqand, and Abū 'Alī made the *khuṭba* (sc. at Bukhara) for Ibrāhīm b. Aḥmad and remained there for some time. The people of Bukhara laid plans for seizing Abū 'Alī and all his entourage. When he got news of this, he left the city next day and ordered all his troops to leave also. They carried off all the cotton and linen cloth and sets of clothing, and left [N 35] with the intention of setting the city on fire. The leading citizens came forth and sought the intercession of God, He is Mighty and Exalted. They instilled fear into Abū 'Alī and he desisted. When he perceived that the feelings of the citizens were unfavourable to him, he set up Abū Ja'far (i.e. Nūḥ's brother Muḥammad b. Naṣr b. Aḥmad) as ruler, made appointments to all departments of the Dīwān, and himself departed by the R.khna[44] road. [M 228] He gave out that he was making for Samarqand, but [actually] went to Nakhshab. He then sent back all his senior officers and troops (i.e. to Khurasan) and himself went to Chaghāniyān.

When Abū 'Alī departed, Ibrāhīm and Abū Ja'far Muḥammad b. Naṣr sent a messenger to Amir Nūḥ seeking from him a guarantee of protection; he granted them this and accepted their excuses. He returned to Bukhara in person in the month of Ramaḍān of the year 335 [/March–April 947].

In this same year, Muṭī' succeeded to the caliphate.

The Praiseworthy Amir appointed Manṣūr b. Qarategin as commander-in-chief in Khurasan. From Bukhara, Manṣūr arrived in Merv, where was Aḥmad b. Muḥammad b. 'Alī al-Qazwīnī. He came into Manṣūr's presence and rendered to him service. Manṣūr proceeded from there to Nishapur, whilst Abū 'Alī was during all this time in Chaghāniyān. Abū ʿAlī then got word that Amir Nūḥ had got together an army and was planning to attack him. Abū ʿAlī acted decisively, came to Balkh and remained there for some time. He then set out with his army for Bukhara. The Praiseworthy Amir and all his troops fell back before him. At Kharjang[45] the two sides came together in Jumādā I of the year 336 [/November–December 947] and a battle ensued that lasted from the time of the afternoon worship till the close of day. Nūḥ and his senior commanders returned to Bukhara. Abu ʾl-Ḥārith b. Abu ʾl-Qāsim, the treasurer Qut-tegin,[46] Abū ʿAlī b. Isḥāq and Aḥmad the brother of Bārs were stationed [N 36] there confronting Abū ʿAlī till the morning. Ibrāhīm b. Abu ʾl-Ḥasan was taken prisoner, together with several others of Abū ʿAli's followers. Abū Isḥāq Ruzgāni[47] sought a guarantee of protection and came over with a numerous force of Daylamīs. Abū ʿAlī retreated in flight to Chaghāniyān. The General Bāyjūr (?) was killed in the battle. ʿAlī b. Aḥmad b. ʿAbdallāh was captured in the environs of Samarqand and Aḥmad b. al-Ḥusayn/al-Ḥasan al-ʿUtbī at Nakhshab; they were set on camels and brought into Bukhara by day. [H 157] They were brought to the city gate and each of them was beaten with a hundred strokes, was put in fetters and forcibly made to disgorge his wealth (*muṣādara*). Abu ʾl-ʿAbbās Muḥammad b. Aḥmad [M 229] died in the course of this, but Aḥmad b. al-Ḥusayn/al-Ḥasan was released after enduring these tortures for a considerable time.

Abū ʿAlī now sought help from the Amir of Khuttalān. He himself gathered together an army, marched on Tirmidh, and crossed the Oxus and came to Balkh. From there he headed for Gūzgānān and, according to the preconceived arrangement, met up with the Amir of Khuttalān at Simingān. When he reached Tukhāristān, the news came that the army of Bukhara had invaded Chaghāniyān, had burnt the Iron Gate (*dar-i āhanīn*)[48] and had devastated the whole of Abū ʿAlī's property and possessions. He immediately took the Mīla road and crossed the Oxus back again. He sent out separate detachments of troops in all directions and blocked the way for the army of Bukhara. Their position became parlous, and they had no access to any food and fodder. When Abū ʿAlī reached the village of K.m.kānān (?), it being at a distance of two parasangs from [the town of] Chaghāniyān, a battle took place there in the month of Rabīʿ I of the year 336 [/September–October 947]. The Praiseworthy Amir's army secured the victory over Abū ʿAlī, and he retreated to Shūmān, twelve parasangs beyond Chaghāniyān [town]. The army of Bukhara entered Chaghāniyān and plundered the town, including Abū ʿAlī's palaces and residences. At this point, Abū ʿAlī received reinforcements from the Kumījīs and from the Amir of Zhāsht[49] Jaʿfar b. Sh.mānīqwā (?) and the army of Īlāq, and, in the space of a day, they came to Wāshgird.[50] The Amir of Khuttalān, Aḥmad b. Jaʿfar, [N 37] also sent his commander-in-chief Bajkam with a numerous army, and the way for the army of Bukhara was now blocked and their communications with the capital severed. Peace negotiations were opened up and a contractual agreement (*muwāḍaʿat*) was reached that Abū ʿAlī should send his son Abu ʾl-Muẓaffar ʿAbdallāh b. Aḥmad to Bukhara as a hostage, and this was done. This happened in Jumādā II of the year 337 [/December 948].

When Abu ʾl-Muẓaffar came to Bukhara, the Praiseworthy Amir ordered that the city should be decked out in a festive manner, and he was escorted into the city with pomp and ceremony. The Amir further ordered that he should be lodged in the palace; he invited him to the royal table and ordered him to be given a special robe of honour, including the donning of a cap. [H 158, M 230]

A self-styled prophet (*mutanabbi*) from the region of Chaghāniyān and the district of Bāsand[51] had led an uprising, and he headed for the Iron Gate. He styled himself the Mahdī and a prophet. He had first publicly made his claims in the year 322 [/934], and considerable numbers of people had gone to join him and adopted his doctrines. This Mahdī used to have a sword in his belt, and with it would attack anyone who opposed him. He was a crafty individual and up to tricks of all kinds. Thus he would put this hand into a cistern filled with water and bring out from it a fistful of dinars. A great number of people used to eat at his table, but it never made any diminution in the amount of food there. People would drink water from his goblet till their thirst was quenched, but that goblet never became empty. Each person from his circle of retainers would eat just a single date per day, and that would be enough for him. When news of this spread through those regions, large numbers of the ignorant common people flocked to join him.[52]

A letter reached Abū ʿAlī Chaghānī from Bukhara instructing him to deal with the matter of that self-styled prophet. Abū ʿAlī despatched Abū Ṭalḥa Jaʿfar b. Mardānshāh. This Mahdī [N 38] was at the village of Wardī.[53] He retreated into the mountains, but an attack was launched against him which dislodged him from the mountains. His head was chopped off, and Abū Ṭalḥa sent it to Abū ʿAlī in a horse's nosebag. Abū ʿAlī was at that moment in Shūmān, and he gave orders that the head should be publicly displayed to all the persons who had followed the would-be prophet, and then he forwarded it to Bukhara.

Abu 'l-Muẓaffar was meanwhile residing at Bukhara. One day he mounted his horse and was riding on, but inadvertently the horse threw him. His head landed against a stone, his brains were spattered out and he died. The Praiseworthy Amir was distressed and gave orders that the dead man should be enshrouded in a handsome fashion, and he sent his funeral bier back to Chaghāniyān, with the Royal Purveyor of Drinks (*sharāb-dār*) Naṣr being charged with performing the rites of mourning and consolation with Abu ʿAlī.

Only two months after Abu 'l-Muẓaffar's death, Manṣūr b. Qarategin died at Nishapur. The Praiseworthy Amir bestowed the office of commander-in-chief of Khurasan on Abū ʿAlī Chaghānī and sent him an investiture diploma and a standard. He gave him all the lands south of the Oxus (*mā dūn al-nahr*) and bestowed Chaghāniyān and Tirmidh on his son Abū Manṣūr Naṣr b. Aḥmad. [M 231] Abū ʿAlī came to Nishapur in Dhu 'l-Ḥijja of the year 340 [/May 952], and in the year 341 [/952–3] all affairs in Khurasan were peaceful and orderly.

In the year 342 [/953–4] Abū ʿAlī marched on Ray and besieged Ḥasan-i Būya[54] in the town. Wushmgīr b. Ziyār sent reinforcements for Ḥasan-i Būya. The besiegers were unable to make any headway. At this point, the riding beasts at Ray were hit by a fatal murrain and only a few beasts survived. Negotiators from each side met together and made peace on the basis that [Ḥasan-i] Būya should pay an annual tribute of 200,000 dinars and that Abū 'Alī should withdraw. Ḥasan sent to him 'Abbās b. Dāwūd as surety for this sum of money.

Abū 'Alī returned to Nishapur. However, the Praiseworthy Amir became suspicious that Abū 'Alī might perhaps have colluded with al-Ḥasan-i Būya. Abū 'Alī [N 39, H 159] sent emissaries and explained what he had been doing, but the feeling of rancour was not dispelled from the Praiseworthy Amir's mind. Abū 'Alī Chaghānī then sent a deputation of shaykhs, professional attesters and leading citizens of Nishapur to Bukhara so that they might set forth the justification for his action and explain that he was guiltless of the suspicions the Praiseworthy Amir held. But before this group of trustworthy persons from Nishapur [attesting Abū 'Alī's innocence] could reach Bukhara, the Praiseworthy Amir fell ill. His sickness became acute, and in the month of Rabī' II of the year 343[/August 954] he died from it.[55]

The Rightly-Guided One (*al-rashīd*)
Abu 'l-Fawāris 'Abd al-Malik (I) b. Nūḥ (I)

Nūḥ b. Naṣr had four sons: 'Abd al-Malik, Aḥmad, Naṣr and 'Abd al-'Azīz. He had had allegiance done to them as his covenanted heir in that successive order, 'Abd al-Malik being the oldest. 'Abd al-Malik succeeded to power in the month of Rabī' II of the year 343 [/December 954]. He appointed as his vizier Abū Manṣūr Muḥammad b. 'Uzayr, and as his commander-in-chief Abū Sa'īd Bakr b. Mālik. The latter came to Nishapur in Sha'bān of the year 343 and established there a benevolent and just regime. [M 232]

Then the news arrived that Muṭī' had given the governorship of Khurasan to Abū 'Alī Chaghānī. This information enraged Bakr b. Mālik. He marched out with his army and encamped at the village of Āzādwār in the rural district of Juwayn, and formulated the plan of moving on from there with his army to give battle. His commanders, however, objected that 'Fodder is in short supply, the army is without provisions and it's not possible to engage in battle.' So Bakr b. Mālik wrote a letter to the Rightly-Guided Amir 'Abd al-Malik b. Nūḥ explaining this state of affairs and seeking money from him. The Rightly-Guided Amir sent back [to him] Ismā'īl b. Ṭoghān (text, *t.gh.yān*) but did not send the required money. [N 40] When this news reached Khurasan, the province was plunged into a disturbed state. Taking advantage of this, Ḥasan Būya sent Abu 'l-Faḍl[56] Ibn al-'Amīd against Isfahan, and Ibn al-'Amīd engaged in warfare, seized the Son of Mākān and consigned him to the fortress of Arrajān, after which no-one ever saw him again. This conquest of Isfahan took place in the month of Rabī' I of the year 344 [/June–July 955].

Ḥasan-i Būya now marched against Gurgān. News of this reached Bakr b. Mālik, and Ḥasan [b.] Fīrūzān moved to the confines of Jājarm. When 'Abd al-Malik b. Nūḥ heard about these happenings, he gathered together military forces and despatched them to Bakr b. Mālik at Āzādwār. Ḥasan-i Būya and Abū 'Alī did not stay to deliver battle to Bakr, but retreated to Ṭabaristān. Abū Sa'īd [Bakr b.] Mālik summoned Abu 'l-Ḥasan Muḥammad b. Ibrāhīm b. Sīmjūr to be military governor (*shiḥna*) at Nishapur. A letter from Ḥasan-i Būya and Abū 'Alī Chaghānī reached 'Alī b. al-Marzubān seeking a peace settlement with Abū Sa'īd Bakr b. Mālik. Ḥasan engaged

[H 160] that he would regularly send an annual tribute of 200,000 dinars from Ray and the districts of Jibāl plus additional presents, and would provide hospitality and feasting (?),[57] and he would not molest Wushmgīr in regard to Ṭabaristān. ʿAlī b. al-Marzubān acted as an intermediary, and on this basis peace was made. Ḥasan sent the tribute and the presents stipulated in the peace agreement. The danger of bloodshed was averted and the causes of emnity removed, and affairs in Khurasan became settled and ran smoothly. [M 233]

Muṭīʿ wrote a letter to Ḥasan-i Būya. This peace made on the basis of a contractual agreement was displeasing to him, and he said, 'That's the pay allotment for the army of Khurasan due each year according to the agreement made in the year 344 [/955–56].' Abū ʿAlī fell ill and died at the end of Rajab of the year 344 [/19 November 955] and his bier was carried back to Chaghāniyān.

Bakr b. Mālik used to treat his troops with disdain and [N 41] used to stint them in what was their due until they grew to hate him. They returned to Bukhara and laid their complaints before ʿAbd al-Malik. Bakr b. Mālik came to the royal court at Bukhara in Ramaḍān of the year 345[/December 956–January 957] because he, in company with thirty-seven other commanders, was going to be invested with a robe of honour, so that they might then go back to Farghāna. When Bakr b. Mālik came along, performed the due obeisance and sought an answer (i.e. to his request for entry to the palace), Qut-tegin the treasurer was on his right and the Ḥājib Alptegin on his left. He requested that he might mount, but the Ḥājib Alptegin knocked him to the ground. They attacked him with their swords and spears and killed him at the Gate of the Government Headquarters (*dar-i sulṭān*), and carried off his [severed] head. They clapped in bonds Abū Manṣūr b. ʿUzayr and set up Abū Jaʿfar b. Muḥammad [b.] al-Ḥusayn [ʿUtbī][58] in the vizierate, whilst Abu 'l-Ḥasan Muḥammad b. Ibrāhīm [Sīmjūrī] was appointed commander-in-chief of Khurasan. The Ḥājib Ibrāhīm b. Alptegin was sent to Abu 'l-Ḥasan with the investiture diploma and standard for a commander-in-chief in the year 347 [/958–9].

Abū Jaʿfar ʿUtbī was continually alighting on sources of wealth that he could appropriate for himself and exerting himself to the utmost in searching out money for the treasuries, until people complained volubly about him, and in the months of the year 348 [/959–60] Abū Jaʿfar was deprived of the vizierate, which was now given instead to Abū Manṣūr Yūsuf b. Isḥāq.

At Nishapur, the Amir Abu 'l-Ḥasan Muḥammad b. Ibrāhīm committed numerous oppressive acts, and complaints about his tyranny were continually reaching the court in Bukhara. Hence in Jumādā II of the year 349 [/August 960] he was dismissed and the post of commander-in-chief given to Abū Manṣūr Muḥammad b. ʿAbd al-Razzāq. Abū Naṣr Manṣūr b. Bāyqarā was sent to him with an investiture diploma, a standard and a robe of honour. [H 161, M 234]

When that investiture diploma reached Abū Manṣūr b. ʿAbd al-Razzāq, he got a firm grip on the Cis-Oxanian lands (*wilāyat-i mā dūn al-nahr*) and established laudable practices. [N 42] He held sessions for hearing complaints of injustice, personally acted as an arbiter between opposing parties and dispensed justice in cases between the subjects. Abū Manṣūr was an upright man, knowledgeable about customs and conventions, pleasant company and characterised by an abundance of good deeds.[59]

At the court, the Ḥājib Alptegin always acknowledged Abū Manṣūr's suitability[60] for his post. But Alptegin spoke up about Yūsuf b. Isḥāq's mismanagement of affairs until the latter was deprived of the vizierate, which was given to Abū ʿAlī Muḥammad b. Muḥammad al-Balʿamī.[61] After some time, Alptegin perceived that ʿAbd al-Malik's attitude towards him had changed. He was now less and less[62] rendering service and participating in court life. ʿAbd al-Malik ordered him to go to Balkh (i.e. as governor there). Alptegin protested, 'In no way will I become a mere local governor and tax collector after having been the Chief Ḥājib.' So he was given the post of commander-in-chief in Khurasan, with Abū Manṣūr dismissed from that office. Abū Manṣūr went to Ṭūs and Alptegin came to Nishapur on 20 Dhu 'l-Ḥijja of the year 349 [/10 February 961]. Alptegin's vizier was Abū ʿAbdallāh Muḥammad b. Aḥmad al-Shiblī.

There was an agreement between Alptegin and Abū ʿAlī Balʿamī that each would act as the other's representative, and Balʿamī used never to do anything without Alptegin's knowledge and counsel. Alptegin had sent some presents for the Rightly-Guided Amir ʿAbd al-Malik, included amongst them being some horses and other things. They were brought into the Amir's presence after the noon worship. ʿAbd al-Malik was an enthusiast for polo-playing in the open parade ground. He had drunk a certain amount of wine, and he successively mounted the horses which had been given to him as presents. One of them bucked when ʿAbd al-Malik was on him and threw him off, and his head and neck were smashed to pieces. They bore away his corpse, and they gave him the honorific title of 'The Rightly-Guided One'.[63]

The Upright One (*al-sadīd*) Abū Ṣāliḥ Manṣūr (I) b. Nūḥ (I)

The Rightly-Guided One and the Upright One were sons of the Praiseworthy Amir Nūḥ. When that accident befell the Rightly-Guided One, Abū ʿAlī Balʿamī immediately wrote a letter to [M 235] Alptegin with the news of what had happened to the Rightly-Guided One and asking him who, in his view, was the most suitable candidate for the throne. Alptegin wrote back in reply that out of the Rightly-Guided One's sons, one was particularly suitable to succeed.[64] When this reply had gone off, a letter arrived with the information that the members of the Samanid family and the army were all agreed that Manṣūr should be raised to the throne.

When Alptegin read the letter, swift-running camel riders had already crossed the river (i.e. the Oxus). Alptegin then sent a messenger[65] to Abū Manṣūr ʿAbd al-Razzāq with the instructions, 'Get a firm grip on affairs in Khurasan and act according to the friendship which exists between the two of us, as I am firmly convinced you will do.' Alptegin's envoy was still with Abū Manṣūr when a letter arrived from Bukhara dismissing Alptegin and appointing Abū Manṣūr as governor in his place. Abū Manṣūr had also been ordered, 'Don't allow Alptegin to cross the river, but launch an attack on him, and the post of commander-in-chief at Nishapur is yours', and further hopes of favour were offered to him. [H 162]

Alptegin left Nishapur in Dhu 'l-Qaʿda of the year 350 [/December 961–January

962]. Abū Manṣūr despatched an army by the Ṭābarān and Nūqān Gate to Jāha (?).[66] Alptegin had already left. They came upon a certain amount of the remnants of his baggage, which the *'ayyārs* and *sarhangs* plundered, carrying off everything that was there. Following in Alptegin's tracks, Abū Manṣūr came to Jāha, but Alptegin had already reached the bank of the Oxus. Letters sent from Bukhara by the Amir, the Vizier and the head of the palace household (*wakīl-i dar*) reached Alptegin's senior officers (*sarhangān*) denouncing Alptegin for acting wrongfully. When Alptegin saw what the situation was, he set fire to the army camp until the whole of it was consumed. Then he told his personal ghulāms, [N 44] 'You all see what lies before us – sword blows, imprisonment and the violent extortion of wealth – and behind us – killing, captivity and the sword. The right course is that we should make for Balkh.' He went from there to Balkh and then left that city by the Khulm road.

When the Upright One got news of Alptegin's flight, he sent against him B.b.dāḥ (?),[67] and B.b.dāḥ caught up with Alptegin at the pass (*dara*) leading to Khulm. Alptegin had with him 700 ghulāms, and they gave battle to 12,000 opponents, killing the greater part of them. In the end, B.b.dāḥ turned and fled back to Bukhara. Alptegin went to Tukhāristān and from there to Ghaznin. He remained there for a period of time and it was there that he died.[68] [M 236]

Abū Manṣūr b. 'Abd al-Razzāq knew that he would not be left in that post (i.e. of commander-in-chief) and that he would be dismissed. He returned to Merv, but the *sarhangs* of Merv shut the gates of the town in his face. He passed on from there and [now] allowed his troops full licence. The troops were indulging in plundering and seizing people's wealth, and in this fashion he headed for Nasā and Bāvard. The headman (*ra'īs*) of Nasā had just died; Abū Manṣūr arrested his heirs and seized the wealth. He sent a letter to Ḥasan b. Būya seeking an agreement with him; he invited him to Gurgān, and Ḥasan-i Būya set out from where he was.

Wushmgīr gave the physician Yuḥannā 1,000 dinars in gold, and he administered poison to Abū Manṣūr. That unjust and violent behaviour on Abū Manṣūr's part redounded on his own head;[69] the poison worked in him and he perished as a result of it. The post of commander-in-chief (i.e. of Khurasan) was given to Abu 'l-Ḥasan Muḥammad b. Ibrāhīm [Sīmjūrī] for a second time, in Dhu 'l-Ḥijja of the year 350 [/January–February 962]. Abu 'l-Ḥasan took up his post and treated the subjects very benevolently, spread widely his justice, followed beneficent governmental ways and put into practice laudable policies. He used always to cultivate the learned classes, and turned completely away from those evil ways that he had previously followed and from which the subjects had much suffered; he now conciliated people, put aside that evil disposition and [N 45] abandoned reprehensible practices.

The order reached Abu 'l-Ḥasan to attack Abū Manṣūr b. 'Abd al-Razzāq. When Amir Abu 'l-Ḥasan sallied forth to engage him in battle, he came upon Ḥasan-i Būya's army at N.m.kh.k.n[70] and Khabūshān. Abu 'l-Ḥasan came up in pursuit of him, and battle was joined by the two sides. [H 163] That poison administered to Abū Manṣūr had done its work and he was in an afflicted state, with his eyesight also badly affected. Abu 'l-Ḥasan's army proved victorious and Abū Manṣūr's troops fled. In the course of this flight, Abū Manṣūr said to his troops, 'I've got to dismount.'

They replied, 'There's no time for that.' He repeated, 'I've got to take a rest.' They left him there alone and went off, and he himself dismounted. Straightway, a cavalry troop of Aḥmad b. Manṣūr b. Qarategin arrived; a Ṣaqlābī ghulām came upon him, severed Abū Manṣūr b. 'Abd al-Razzāq's head and pulled off his signet ring, and laid them before his master. [M 237]

Amir Abu 'l-Ḥasan was now in a firm, settled position. He remained at Nishapur for five years and did not go anywhere else. Then he received a letter from Bukhara instructing him to go to Ray and campaign there. Wushmgīr sent his secretary 'Alī Dāmghānī, and he himself followed on after him. During the journey, he went out hunting. A wild boar felled him to the ground, he was badly injured and died on the spot. He was brought to Gurgān on 14–15 Dhu 'l-Ḥijja of the year 356[/20–1 November 967].

With Wushmgīr dead, there was no point in going to Ray. The army of Khurasan clamoured for its pay. Amir Abu 'l-Ḥasan sent a letter to Manṣūr b. Nūḥ asking for money; Manṣūr replied that the army's pay would have to be taken from Bīsutūn, son of Wushmgīr. When Bīsutūn heard this, he headed for Ṭabaristān, on the plea that his money was laid up there. But he secretly concerted a plan of action with Ḥasan-i Būya. The latter sent his *'āriḍ* 'Alī b. al-Qāsim to Āmul, [N 46] Bīsutūn then arrived there and he made that arrangement between them firm.

The robe of honour sent by Muṭī' reached Bīsutūn, together with a standard for the governorship of Ṭabaristān, Gurgān, Sālūs and Rūyān, and he had awarded him the honorific title of *Ẓahīr al-Dawla* 'Upholder of the State'. Amir Abu 'l-Ḥasan returned to Nishapur, and he was now accused of impotence and weakness. Sālār b. Shīrdil and Shahriyār b. Zarrin-kamar had come to Amir Abu 'l-Ḥasan's court, and he welcomed and treated them handsomely. Then Bīsutūn died at Astarābād in Rajab of the year 367 [/February–March 978]. Signs of weakness in Abu 'l-Ḥasan's grip on state affairs became apparent to the ruling authority (*sulṭān*), one of the manifestations of this being that Gurgān, Qūmis, Sālūs and Rūyān slipped from his control.

Manṣūr b. Nūḥ then sent Ash'ath b. Muḥammad al-Yashkurī to Nasā so that he might proceed from there to Gurgān, and he despatched Naṣr b. Mālik to Gurgānj[71] so that he might conquer it. He was also putting into effect plans regarding Abu 'l-Ḥasan. When [news of this] reached Abu 'l-Ḥasan, he got busy devising stratagems. He came to Bukhara, and through the intimates of Manṣūr secured intercession, and as a result he was able to dispel that rancour from Manṣūr's heart and fend off from himself that intended harm. The function of vizier had come to be shared between Abū 'Alī Bal'amī and Abū Ja'far 'Utbī over a certain period, but then Abū 'Alī Bal'amī died in Jumādā II of the year 363 [/March 974].[72] [H 164, M 238]

Amir Abu 'l-Ḥasan was a very crafty and ingenious person, and he now brought into play stratagems. He returned to Nishapur with the post of commander-in-chief [and] as holder of the governorship of Merv. A *sarhang* from the province of Herat, a certain Abū 'Alī Muḥammad b. al-'Abbās Tūlakī, raised a rebellion. He put in order and garrisoned the fortress of Tūlak,[73] and a body of troops gathered round him. Amir Abu 'l-Ḥasan appointed Abū Ja'far Ziyādī to go and attack Tūlakī. Abū Ja'far found Tūlakī in the fortress of Tūlak. Tūlakī then came forth under a guarantee of protection, and Abū Jaʿfar brought him back to Nishapur. This same Abū Jaʿfar Ziyādī marched into Ghūr and [N 47] conquered several of the fortresses there.[74] In the year 369 [/979–80] he went on to Sistan in order to aid Ḥusayn b. ʿAlī b. Ṭāhir al-Tamīmī, who was engaged in continuous warfare with Khalaf b. Aḥmad.[75] Amir Abu 'l-Ḥasan also proceeded there, following after him; they engaged in warfare for some time and then they returned (i.e. to Khurasan) in the year 373 [/983–4].

The Commander of the Faithful al-Ṭāʾiʿ li'llāh succeeded to the caliphate in the year 374 [/984–5].[76] Abū Jaʿfar ʿUtbī entered into correspondence with Abu 'l-Fatḥ[77] Ibn al-ʿAmīd. Abu 'l-Fatḥ was delighted at this, and the two viziers engaged in negotiations and cleared up the causes of emnity between the Buyids and Samanids. The sequence of hostile acts was ended, warfare ceased, and affairs became orderly and settled. The Buyid house acknowledged its obedience to Manṣūr b. Nūḥ and put a stop to acts of provocation. The land was no longer plagued by acts of violence and the populace now enjoyed peace. Each year the stipulated tribute of 200,000 dinars and the additional presents were brought to Khurasan from Ray and the districts of Jibāl.

Ḥasan-i Būya eventually fell ill. He bestowed his kingdom on his sons. Abū Shujāʿ [ʿAḍud al-Dawla] Fanākhusraw had a private meeting with him, and Ḥasan passed on to him all his secrets. He died at Ray on 5 Muḥarram of the year 366 [/3 September 976].

Abū Jaʿfar ʿUtbī did laudable things in Khurasan. Yūsuf [b. Isḥāq] was brought back again and appointed vizier, but died in Dhu 'l-Qaʿda of the year 363 [/July–August 974],[78] and the vizierate was then given to Abū ʿAbdallāh [M 239] Aḥmad b. Muḥammad al-Jayhānī in the year 365 [/975–76]. At this time Manṣūr b. Nūḥ fell ill. The malady grew worse and he died of it on 11 Shawwāl of the year 365 [/12 June 976]. He was given [posthumously] the honorific title of 'The Upright One'.[79] [N 48]

The Well-Pleasing One (*al-raḍī, al-riḍā*)
Abu 'l-Qāsim Nūḥ (II) b. Manṣūr (I)

When Nūḥ b. Manṣūr succeeded to power, he had not yet attained mature years. He reigned for twenty-one years and nine months. He made his close intimates the Amir Abu 'l-Ḥasan [Sīmjūrī] [H 165] and Abu 'l-Ḥārith Muḥammad b. Aḥmad b. Farīghūn,[80] and through them he acquired strong backing. He entrusted his affairs to Fāʾiq of the royal guard (*al-khāṣṣa*) and the Ḥājib Tāsh. When he assumed power, he sent Abū ʿAbdallāh b. Ḥafṣ, the commander (*sālār*) of the Bukhara ghāzīs, on a mission to the Amir Abu 'l-Ḥasan and awarded him (i.e. Abu 'l-Ḥasan Sīmjūrī) the honorific title of *Nāṣir al-Dawla* ('The One who Renders the State Victorious').[81] He further sent him an investiture patent and robe of honour for the post of commander-in-chief and for the levying and collection of regular and extraordinary taxation (*ʿamal-i maʿūnat wa aḥdāth*) at Nishapur and Herat and in Quhistān. By the agency of [Abū] ʿAbdallāh the Ghāzī he sent to him the following verbal message:

> We have raised you to a higher level of closeness in our service than you expected, since we have discerned in you signs of trustworthiness and indications of right conduct; take care not to do anything to spoil our good opinion of you. We have bestowed on you three things that none of our predecessors ever granted. One is that we have made you one of our circle of intimates, and this will be an indication of the firmness of our confidence in you and what has impelled us to increase your noble status and high rank. Second is a further allocation of territory for your governorship, and this will be an indication of how highly we value your position and achievements. Third is the award of honorific titles for you, to be used when you are formally addressed and in correspondence, so that you will have an exalted status amongst your contemporaries and peers.

When this investiture patent, robe of honour and message reached Abu 'l-Ḥasan, he was overjoyed. He entertained the envoy lavishly and sent presents for the royal princes, according to their statuses. Then he despatched Abū ʿAbdallāh the Ghāzī homewards.

Abu 'l-Ḥusayn ʿAbdallāh b. Aḥmad ʿUtbī was appointed vizier in Rabīʿ II of the year 367 [/November–December 977]. When the Well-Pleasing Amir [N 49] expressed his desire to appoint Abu 'l-Ḥusayn ʿUtbī as his vizier, [M 240] he sent a letter to Amir Abu 'l-Ḥasan seeking his advice. The latter sent back a reply that Abu 'l-Ḥusayn was too young for the post.[82] When Abu 'l-Ḥusayn heard these contemptuous and deprecatory words of Amir Abu 'l-Ḥasan, he sought his revenge. He started spreading tales about Amir Abu 'l-Ḥasan's defects and reprehensible actions. He kept on saying continually that 'Abu 'l-Ḥasan is useless and will never achieve anything. He has brought Khurasan to ruin. All he cares about is mulcting people and extracting taxation with violence. To make an intimate counsellor of him is *n.m.w.ḥ.t.*'[83] He said so much in this vein that the Well-Pleasing Amir dismissed Abu 'l-Ḥasan and sent him a letter terminating his appointment.

Abu 'l-Ḥusayn ʿUtbī ordered the envoy to communicate the letter dismissing Abu 'l-Ḥasan publicly and in a loud voice. When the envoy reached Nishapur, Amir Abu 'l-Ḥasan had at the time taken up his position amongst his array of troops. The envoy read out this message in accordance with the vizier's instructions. Amir Abu 'l-Ḥasan became indignant and filled with anger, and said, 'I'm the governor of Khurasan and the commander-in-chief of the army is my son Abū ʿAlī. By God, I'll make them see stars!',[84] and he had the drums beaten and brought out his army for action.

When news of this reached Abu 'l-Ḥusayn ʿUtbī, he became despairing and repented of what he had said. He kept worrying whether the Amir would be pleased with him or would charge him with responsibility for this reprehensible action, clap him in bonds and imprison him. The next day, a letter brought by an agent of the postal and intelligence service arrived with the information that Abu 'l-Ḥasan had regretted his initial reaction and had accepted what was decreed regarding his governorship and his dismissal. Amir Abu 'l-Ḥasan sent a group of trusted citizens of Nishapur with Bū Naṣr Aḥmad b. ʿAlī Mīkālī,[85] seeking the Vizier's pardon for his action. Abu 'l-Ḥusayn was filled with joy. Amir Abu 'l-Ḥasan summoned into his presence Aḥmad [H 166] b. al-Ḥusayn, who had come on the mission (i.e. to Nishapur); he sought pardon and sent him back in a handsome fashion.

The Well-Pleasing Amir Nūḥ then gave the post of commander-in-chief of the army to the Ḥājib Abu 'l-'Abbās Tāsh and awarded him the honorific title of *Ḥusām al-Dawla* ('Sword of the State'). Tāsh reached Nishapur in mid-Sha'bān of the year 371 [/14–15 February 982] and remained there for a year. Abu 'l-Ḥusayn 'Utbī [N 50] showed favour for Tāsh and solicitude because the latter had been one of his father's ghulāms. Abu 'l-Ḥusayn sent Fā'iq, Qābūs [b. Wushmgīr][86] and several [M 241] other senior commanders to Gurgān in order to combat Būya (i.e. Mu'ayyid al-Dawla), and himself set off on the road to B.y.h (?).

'Alī b. al-Ḥasan b. Būya (i.e. Mu'ayyid al-Dawla) prepared to launch a military campaign on behalf of his brother (i.e 'Aḍud al-Dawla). First of all, he attacked 'Alī [b.] Kāma and put him to flight, and himself proceeded to Astarābād. The Khurasanian troops were busy plundering. Tāsh recalled 'Alī [b.] Kāma. Abū Shujā' Fanā-Khusraw (i.e. 'Aḍud al-Dawla) sent reinforcements for his brother [Mu'ayyid al-Dawla] Būya to the number of 7,000 men, 4,000 of them coming from one direction and 3,000 from another direction. When the Buyid reinforcements arrived, they engaged Tāsh's forces and put them to flight. Tāsh went to his army camp and gave orders that it should be set on fire, and himself departed. Just when the army of Būya b. al-Ḥasan was about to pursue the fugitives into Khurasan, the news reached them of Fanā-Khusraw's death. The Buyid army halted and did not invade Khurasan; if this [death] had not occurred, they would have destroyed Khurasan and Tāsh.

A letter reached Amir Abu 'l-Ḥasan from Bukhara telling him to put on a *durrā'a* and remain at home.[87] He did this, and gave command of the army to his son Amir Abū 'Alī and sent him to reinforce Ḥusayn b. Ṭāhir in Sistan. The Amir of Khurasan made over to him Pūshang, and Abū 'Alī departed. When this news reached Amir Khalaf in Sistan, he designated the ghulāms formerly of the following of Bāytūz and the free troops, amounting to 4,000 cavalrymen, plus four elephants, to attack Amir Abū 'Alī.[88] The latter had [only] 1,000 cavalrymen. Battle was joined and large numbers of persons killed, and those four elephants were captured.

When this news reached Bukhara, praises were heaped on Abū 'Alī, and he was further awarded the province of Bādghīs. A reconciliation between him and Tāsh was effected. Amir Abu 'l-Ḥasan had written to Fā'iq with complaints about Abu 'l-Ḥusayn 'Utbī and recounting the story of that uttering of abuses and displaying of contempt. [H 167] Fā'iq replied, 'I'll devise some stratagem to deal with this.' [N 51] He then suborned a group of those royal ghulāms who had no fear of God [M 242] and gave each one of them money. They murdered Abu 'l-Ḥusayn 'Utbī, and he was buried at the side of his father. Things fell into disarray. Tāsh was summoned back to the capital. He set out for there with the intention of wreaking vengeance for the death of Abu 'l-Ḥusayn 'Utbī, but found no opportunity for this.[89]

Abu 'l-Ḥusayn Muḥammad b. Muḥammad al-Muzanī was then appointed vizier, and affairs settled down. Amir Abū 'Alī sought from Tāsh the office of deputy for him at Nishapur, and Tāsh gave it to him; but Tāsh's action here proved to be a mistake. On Abu 'l-Ḥusayn 'Utbī's death, Tāsh's position became weak. Fā'iq and Abu 'l-Ḥasan moved against him, and they incited people so that they were continually complaining of Tāsh's tyrannical deeds. Fā'iq, Abū 'Alī and Abu 'l-Ḥasan conspired together; Abū 'Alī seized Tāsh's tax officials and confiscated large sums of money from them.

Abu 'l-Ḥusayn Muzanī was arrested; he very soon fell ill and died. Abū Muḥammad 'Abd al-Raḥmān b. Aḥmad al-Fārisī was made vizier. The ascendancy in the state of Abū 'Alī and Fā'iq grew very strong. In the end, they decided that Tāsh should have Nishapur; Fā'iq should have Balkh; Abū 'Alī should have Herat; and Abu 'l-Ḥasan should have Bādghīs, Ganj Rustāq and Quhistān.

Tāsh went to Nishapur, but his detractors took the opportunity to denigrate him, and they kept on making provocations, stirring up trouble and bringing false testimonies until Tāsh was dismissed from office. 'Abd al-Raḥmān was deprived of the vizierate in the month of Rabī' I of the year 376 [/July–August 986]. The post of commander-in-chief in Khurasan was given to Amir Abu 'l-Ḥasan, and Nasā and Bāvard given to Tāsh. When the latter heard the news of his dismissal (i.e. from the supreme command in Khurasan), he remained at Sarakhs and made no move as yet to go to Nasā. Abū Sa'īd Shaybī and 'Abdallāh b. Muḥammad b. 'Abd al-Razzāq were at Nishapur.

When Amir Abu 'l-Ḥasan [N 52] arrived, they decorated the town. They went to Tāsh, and . . . they saw how well set-up and arrayed he was. Amir Abu 'l-Ḥasan entered Nishapur. Tāsh came along and shut himself up in the citadel. 'Alī b. Ḥasan b. Būya (i.e. Fakhr al-Dawla) sent military help to Tāsh. Fighting broke out. Abu 'l-Ḥasan abandoned the town and fell back to Quhistān. He (sc. Tāsh) sought help from Abu 'l-Fawāris b. Abī Shujā' (i.e. Sharaf al-Dawla Shīrzīl b. 'Aḍud al-Dawla), [M 243] who sent a force of 2,000 men. Fā'iq now arrived. They proceeded to Nishapur, and they defeated Tāsh, this defeat being on 7 Sha'bān of the year 377 [/2 December 987].

They took prisoner large numbers of Daylamīs. Manṣūr b. Muḥammad b. 'Abd al-Razzāq was involved, and he was taken captive also. All were sent to Khurasan. Manṣūr was set on an ox and brought into Bukhara by day. Tāsh fled to Gurgān. 'Alī b. al-Ḥasan b. Būya received him handsomely and bestowed many presents on him, and himself returned to Ray, entrusting Gurgān, with its harvest of grain and its taxation, to Tāsh. Tāsh died in Gurgān in the year 378 [/988–9].

Abū 'Alī Muḥammad b. 'Īsā al-Dāmghānī was then appointed vizier on 10 Rabī' II of the year 378 [/28 July 988]. [H 168] The royal guard now favoured Abū Naṣr [b. Aḥmad b. Muḥammad b.] Abū Zayd, but in the end Bū 'Alī Dāmghānī was given the vizierate for a second time. He functioned thus as vizier until the Khān (i.e. Hārūn or Ḥasan Bughrā Khān, the Qarakhanid Ilig Khān) came to Bukhara. When the Khān left, he took Dāmghānī with him. He passed away at Samarqand on 1 Rajab of the year 382 [/2 September 992].

One day, Amir Abu 'l-Ḥasan went to the Khurramak Garden. He was enamoured of a slave girl and slept with her. He had fallen asleep across her abdomen and then died, this being in Dhu 'l-Ḥijja of the year 378 [/March–April 989]. Amir Abū 'Alī was at that time at Herat, whilst [his brother] Abu 'l-Qāsim was in charge of Nishapur. Troublemakers sowed dissension between the brothers. When Abu 'l-Qāsim learnt of this, he came from Nishapur to Herat in the year 379 [/989–90], bringing Amir Abu 'l-Ḥasan's treasury and ghulāms to Abū 'Alī there. [N 53]

Nūḥ b. Manṣūr now in the year 381 [/991–2] appointed Abū 'Alī commander-in-chief, sent him an investiture patent, a standard and a robe of honour, and gave him the honorific title of *'Imād al-Dawla* ('Pillar of the State'). Fā'iq came back to Bukhara without having received any permission for this. The Ḥājib Inanch[90] (? text *'.n.j*) and Begtuzūn engaged in battle with him; they defeated Fā'iq and he fled to Balkh. Chaghāniyān was bestowed on Abu 'l-Ḥasan Ṭāhir b. al-Faḍl. [M 244]

Amir Ṭāhir b. al-Faḍl came forth, and Abu 'l-Muẓaffar [Muḥammad b. Aḥmad] went to Fā'iq, who provided him with military assistance. He engaged in battle with Ṭāhir b. al-Faḍl, and in the course of that battle Ṭāhir was killed. When Abū Mūsā Hārūn, son of the Ilig Khān,[91] came from Turkistan to Ispījāb there was a military engagement. He captured Fā'iq's senior commanders at Khartang.[92] Fā'iq sought the Khān's protection and entered Bukhara with him. Nūḥ b. Manṣūr went into hiding. Fā'iq sought a grant of Balkh from the Khān. The Khān gave it to him and himself went back.

Amir Abū 'Alī possessed numerous troops and weapons and an ample treasury. He intervened in the territory of the Amir of Khurasan and seized control of the whole of the lands this side of the Oxus. He took possession of the proceeds of the land-tax, the tolls on local trade (*ajlāb*), the regular taxes and extraordinary levies (*ma'āwin wa aḥdāth*) and the revenues from crown lands, and he inflicted every humiliation possible on Amir Nūḥ. He assumed unilaterally the honorific title of *Amīr al-Umarā' al-Mu'ayyad min al-Samā'* ('Supreme Commander, the Divinely-Aided One'), whilst retaining the name of Nūḥ in the *khuṭba* made from the mosque pulpits.[93]

When the Ilig came to Ispījāb, Abū 'Alī sent a message to him and offered him his support. The Ilig came to Bukhara and encamped at the Jūy-i Mūliyān[94] in Rabī' I of the year 382 [/May–June 992]. Nūḥ wrote a letter and sent it with an envoy to Abū 'Alī, instructing him to to come, since the Khān had appeared; Abū 'Alī paid no heed at all to that letter. Nūḥ sought troops from him, but he did not respond. The Khān fell ill for a while with haemorrhoids and turned back homewards. On leaving, he entrusted the realm to 'Abd al-'Azīz b. Nūḥ b. Naṣr, to whom a splendid robe of honour was awarded; the Khān said to him, 'We have deprived Nūḥ of his realm and have entrusted it to you.'[95] The Ilig reached Quchqār-bāshī[96] [H 169] and there died. Nūḥ had exiled to Khwarazm from his kingdom 'Abdallāh b. Muḥammad b. 'Uzayr. When Nūḥ came to Āmūy, he recalled him and restored to him his former office. On several occasions Nūḥ sent letters to Abū 'Alī, summoning him and seeking financial help and troops, but Abū 'Alī made no reply whatever, and displayed overweening pride and rebelliousness until the day when God, He is Exalted and Magnified, showed favour for Nūḥ's cause and, [M 245] without the latter's having to seek help from anyone, vouchsafed His favourable intervention. Nūḥ returned to Bukhara.[97]

Amir Abū Manṣūr Sebüktegin, following on after the Ḥājib Alptegin, had established his control over Ghazna, Gardīz, Parwān, Kabul, Bust and those regions which Qarategin's ghulāms held.[98] Amir Sebüktegin's role and status became exalted and he became renowned. When Abū ʿAlī's harsh and contemptuous treatment of the Well-Pleasing Amir increased in intensity, Amir Nūḥ wrote a letter to Sebüktegin, may God have mercy on him, embodying his complaints about Abū ʿAlī and summoning him (i.e. to furnish aid). Amir Sebüktegin proceeded to Kish and Nakhshab, and made all the required pledges [to Nūḥ]. Abū ʿAlī moved from Merv to Nishapur in Rajab of the year 383 [/August–September 993]. Letters reached him from Amir Sebüktegin filled with a mixture of promises and menaces, but these were of no avail. Abū ʿAlī obstinately stood his ground and maintained his disregard for authority. However much he was proffered copious advice, his pride and rebelliousness only increased.

When Abū ʿAlī went beyond bounds in his rebelliousness, it was impossible to tolerate this any further. Nūḥ moved from Bukhara to Merv and from there to Herat with his army, of which Amir Sebüktegin was commander. Abū ʿAlī moved from Nishapur to Herat. Outside the town, he set up his army camp with his brothers, Fā'iq and other amirs, and envoys appeared with the aim of making peace between the opposing sides. However, Abū ʿAlī's senior commanders opposed this and said, 'Nūḥ and Sebüktegin are convinced[99] that we shall be victorious.' [N 55] The next day, Nūḥ's and Sebüktegin's troops seized the source of the water supply for Herat (? *sar-i ʿayn- Harāt*).

When Abū ʿAlī and his troops saw what was happening, they repented of their decision, but it was too late. Abū ʿAlī had an intelligence agent (*ṣāḥib-khabar*) (i.e. in Sebüktegin's camp); Amir Sebüktegin was fully aware of this man's presence, but since he deemed it expedient not to expose him, he revealed nothing. One day, a trusty messenger arrived and told Amir Sebüktegin, 'Dārā b. Qābūs[100] is intending to come over to your side when on the battlefield; I will go and escort him back.' Amir Sebüktegin was delighted at this news. He summoned that spy on pretext of giving him orders about some matter, and then spoke with one of the boon-companions of his entourage, in such a way that the spy would overhear, saying that 'Abu 'l-Qāsim Sīmjūr, Fā'iq and Dārā are all planning to come over to our side, [M 246] and one of them has undertaken to arrest Abū ʿAlī and hand him over to us,' after which the Just Amir (i.e. Sebüktegin) turned his attention to something else.

The spy reported back to Abū ʿAlī. The latter became fearful and now desired a peace agreement, after not having [previously] given any reply. He hoped that someone might come offering a peace agreement, but no-one came. Next morning, signs of treachery and betrayal became apparent within his army, and he was convinced that they would flee the battlefield. Contingents of ghulāms and banners came into view from every side, and there were so many enraged elephants, cavalrymen and infantrymen that the actual earth's surface could not be seen. Abū ʿAlī had taken up his position on an eminence. He saw that Dārā had gone over to the other side. He realised that the spy's information had been correct, and his fearfulness grew stronger. [H 170]

Then there arose the sound of drums, trumpets, barrel-shaped drums and kettledrums,[101] trumpets with tapered tubes (*gāv-dum*), cymbals, the jangling ornaments and bells of elephants, deep-toned trumpets (*karranāy*) and conches (*sapīd-muhra*), together with the shouting of warriors and the noise of horses, to such a pitch that the world grew dark. The wind arose, with dust and stones swirling in it. Abū ʿAlī fled with a body of his ghulāms, abandoning everything left there in his encampment. This battle took place in the year 384 [/994].

Then the Amir of Khurasan [N 56] and Sebüktegin's troops joined forces and fell upon Abū ʿAlī's army camp, plundering all the valuables and impedimenta there. Abū ʿAlī and his forces fled and entered Nishapur by night. The Well-Pleasing Amir Nūḥ awarded Amir Sebüktegin the honorific title of *Nāṣir al-Dīn wa 'l-Dawla* ('The One who Secures Victory for the Faith and the State') and his son Abu 'l-Qāsim Maḥmūd b. Nāṣir al-Dawla the title of *Sayf al-Dawla* ('Sword of the State').[102] Amir Maḥmūd remained for some time at Herat with Amir Nūḥ in order to finish those items of business there, and from Herat proceeded back to Nishapur.

When Abū ʿAlī Sīmjūrī realised his own wretched and humiliating position, he came forward offering his apologies, but these were not accepted, and in despair he left for Gurgān. In the year 385 [/995] the Ṣāḥib Abu 'l-Qāsim [Ismāʿīl] Ibn ʿAbbād[103] died at Ray. Amir Nūḥ went back to Bukhara, Amir Sebüktegin was at Herat and Pūshang, whilst Amir Maḥmūd was at Nishapur engaged in getting a firm grip [M 247] on affairs in that region.

Abū ʿAlī and Fā'iq came with a powerful army in the year 385. Amir Maḥmūd moved to Herat and joined up with his father, and they sought reinforcements from all quarters. Abū Naṣr [Aḥmad b.] Abū Zayd was despatched as an envoy to the ruler of Sistan Khalaf b. Aḥmad. Khalaf came with a fully equipped army, and the Amir [Abu 'l-Ḥārith Muḥammad b. Aḥmad b.] Farīghūn came from Gūzgānān. The Khalaj Turks[104] were likewise summoned. Khalaf was left at Pūshang, and his son Ṭāhir was taken along with the army. A battle took place in the region of Ṭūs at the village of Andarikh. Abū ʿAlī was routed, the prisoners he had taken were now released and his army camp was plundered.

Abū ʿAlī went to Ray via the Ṭabas road. ʿAlī b. al-Ḥasan b. Būya welcomed and made much of him, allotting him a monthly stipend [H 171] of 50,000 dirhams. Whenever he was invited to a feast, a horse with fine accoutrements would be sent along, and all that would be left for him to retain. Subsequently, Abū ʿAlī became discontented with his lot [N 57] and came back to Nishapur in disguise on account of a love affair with a woman. Amir Maḥmūd arrested and imprisoned him, but he managed to escape from his bonds and headed for Khwārazm. When he reached Hazārasp he encamped in a garden. The Khwārazm Shāh Abū ʿAbdallāh's stewards came, and set out fitting hospitality and food for Abū ʿAlī, and it was said that the Khwārazm Shāh was coming in person the next day.[105] Whilst everyone was asleep, the Khwarazmians came in and Abū ʿAlī was seized, placed in bonds, taken back to Khwarazm and imprisoned.[106]

There was a long-standing animosity (*taʿaṣṣub*) between the people of Gurgānj and those of Khwarazm (i.e. of the city of Kāth or Madīnat Khwārazm). The Amir of Gurgānj Ma'mūn sent an army. A battle ensued at [Madīnat] Khwārazm and the Khwārazm Shāh Abū ʿAbdallāh was taken prisoner. Abū ʿAlī Sīmjūrī was released from his jail. All were brought back to Gurgānj, and Abū ʿAlī al-Ma'mūn was hailed as Khwārazm Shāh. Ma'mūn was continually showing great favour to Abū ʿAlī [M 248] and gave him rich presents of money, and Abū ʿAlī's position now improved.[107]

Nūḥ's envoy came to Abū ʿAlī with many attractive words and promises of favour, and had invited him back. Abū ʿAlī went to Bukhara. ʿAbdallāh b. [Muḥammad b.] ʿUzayr and Begtuzūn[108] met and came back with him, but when they were inside Nūḥ's palace, Abū ʿAlī was seized, together with eighteen of his brothers and senior commanders, fettered and consigned to the citadel, this in the year 386 [/996].

When Amir Sebüktegin heard this news about Abū ʿAlī, he made a request to the Well-Pleasing Amir Nūḥ for him to be handed over. So Nūḥ sent Abū ʿAlī, his ghulām Il-Mengü, Amīrak Ṭūsī and Abū ʿAlī's son Abu 'l-Ḥusayn to Amir Sebüktegin in Shaʿbān of the year 386 [/August–September 996]. Sebüktegin then despatched these four persons to the fortress of Gardīz, which was a highly secure place, and imprisoned them there, and in the year 389 [/999] all four of them were killed. The Well-Pleasing Amir Abu 'l-Qāsim Nūḥ fell ill, and passed away on Friday, 14 Rajab of the year 387[109] [/23 July 997].[110]

In Shaʿbān of this year [/August–September 997], Abu 'l-Ḥasan [Fakhr al-Dawla ʿAlī b. Ḥasan] b. Būya also died. Amir Sebüktegin fell sick at Balkh. He set out for Ghaznīn but died en route, this event taking place in Shaʿbān of the year 387. When the Well-Pleasing Amir Nūḥ died, they gave him this designation of 'The Well-Pleasing One'.

Abu 'l-Ḥārith Manṣūr (II) b. Nūḥ (II)

The Well-Pleasing Amir Nūḥ b. Manṣūr had made his son Manṣūr the designated heir, and when Nūḥ died, Manṣūr succeeded to his throne when he had not yet achieved the age of maturity. His vizier was Abu 'l-Muẓaffar Muḥammad b. Ibrāhīm al-Barghashi. Fā'iq was in control of everything else. [H 172]

Al-Qādir bi'llāh Abu 'l-ʿAbbās Aḥmad b. Isḥāq b. al-Muqtadir succeeded to the caliphate and invested Abu 'l-Ḥārith with rule over Khurasan. Abū Manṣūr ʿAbdallāh b. Muḥammad b. ʿUzayr [M 249] said to Abū Manṣūr Muḥammad b. al-Ḥusayn b. Mut, '. . .[111] with me so that the supreme military command over the lands south of the Oxus may be entrusted to you' (i.e. they were planning a revolt). They also summoned the aid of the Ilig,[112] who came to them bringing military assistance and encamped at the gate of Samarqand. Abū Manṣūr came out to meet the Ilig with a small detachment of troops and brought him back to his camping place. When the Ilig's cavalrymen arrived, the Ilig ordered that Abū Manṣūr [ʿAbdallāh b. Muḥammad] b. ʿUzayr should be seized and placed in bonds. He summoned Fā'iq from Samarqand, placed him over the vanguard of his troops [N 59] and ordered him to go to Bukhara.

When Amir Abu 'l-Ḥārith got news of these events, he went to Āmūy. When Fā'iq arrived, he reproached Abu 'l-Ḥārith for the loss of the kingdom. Abu 'l-Ḥārith then appointed Begtūzūn commander-in-chief in Khurasan. He despatched him thither and himself returned to Bukhara. Fā'iq came out one stage to meet him, and they entered Bukhara together.

At this time, Amir Maḥmūd was at Nishapur. He heard about the death of his father and also that his brother Ismāʿīl b. Nāṣir al-Dīn had appropriated his father's legacy and position, including the governorship of Ghaznīn. Amir Maḥmūd set out for Ghaznīn. He and his brother clashed in a battle at the gate of Ghaznīn. He defeated his brother and took him prisoner, routed his army and occupied the town of Ghaznīn.[113]

Abu ʾl-Qāsim Sīmjūrī had inflicted a defeat on the Turks.[114] He then formed the intention of attacking Begtuzūn, and proceeded to Nishapur. Begtuzūn marched out and gave battle in the month of Rabīʿ I of the year 388 [/March 998], defeated Abu ʾl-Qāsim, and seized his wealth and possessions. Abu ʾl-Muẓaffar Barghashī was deprived of the vizierate at Bukhara, and in his place Abu ʾl-Qāsim al-ʿAbbās b. Muḥammad Barmakī was set up provisionally until someone properly qualified should appear.

When Abu ʾl-Qāsim was killed, Abu ʾl-Ḥusayn b. Muḥammad b. ʿAlī al-Ḥamūlī was set up provisionally until someone properly qualified should appear. Abu ʾl-Ḥusayn proved useless, so the vizierate was given to Abu ʾl-Faḍl Muḥammad b. Aḥmad al-Khunāmatī[115] – this place Khunāmat is one of the villages of the Bukhara region[116] – and he was confirmed in the vizierate. [M 250]

When Amir Maḥmūd had cleared up affairs at Ghaznīn, he got his forces ready and set out for Nishapur. Begtuzūn realised that he could not prevail against Maḥmūd, and withdrew to Nasā and Bāvard. Amir Abu ʾl-Ḥārith [N 60] moved against him, but Begtuzūn and Fāʾiq joined together, deposed Abu ʾl-Ḥārith and blinded him at Sarakhs on Wednesday, 12 Ṣafar of the year 389 [/2 February 999].[117] [H 173]

Abu ʾl-Fawāris ʿAbd al-Malik (II) b. Nūḥ (II)

Begtuzūn, Fāʾiq and a section of the royal guard came together and set Abu ʾl-Ḥārith's brother ʿAbd al-Malik b. Nūḥ on the throne. They sought from him an accession payment (*māl-i bayʿat*) and he handed it over. At this juncture, Amir Maḥmūd, may God have mercy on him, came to Merv seeking to avenge Abu ʾl-Ḥārith and to engage in war. Envoys met together and a peace agreement was made on the basis that Maḥmūd should have Herat and Balkh with all their revenues and treasuries. Amir Maḥmūd, may God have mercy on him, distributed 2,000 dinars in alms for the poor, and went back according to the terms of the peace agreement. He rendered thanks to God, He is Mighty and Exalted, that no blood had been shed.

Whilst Amir Maḥmūd was on the way back, the royal ghulāms attacked and plundered his baggage train, this being at the instigation and prompting of Dārā b. Qābūs. The Amir Naṣr b. Nāṣir al-Dīn, the commander-in-chief, who was the brother of Amir Maḥmūd, may God have mercy on them, came back and engaged in war. Begtuzūn was routed and returned to Bukhara in a wretched condition. Fāʾiq died in Shaʿbān of the year 389 [/July–August 999] and Begtuzūn was left in a state of deep regretfulness (i.e. for his actions).

The Ilig Abu ʾl-Ḥasan b. Naṣr,[118] the [Great] Khān's brother, came to the gate of Bukhara. He kept giving out that everything he did was out of friendship for ʿAbd al-Malik b. Nūḥ, but in reality meant the opposite, and the sons of Nūḥ were fearful of his evil intentions. The next morning they went to greet him, and they were arrested. He made them prisoners, put them in bonds and transported them to Uzgend,[119] and he seized all their wealth and possessions. Their period of power came to an end and the age of their rule [N 61] passed away. [M 251]

The Ilig entered Bukhara on Monday, 10 Dhu 'l-Qaʿda of the year 389 [/23 October 999] and established himself in the government headquarters. Abu 'l-Fawāris ʿAbd al-Malik had gone into hiding. The Ilig ordered that a search for him should be made and he was brought forth. A veil was thrown over his head, and in that guise they brought him out of Bukhara into the Ilig's presence. The latter ordered that he should be placed in bonds and transported to Uzgend. It was there, in the captivity of the Ilig, that he passed away.[120] God is Most High and Exalted! [M 252]

PART FOUR: THE EARLY GHAZNAVIDS

[Chapter Thirteen Concerning the Historical Accounts of Yamīn al-Dawla and His House]

The person who has put this book together, Abū Saʿīd ʿAbd al-Ḥayy b. al-Ḍaḥḥāk b. Maḥmūd Gardīzī, relates: Since we have finished with the stories and historical narratives of the prophets, the kings of the Chaldaeans,[1] the kings of the Persians, the Islamic caliphs and the governors of Khurasan, we have set about relating the exploits of Yamīn al-Dawla, may God's mercy be upon him, in a summary and condensed fashion. [This is] because of all the historical narratives that we have read, none have that important status that the reports about him have. For we have either heard those narratives through oral transmission or have read them in books. It may well be that authors and relaters of narratives handed down orally have set down less or more in those compositions and histories, and have said things out of an attempt to create a remarkable effect or to make the book more impressive. [H 174] But these historical narratives of ours are mainly based on what we have seen personally: what Amir Maḥmūd, may God have mercy on him, did in India; how he reduced fortresses in Nīmrūz (i.e. Sistan), Khurasan and ʿIrāq[-i ʿAjam] (i.e. Western Persia); how he traversed fearful deserts, mountains and tracks; how he undertook military campaigns there; how he subdued mighty monarchs – things the like of which no-one ever saw or heard about, for warfare and strategies like these may only be regarded as superhuman achievements.

In particular, it so happens that for this lord of the world, the exalted Sultan ʿIzz al-Dawla wa-Zayn al-Milla, Sayf Allāh, Muʿizz Dīn Allāh Abū Manṣūr ʿAbd al-Rashīd b. Yamīn al-Dawla wa-Amīn al-Milla Abi ʾl-Qāsim Maḥmūd b. Nāṣir al-Dīn wa ʾl-Dawla, [N 62] may God prolong his life and perpetuate his power, make firm his kingship and humble his enemies, royal power passed into his hands without any effort. Whenever he purposed anything he immediately achieved his desire without any hindrance or delay. So many thousands of people here became obedient and submissive to him without his shedding any blood, without any lusting for gain, without any pain or injury, without any great lapse of time, and without any trickery or deceitfulness. May his power be always firmly established, his banner always victorious and his enemy always brought low! [M 253] May his friend always be rendered joyful and all tribulations dispelled far from his sphere of life!

From all the historical narratives concerning the imperial power of this house, may God make perpetual its continuance, I have now chosen whatever is most pleasing and remarkable and have set it down here. I have kept it as brief and concise as possible; if I had been concerned with producing a commentary on events, it would have come out much fuller. I have then made a selection from those historical accounts, and have set it down here, with God Most High's permission. [H 175]

The Reign of the Most Exalted Amir, Sayyid Yamīn al-Dawla wa-Amīn al-Milla wa-Kahf al-Islām Abu 'l-Qāsim Maḥmūd, Son of Nāṣir al-Dīn wa 'l-Dawla Sebüktegin, God's Mercy upon Them!

Maḥmūd, may God have mercy on him, completed the conquest of Merv and became Amir of Khurasan. He came to Balkh, and was still there when an envoy from Baghdad sent by al-Qādir bi'llāh came to him with an investiture patent for Khurasan, a standard, a splendid robe of honour and a crown. Qādir also bestowed on him the honorific titles of *Yamīn al-Dawla wa-Amīn al-Milla* ("Right Hand of the State and Trusted One of the Religious Community"), Abu 'l-Qāsim Maḥmud, Friend (*walī*) of the Commander of the Faithful'. When the investiture patent and standard arrived, Amir Maḥmūd sat down on the throne of sovereignty, donned the robe of honour and placed the crown on his head, and held public audience for both high [N 63] and low, this being in Dhu 'l-Qa'da of the year 389 [/October–November 999).[2]

Then in the year 390 [/1000] he left Balkh for Herat. From there he went to Sistan and besieged Khalaf b. Aḥmad in the fortress of Ispahbad. Khalaf sent envoys to negotiate and made peace with Amir Maḥmūd, promising to hand over 100,000 dinars as tribute and to make the *khuṭba* in Maḥmūd's name.[3]

When Amir Maḥmūd had completed this task, he went on to Ghaznīn and from there to India, where he seized many fortresses.[4] On his return from there, the Khān sent an envoy and made a marriage alliance with Maḥmūd. The two rulers came to a solemn agreement (*muwāḍa'at*) that Transoxania should be held by the Khān (i.e. the Ilig Naṣr), whilst Amir Maḥmūd should have the lands south of the Oxus. Maḥmūd came to Nishapur at the end of Jumādā I of the year 391 [/27 April 1001].[5] [M 254]

The Samanid Abū Ibrāhīm [Ismā'īl al-Muntaṣir][6] attacked the commander-in-chief Amir Naṣr, son of Nāṣir al-Dīn [Sebüktegin], may God have mercy on the two of them. He put Amir Naṣr to flight and captured the Hindu youth (? *hindū-bachcha*),[7] this on Wednesday, the last day of Rabī' I of the year 391 [/27 February 1001]. Abū Ibrāhīm consolidated his position at Nishapur, and Amir Maḥmūd, God's mercy be upon him, led an expedition against him. Abū Ibrāhīm withdrew to Isfarā'in and Kirmān (?)[8] and from there to Gurgān, but then came back to Nishapur a second time. Amir Naṣr marched out from Nishapur to Būzgān. [Abū] Ibrāhīm's army came up after him, but the commander-in-chief Amir Naṣr put it to flight. The headman (*ra'īs*) of Sarakhs indicated to Abū Ibrāhīm that he would attack Amir Naṣr and that he, the headman, would provide him with military assistance. They both proceeded there and Amir Naṣr likewise, and they met in battle. Abū Ibrāhīm was defeated, and the Ḥājib Tūztāsh[9] and Abu 'l-Qāsim Sīmjūrī were both captured.

Abū Ibrāhīm fell back to Bāvard, [N 64, H 176] and from there went to the Ghuzz Turks and was staying amongst them. The Turks agreed to march out with him to battle. Their chief, the Yabghu, became a Muslim and became linked to Abū Ibrāhīm through a marriage alliance.[10] The two of them marched to Kūhak and gave battle to Sübāshītegin, defeating him. The Ilig came to Samarqand. They attacked him at that hill[11] and captured eighteen of his senior officers. The Ghuzz carried off the prisoners (i.e. for themselves).[12] Abū Ibrāhīm fell into despair. With a force of 300 cavalrymen and 400 infantrymen he went to the Oxus crossing-place at Darghān[13] and crossed over, the ice being firm. A force came after him in pursuit and tried to cross over the river, but the ice broke and all of them were drowned. [Abū] Ibrāhīm dallied at Āmūy. He sent the troop commander (*naqīb*) Maris[14] to Amir Maḥmūd on a mission, with the message, 'I am unable to prevent the ruin of the Samanid house except with your own help. Take thought about what you think will be the best course, and I'll follow it.' When the troop commander Maris set off, Abū Ibrāhīm went to Merv, and when he entered Kushmayhan,[15] he sought help from his sister's son, Abū Ja'far, but the latter refused this, treated the envoy with contempt and marched out to give battle to Abū Ibrāhīm and [M 255] defeated him, so that Abū Ibrāhīm fell back on Bāvard.

When Maris came into Amir Maḥmūd's presence, the Amir treated him handsomely and lavished favour on him. He sent him back with a considerable sum of money and promised him whatever he wanted. He wrote a letter to Abū Ja'far ordering him to provide assistance as far as he could and to seek forgiveness (i.e. from Abū Ibrāhīm). Abū Ibrāhīm went to Bukhara and from there to Sogdia. The Son of the Standard-Bearer (*pisar-i 'alamdār*), who was commander of the *'ayyār*s of Samarqand with a force of 3,000 men, and the elders of Samarqand, rallied to him [with 300 ghulāms].[16] The Great Khān came to combat him, but the allied forces defeated him in Sha'bān of the year 394 [/May–June 1004]. The Son of [N 65] Surkhak defected from Abū Ibrāhīm's camp to that of the Khān and joined his side.[17] Then he wrote a letter to [Abū] Ibrāhīm containing many fine words and pledges to him; but all that was a tissue of lies which he had concocted together with the Khān.[18] When the Khān received the news that the Samanid (i.e. Abū Ibrāhīm) had been defeated, he seized control of all the Oxus crossing-points and stationed men at them. When Abū Ibrāhīm heard this news, he fled with just eight men, and came to the encampment of the Son of Buḥayj, one of the Arabs nomadising in the desert around Merv. There was a local governor and tax collector (*bundār*) called Māhrūy, and he gave orders that a watch should be kept on Abū Ibrāhīm's route [and when darkness fell, they killed him], this being in Rabī' II of the year 395 [/January–February 1005]. The rule of the Samanid house came to an end at one stroke.[19]

When Amir Maḥmūd heard about the killing of Abū Ibrāhīm, he immediately despatched Arslān Jādhib to plunder the Son of Buḥayj's camp, [H 177] and Māhrūy and the Son of Buḥayj were killed in a most contemptible fashion.

When Amir Maḥmūd had reached Nishapur, the ghulāms had broken out in a revolt. He straightway got news of it and took steps energetically to deal with it. He made preparations to seize and punish them. They were filled with fear; some were captured and others fled. Amir Maḥmūd [M 256] pursued the fugitives; some he killed, some he took captive and some fled to join the Samanid (i.e. Muntaṣir). At this juncture, Abu 'l-Qāsim Sīmjūrī also took to flight [and joined up with] the Samanid.

Amir Maḥmūd returned to Herat on 5 Ramaḍān of the year 391 [/29 July 1001]. From there he proceeded to Ghaznīn, and from there on to India with a large army and encamped at the town of Peshawar with 10,000 ghāzīs. [N 66] The King of India Jaypāl (Jayapāla)[20] encamped with his army facing Amir Maḥmūd, having brought along for the battle 12,000 cavalrymen, 30,000 infantry and 300 elephants. The two sides deployed their forces in battle line and launched into the fight. God, He is Magnified and Exalted, vouchsafed His help to the Muslims, and Amir Maḥmūd emerged victorious. Jaypāl was vanquished and the unbelievers extirpated. In the course of that battle the Muslims killed 5,000 of the infidels and captured Jaypāl with fifteen of his sons and brothers. A vast amount of booty was taken, comprising money, slaves and beasts.

It is related that around Jaypāl's neck was a necklace set with jewels, which experts valued at 180,000 dinars, and they found similar precious necklaces around the necks of other Indian senior commanders. This battle took place on Saturday, 8 Muḥarram of the year 393 [/17 November 1002]. From there Maḥmūd went to Wayhind and conquered the greater part of that region. When spring came along, Amir Maḥmūd returned [to] Ghaznīn.[21]

In Muḥarram of the year 393 [/November–December 1002] he went to Sistan. Khalaf b. Aḥmad shut himself up in the fortress of Ṭāq, which was a heavily fortified place. Amir Maḥmūd held back from battle, but when the right moment came along, he gave orders for the elephants to be hurled against the gate of the fortress of Ṭāq. Khalaf was filled with terror and asked for quarter. He came forth and laid all the keys of his treasuries before Amir Maḥmūd. The latter treated him handsomely and spoke kind words to him, asking him where he would like to be sent (i.e. exiled). Khalaf [M 257] replied, 'To Gūzgānān', so Maḥmūd despatched him thither. The death[22] of Amir Khalaf took place at Dahak.[23]

When Amir Maḥmūd returned to Ghaznīn, he led an expedition against Bhatinda (Bhāṭiya).[24] He marched by way of Wālishtān and [N 67] and Ḥiṣār, and reached Bhatinda. [H 178] He was engaged in fighting there for three days. Bajī Rāy[25] prepared an army at Bhatinda, and sent it to give battle to Amir Maḥmūd whilst he himself, with a numerous force, proceeded to the bank of the river Sāsind.[26] When Amir Maḥmūd received news of this, he despatched a numerous force of cavalry against him. When they made contact, they captured all that body of troops with Bajī Rāy. When Bajī Rāy saw what the situation was, he drew his short sword and killed himself. The victors carried off his head, and all those troops of his were taken prisoner and brought before Amir Maḥmūd. The latter was filled with great joy, and ordered that all the infidels should be put to the sword. Large numbers were killed, and 280 elephants captured.

When Amir Maḥmūd returned from Bhatinda, news arrived that the people of Sistan had broken out in rebellion. He set out for Sistan, and when he came to there, all the Sistani leaders took refuge in the fortress of Ūk.[27] The Amir launched an attack lasting just one day and captured the chief of the rebels. All the Sistanis offered their submission, and Maḥmūd returned to Ghaznīn victorious and triumphant.

From Ghaznīn he set off on an expedition against Multān. The Amir thought that, if he went by the direct road, Dāwūd, son of Naṣr, the Amir of Multān, would become aware of the attack and be ready to resist it, so he went by a different route. Jaypāl's son Anandpāl (Ānandapāla) blocked the way and refused Amir Maḥmūd transit across his territory. Amir Maḥmūd gave his troops free rein, and they fell upon Anandpāl's territories and busied themselves with seizing people and things, killing and plundering. Anandpāl fled into the mountains of Kashmir. Amir Maḥmūd took the main route into India to Multān and besieged that place for seven days, until negotiations took place between the two sides, and a peace agreement was reached on the basis that twenty [N 68] million dirhams would be handed over annually from the province of Multān. On these terms the peace agreement was concluded, and Amir Maḥmūd returned homewards. This took place in the year [3]96 [/1005–6].[28]

Amir Maḥmūd then heard that the Turks (i.e. the troops of the Qarakhanids) had crossed the Oxus, had entered Khurasan and [M 258] had spread out through the land.[29] The Amir rushed back from Multān to Ghaznīn in double-quick time (*ba-'ahdī nazdīk*). The Turk Sübāshītegin had come to Herat and taken possession of it, and had sent a cavalry force to Nishapur in order to seize control of that region. Amir Maḥmūd's governor Arslān Jādhib had withdrawn from Nishapur. The Turks had not yet consolidated their position when the news came that Amir Maḥmūd had returned from India and had reached Balkh. The Khān's troops pulled back in order to join up with the Khān himself, but Amir Maḥmūd's agents had seized control of their intended routes. The Turks were filled with alarm and were retreating to the regions of Marv al-Rūd, Sarakhs, Nasā and Bāvard, with Arslān Jādhib all the time pursuing them from town to town. Those who fell into Arslān Jādhib's hands he would either make captive or kill. [H 179]

Amir Maḥmūd sent the Ḥājib Altuntāsh to reinforce him. The Turks then sought a way out. Some of them went to the river crossing-place, and one group of them took a bold decision and tried to cross the Oxus, but the greater part of them was drowned. The Cis-Oxanian lands were thus cleared of them. Information reached Amir Maḥmūd that a substantial force of the Turks had proceeded to the bank of the Oxus but would not be able to cross (?).[30] Drums which were the signal for attack were beaten and elephant accoutrements jangled.[31] When the Turks who had been left there heard that clamour, they threw themselves into the river out of terror and were drowned. Ghāzī, the master of the stables (*ākhur-sālār*), was killed there in . . . who fought.[32] Amir Maḥmūd had the intention of engaging them, but since his troops had become exhausted from fighting, [N 69] he thought that, if his troops carried on combatting the enemy, the Turks might in desperation fight for their lives, and it might happen that some adverse effects might mar[33] this victory and triumph.

When Sübāshītegin came into the Ilig's presence, the latter upbraided him violently, but the senior officers replied that it was impossible for anyone to withstand those elephants, weapons and matériel, and warriors. After these events, the Ilig sent agents to all parts of Transoxania and sought to assemble an army, and he ended up with a force of 40,000 cavalrymen. With that army he crossed the Oxus and reached Balkh. Amir Maḥmūd marched thither and the armies clashed on the plain of Katar.[34] When the armies [M 259] formed up in their battle lines, Amir Maḥmūd performed two *rak'at*s of the worship and prayed to God, He is Magnified and Exalted, for victory. Then he turned his attention to the battle. He gave orders that all the elephants should be enraged and sent forward in an attack. The Turks were immediately defeated, and Amir Maḥmūd's army killed large numbers of them and took many captives. Those who fled were drowned in the Oxus, and their horses and weapons seized as booty. This victory took place on Sunday, 22 Rabīʿ II of the year 398 [/5 January 1008].[35]

When Amir Maḥmūd had completed this campaign, news arrived that Shūkpāl (Sukhapāla), the king's (i.e. Jaypāl's) grandson, who had been held captive at Nishapur by Abū ʿAlī Sīmjūr and had become a Muslim, had now apostasised. Amir Maḥmūd set out to attack him, and captured him in the mountains of K.sh.n.w.r.[36] Shūkpāl offered to pay an indemnity of 400,000 dirhams. Amir Maḥmūd handed that sum over to Tegin[37] the Treasurer and held Shūkpāl in captivity until he died in it. From there he marched into India in the year 399 [/1008–9]. He attacked Anandpāl and defeated him, and he captured thirty elephants [H 180] whilst the army took much booty. From there he went to the fortress of Bhīmnagar [N 70] and besieged it. Fighting went on for three days until the defenders came out under a guarantee of safe conduct and opened the gate. Amir Maḥmūd and a detachment of his personal guard entered the fortress and seized the treasuries of gold, silver and diamonds and everything which had been deposited there in the time of Bhīm of the Pāndu'a dynasty. In that fortress they found quantities of wealth whose extent was hardly conceivable, and from there he returned to Ghaznīn. The throne made of gold and silver was set up at the palace gate, and he gave orders for all that wealth to be openly displayed and spread out for all the troops and the masses of people to see. This was in the year 400 [/1009–10].[38]

When it was the year 401 [/1010–11], he led an attack from Ghaznīn on Multān. He proceeded there and annexed what remained of that province in its entirety. He seized the greater part of the Carmathians there: [M 260] some of these he killed, he cut off the hands of some and inflicted exemplary punishment, and some he imprisoned in various fortresses until they all died there. In this same year, he seized Dāwūd b. Naṣr, brought him back to Ghaznīn and from there consigned him to the fortress of Ghūrak, where he was held prisoner till he died.[39]

Information reached Amir Maḥmūd that Thānesar was an important place with large numbers of idols there. The Indians accorded it an importance comparable to the position of Mecca for the Muslims, and they venerated the shrine highly. Within the city was a very ancient idol temple containing an idol which was called Chakraswāmī (*j.k.r.s.w.m*). When Amir Maḥmūd heard about this, he felt a strong desire to go there, conquer that region, destroy that idol temple and acquire a great [heavenly] reward for himself. So in the year 402 [/1011–12] he set out from Ghaznīn and [N 71] headed for Thānesar.

When the king of India Trilochanpāl (Trilochanapāla) heard about this, he became alarmed. He sent an envoy to Amir Maḥmūd promising that, if he would desist from his intention and not march against Thānesar, he would give him fifty choice elephants. Amir Maḥmūd paid no heed to those words and set out. He reached the encampment of Rām (Rāma). Rām's troops advanced along the road in great force and took up positions at a place suitable for an ambush, and killed large numbers of the Muslims. When Maḥmūd reached Thānesar, he found that the town had been evacuated. The Muslim troops plundered whatever they found and smashed numerous idols. They carried off to Ghaznīn the idol Chakraswāmī. It was set up at the palace, and lots of people flocked round it to look at it.[40]

In the year 403 [/1012–13] Maḥmūd conquered Gharchistān. He brought forth the Shēr (texts, Shār), ruler of Gharchistān, placed him in bonds and depatched him to the town of Mastang.[41] [H 181]

When the year 403 reached its end (i.e. in July 1013), Abu 'l-Fawāris [Qawām al-Dawla] b. Bahā' al-Dawla came from Kirman to Amir Maḥmūd at Bust seeking the Amir's protection from his brother Abū Shujāʿ [Sulṭān al-Dawla], and was in Ghaznīn for three months. Amir [M 261] Maḥmūd wrote letters regarding this matter and admonished the two parties, and in the end they came to a peaceful solution of their differences, and Abu 'l-Fawāris's brother further undertook not to engage in any more quarrelling and animosity with his brother. Abu 'l-Fawāris returned to Kirman and reassumed his rule there in security and peace.[42]

Also in the course of this year, an envoy called Tāhartī arrived from the ruler of Egypt. When the envoy reached Khurasan, the jurists and theological scholars proclaimed that 'This envoy is come to solicit allegiance to the ruler of Egypt, and he's a Bāṭinī!' When Maḥmūd heard about this, he refused to receive that envoy and ordered him to be handed over to Ḥasan b. Ṭāhir b. Muslim al-ʿAlawī, and Ḥasan personally executed Tāhartī at Bust.[43]

In [N 72] the year 404 [/1013–14] Maḥmūd led an army against the fortress of Nandana.[363] When the king of India Trilochanpāl heard about this, he garrisoned that fortress with battle-hardened warriors, giving instructions for its being held, whilst he himself set out for the pass leading into Kashmir and proceeded there. Amir Maḥmūd's troops took up their positions before Nandana, and the sappers (*ḥaffārān*) began digging mines. The Turkish troops were firing arrows up to the top of the walls. When the defenders in the citadel saw warfare being conducted in this manner, they very quickly asked for a guarantee of safety and quarter, and yielded up the fortress. Amir Maḥmūd and a band of his personal guards entered the fortress, and they carried off the wealth and the weapons found there. Amir Maḥmūd appointed Sārïgh castellan of that fortress, and himself set out for the pass into Kashmir where Trilochanpāl was. On hearing of this, Trilochanpāl fled, and Amir Maḥmūd gave orders for all the fortresses along the pass into Kashmir to be seized and plundered. The troops gained from those fortresses large amounts of booty and many slaves, and many infidels became converts to Islam. In this same year, he gave orders for congregational mosques to be built in all the lands conquered from the infidels, and for teachers to be despatched to all places for inculcating in the Indians the rites and duties of Islam. He himself returned to Ghaznīn victorious and triumphant. This capture of Nandana was in the year 405 [/1014–15].[45] [M 262]

When it was the year [40]6 [/1015–16], he led an expedition against Kashmir. He set out for Kashmir from Ghaznīn, but when he reached the pass into Kashmir, the weather grew cold and winter set in. Within the pass there was a very strong and well-fortified castle called Lōhkōt – which means 'Iron Fortress' [N 73] – and this had a water supply and a numerous garrison. He stationed his army beneath that fortress and kept up continuous attacks on it. He was engaged in this for quite a while, but just when he discovered a means of conquering the fortress, extremely cold weather set in, it began to snow and everything became frozen up, so that nothing could be done on account of the cold. Reinforcements for the fortress's garrison arrived from Kashmir by the road across the mountains from there, and [H 182] the garrison received an access of strength. Amir Maḥmūd took all these facts into account and concluded that his troops would not be able to make any headway, so he raised the siege and descended from those mountains and passes to the plain. He got back to Ghaznīn in the spring.[46]

Also in the year 406, a letter arrived from Khwarazm sent by the Khwarazm Shah Abu 'l-ʿAbbās al-Ma'mūn (II) b. al-Ma'mūn (I) seeking the hand in marriage of Yamīn al-Dawla's sister. Amir Maḥmūd agreed to this and gave his sister to the Shah, and she was brought to Khwarazm. Then in the year 407 [/1016–17] a group of intriguers and dregs of the Khwarazm population banded together and stirred up a revolt, in the course of which the Khwarazm Shah, Yamīn al-Dawla's son-in-law, was killed. News of this reached the Amir Yamīn al-Dawla. He went from Ghaznīn to Balkh, and from there led an expedition to Khwarazm. On reaching Jakarband,[47] which is on the frontier with Khwarazm, he deployed his forces for battle. He sent forward Muḥammad b. Ibrāhīm al-Ṭā'ī in command of the army's advance guard. Muḥammad al-Ṭā'ī encamped in a certain place with all his cavalry. At daybreak, the Muslim troops were all engaged in their ritual worship and ablutions when the Khwarazmian commander Khumārtāsh appeared from the desert with a numerous army, attacked them and killed some of Muḥammad al-Ṭā'ī's cavalry.

Amir Maḥmūd was perturbed when he received news of this, and despatched a contingent of the palace ghulāms [M 263] to pursue Khumārtāsh These troops routed Khumārtāsh's army completely and captured him [N 74] and brought him along. There was unparalleled slaughter and wounding. When they reached Hazārasp, the Khwarazmian army, in perfect battle order and armed to the teeth, advanced on Yamīn al-Dawla's army. The latter was drawn up in battle lines, with the right and left, the centre and the wings, properly deployed, and battle was joined. It was not long before the Khwarazmian army was put to flight. The commander of the Khwarazmian army, Alptegin Bukhārī, was captured. Yamīn al-Dawla's troops invaded Khwarazm and seized the [ancient] capital (*shahr-i Khwārazm*, i.e. Kāth).

The first thing that Yamīn al-Dawla did was to order that all the wrongdoers, including Alptegin Bukhārī and others, should be seized and brought before him. Then he ordained that fitting reprisals should be wrought on each one of them. Vengeance was exacted on behalf of those who had claims for revenge: some were chastised and punished, others were clapped in bonds and consigned to imprisonment.

Amir Maḥmūd appointed his Chief Ḥājib Altuntāsh as governor of Khwarazm (*Khwārazm Shāh*), with Khwarazm (i.e Kāth) and Gurgānj entrusted to him, and to the end of his life Altuntāsh acted as Khwarazm Shah, fully obedient and the faithful servant of Amir Maḥmūd and his house.[48] The decisive battle for Khwarazm took place on 5 Ṣafar of the year 408 [/3 July 1017]. From there, the Amir returned to Balkh and stayed there for some time.[49] Prince Mas'ūd was summoned to Balkh, and when Mas'ūd came into his presence he spoke cordially with him, appointed him governor of Herat and despatched him thither, having attached to him Abū Sahl Muḥammad b. al-Ḥusayn al-Zawzanī as his administrator and counsellor (*kadkhudā*), and he likewise sent him to Herat with Mas'ūd. He conferred the governorship of Gūzgānān on Prince Muḥammad, in the same way giving him a robe of honour and speaking cordially with him, and despatched him to Gūzgānān with Abū Bakr Quhistānī (i.e. as his *kadkhudā*). [H 183]

When it was the year 409 [/1018–19], Amir Maḥmūd decided on [N 75] an expedition against [M 264] Qanawj. This was an extensive, populous and rich region, with numerous infidels. He crossed seven hazardous rivers, and when he reached the confines of Qanawj, he sent a letter to a certain K.w.ra (?), who was the ruler of the frontier region; he made his submission and asked for a grant of security and quarter, which the Amir extended to him. From there, he marched to the fortress of Baran (text, *b.r.na*),[50] whose prince was Hardat. The latter took flight and abandoned his followers. Hardat's followers fortified themselves within the fortress, but when the army of Islam appeared on the scene and the defenders saw their splendid panoply of arms, they sent persons to negotiate and redeemed their freedom by handing over a million dirhams and thirty elephants.

From there, the army of Islam moved to Mahāban (text, *m.hāw.n*) where the commander of the fortress was Kulchandra (Kulachand). This fortress was situated on the banks of the river Jumna (text, *j.w.n*). When Kulchandra heard about the Amir Yamīn al-Dawla's approach, he mounted an elephant, the choicest one out of all those he had, and tried to cross the river. Amir Maḥmūd became aware of this and ordered the ways of access to be closed off. When Kulchandra realised this, he slew himself with his own short sword. Yamīn al-Dawla's troops entered the fortress, and they carried off 185 choice elephants and plundered inestimable amounts of wealth. From there, he marched on the fortress of Muttra (Mātūra), which is a great city and *the* idol temple of the Indians. It is said that the birthplace of Krishna (text, *k.sh.n*), son of Bāsdīv, whom the Indians consider as their prophet, was at this place Muttra.

When Amir Maḥmūd came to this region of Muttra, no-one came out to oppose him. He gave orders for his troops to enter that region, and whenever they came across an idol temple, they pulled it down and burnt it. They carried off all the wealth there as plunder. Amir Maḥmūd got wealth from the idol temples and treasuries of that region to an extent which could not be visualised, [N 76] including a sapphire (*yāqūt-i kuḥlī*) weighing 450 mithqāls (!). No-one had ever before seen such a jewel. There were also idols made of gold and silver, unlimited in number and in size. Amir Maḥmūd ordered one golden idol [M 265] to be broken up and the pieces weighed; 98,300 mithqāls of well-worked gold were obtained from it, and an equivalent amount of money and numerous jewels was gained from there. This conquest of Qanawj was on 8 Shaʿbān of the year 409 [/20 December 1018].[51]

When the Rajah (*rāy*) of Qanawj had been captured (?), Amir Maḥmūd speedily returned homewards from there. On the road from Qanawj to Ghaznīn, the treasury of Chandra (text, *ch.n.d*) Rāy was brought before him, containing an immense amount of wealth. There was also a celebrated elephant belonging to this Chandra Rāy, whose fame had become proverbial throughout India. Amir Yamīn al-Dawla had heard of that beast's fame and had formed the intention that he must buy it at any price, since he was avid to get it; and if it were required to give fifty elephants in exchange for it, he would give them for that single elephant. By a fortunate concatenation of circumstances, the elephant stampeded along the road away from Chandra Rāy and, not having any elephant driver on it, went along until it reached the tented enclosure of Yamīn al-Dawla. When Amir Maḥmūd saw it, he gave thanks to God Most High, and he named the elephant Khudādād ('God-Given One'), and from that place he gave orders for the return to Ghaznīn, victorious and triumphant and laden with a vast amount of plunder. [H 184]

Trustworthy authorities assert that they totalled up the amount of plunder brought back from the Qanawj expedition in that year by the Amir Yamīn al-Dawla, as amounting to twenty-odd million dirhams, 53,000 captives and over 350 elephants.

When it was the month of Tīr of the year 410 [/June–July 1019], Amir Yamīn al-Dawla led an expedition against Ganda (text, *n.n.dā*),[52] who had killed Rājyapāl (Rājyapāla) the ruler of Qanawj, having reproached this last for having fled before Maḥmūd's army, and who had undertaken to Trilochanpāl to provide him with assistance [N 77] and an army that would recover for him his kingdom. When news of Maḥmūd's imminent approach reached those lands, Trilochanpāl crossed the Ganges and came to Bārī. Amir Yamīn al-Dawla crossed the river. All those troops clashed together. Trilochanpāl fled with a detachment of Indian troops, and they avoided further contact with Maḥmūd. An attack was then launched on the town of Bārī. The troops found that the inhabitants had fled and the town left empty; they burnt down all the idol temples [M 266] and plundered everything they could find.

From Bārī, the Amir's army headed towards Ganda's kingdom, crossing numerous wide rivers. Ganda had got news of the army of Islam's approach and had got ready for war, assembling round himself extensive forces; it was reported that there were in his army 36,000 cavalrymen, 5,400[53] infantrymen and 640 elephants, together with weapons, treasuries and fodder commensurate for such numbers. When Amir Maḥmūd drew near to Ganda, he drew up his army in battle formation, and set out the right and left, the centre, the two wings, the vanguard and the rearguard, and he sent out scouts. He encamped with resolution and with careful precautions. Then he sent an envoy to Ganda, proffering wise counsel, expressing threats and rousing him to awareness of the situation. He sent verbal messages containing excuses (i.e for attacking him) and admonitions, exhorting Ganda to become a Muslim and thereby render himself immune from all this warfare, aggravation and destruction. Ganda replied, however, that there could be nothing but war between them.

I have heard from certain reliable sources that Amir Yamīn al-Dawla took up a position that day upon an eminence in order to view Ganda's army. He saw a whole world of tents, pavilions and camp enclosures, with cavalry, infantry and elephants. His spirits drooped and he became gripped by regrets, so he sought help from God Most High, asking that He should vouchsafe him victory. That night, God Most High sowed fear and apprehension within Ganda's heart; he got his army to move off and withdraw. The next day, Amir Maḥmūd sent an envoy. When [N 78] the emissary reached Ganda's encampment, he could see no persons about; all military arms and equipment had been left as it was, but the troops had gone, and all the beasts and elephants had been driven off. The envoy went back and reported this to Amir Maḥ mūd, who ordered that possible ambushes should be investigated. They examined where the army had been encamped, but it had entirely departed. Amir Yamīn al-Dawla offered up thanks to God, He is Magnified and Exalted, and gave orders for Ganda's encampment to be plundered. Great amounts of wealth and property of all kinds were carried off. From there he then returned to Ghaznīn victorious and triumphant. On the way back they came to a forest. The troops went into its depths and found there 580 of Ganda's elephants, [H 185] all of which they drove off (sc. as booty) and [M 267] brought back to their own encampment.[54]

News reached Amir Yamīn al-Dawla that there were two valleys, one called the Qīrāt and the other the Nūr, and these were highly defensible and the people there infidels and idol worshippers. Yamīn al-Dawla led an expedition against these valleys with his army, and he gave orders that numerous squads of artisans, including blacksmiths, carpenters and stonehewers, should accompany the troops, hack out roads, cut down trees and break up rocks. When they reached there, they first made for the Qīrāt valley. This is a pleasant place, whose inhabitants were worshippers of the lion, and with a cool environment and copious fruits grown there. When the ruler of the Qīrāt valley heard about this, he came forward and offered his submission, seeking a guarantee of quarter and security. Amir Maḥmūd received him and showed favour appropriate for his status. The ruler of Qīrāt became a Muslim, together with a large number of the people of his land who followed their ruler's example. They accepted teachers and began to learn the duties and requirements of the faith and to observe the *sharī'at*. The people of the Nūr valley, however, were refractory. Amir Maḥmūd ordered the Ḥājib 'Alī b. Il Arslān al-Qarīb to proceed to Nūr. He conquered it, built there a fortress and appointed 'Alī b. Qadïr Rāḥūq (?) as its castellan, commanding him to use force [N 79] and compulsion, and to impose Islam upon the people by the sword. They accepted that willy-nilly, and Islam spread over those lands. This conquest of the Nūr and Qīrāt valleys was in the year 411 [/1020–1].[55]

When the year 412 [/1021–2] came round, he led an expedition against Kashmir, and he invested the fortress of Lōharkōt. He carried out operations against it for a whole month but was unable to make any headway because it was extremely impregnable and well fortified. During the course of this year, Amir Naṣr b. Nāṣir al-Dīn passed away and Amir Yūsuf b. Nāṣir al-Dīn had gone along with Yamīn al-Dawla. Since it proved impossible to reduce the fortress of Lōharkōt, he withdrew from that valley and proceeded to Lahore and Tākīshar.[56] The troops spread out over that piedmont region and were continually engaged in *ghazw*. Then when spring came along, [M 268] the Amir set out back to Ghaznīn.[57]

When it was the year 413 [/1022–3], Amir Maḥmūd led an expedition against Ganda's territories. When he reached the fortress of Gwalior, he invested it and besieged it. He ordered his troops to occupy all the surrounding territory, but since that fortress was so well fortified and impregnable, and was situated upon a rock of hard stone, sappers and miners and operators of ballistas were useless against it, and it was not possible to take it. Amir Maḥmūd remained there four days and nights until the commander of the fortress sent an envoy and sued for peace, offering thirty-five elephants.

In the end Yamīn al-Dawla's army left Gwalior and marched against Kālanjar, Ganda's own stronghold. Ganda was within that fortress with all his troops, personal retainers and family. Amir Maḥmūd [H 186] ordered his troops completely to surround the fortress, and he was deliberating and making plans since this fortress was a lofty and well-fortified place such that no stratagems or valorous deeds could avail to reduce it. Moreover, the fortress was built [N 80] on a hard rock so that there was no possibility of mining and tunnelling beneath it, and there seemed to be no other means of conquering it. The Amir sat down before it and remained there several days. But when Ganda looked out and saw that numerous army, that had seized all possible ways of access to the fortress, he sent out envoys to discuss peace terms. The terms arrived at involved Ganda's paying tribute (*jizya*), sending the customary presents immediately and handing over 300 choice elephants. Ganda was pleased at this peace arrangement. He straightway ordered the 300 elephants to be driven out of the fortress without mahouts. Amir Maḥmūd gave orders, and the Turks and other warriors plunged into those elephants, secured them and mounted them; the defenders were meanwhile watching from the fortress, and were filled with great wonder at their intrepidness.

Ganda afterwards composed poetry in Hindi in praise of Amir Maḥmūd and sent it to him, and the latter ordered the verses to be recited in the presence of all his court poets – Indian, Persian and Arabic ones. All of them showed their approval and averred that no more eloquent and lofty poetry could be uttered. Amir Maḥmūd took great pride in it and ordered that an investiture patent conferring upon Ganda the governorship of fifteen [M 269] fortresses should be written out and sent to him. He added the words, 'This is an award in return for that poetry you uttered about me,' and he further sent with it many additional things – costly presents, jewels and robes of honour. Ganda sent back in return much wealth and jewels on a similar scale. Amir Maḥmūd returned from there victorious and triumphant, and came to Ghaznīn.[58]

In the year 414 [/1023–4], he ordered a review of the army to be held. Fifty-four thousand cavalrymen paraded on the review ground at the plain of Shāhbahār, these in addition to those cavalrymen who were stationed in outlying parts of the realm and who were on garrison duty in the provinces. One thousand, three hundred elephants, with complete outfits of armour and other trappings, that had paraded in that review, came forth to be enumerated. The number of beasts, including camels and horses, was beyond comparison.[59] [N 81]

At the opening of the year 415 [/15 March 1024], Amir Maḥmūd decided to go to Balkh with the intention of going there and staying over the winter. When he reached Balkh, streams of persons complaining about ʿAlītegin were coming to him continually from Transoxania. They were complaining specifically about ʿAlītegin's oppressive measures, that he was committing many inadmissible acts, afflicting people in various ways, and harming both the subjects and the military classes. When these complaints reached a high pitch, Amir Maḥmūd formed the intention of springing into action[60] and delivering those Muslims there from that distress and those tribulations. He wanted to cross the Oxus and reconnoitre those regions, and formulated firm plans for this. He said, 'If we cross the river in boats, some calamity might occur.' He spent some considerable time over the assembling of materials and equipment. What he did was to order the making of stout chains fitting into each other (lit. 'male and female', *nar u māda*), all of them two or three fathoms[61] long. All the chains were encased in cow hides. Boats were brought along and these were fastened together spanning the width of the Oxus by means of those interlocking chains and on frameworks yoked together which had been constructed in the boats. Strong palm tree fibres had been brought from Sistan, [H 187] with each one transported on a camel's back, and the boats were wrapped round with these fibres. The insides of the boats were stuffed with straw, rags, etc., so that cavalrymen, infantrymen, camels, mules and asses could pass over them easily.[62] [M 270] He then brought the army across on that bridge of boats and himself crossed over.

When news of Yamīn al-Dawla's actions reached Transoxania, a great buzz of excitement and perturbation arose amongst the people in those lands and the local princes became apprehensive. The first person to come and make obeisance to the Amir was the ruler of Chaghāniyān,[63] who brought all his troops, appeared before the Amir in person and rendered every form of service possible. After him there came to Amir Maḥmūd the Khwarazm Shah, the Ḥājib Altuntāsh, with all his troops. Amir Maḥmūd [N 82] then ordered a large tented enclosure (*sarāy-parda*) to be set up, one which would accommodate 10,000 cavalrymen. Another such tented enclosure, of crimson Shushtarī brocade, one with a canopy and domed roof of embroidered brocade, was erected for his personal use.

Then he ordered the army to be deployed in its formations, each with its right, left, centre and two wings, and with an armoury (*zarrād-khāna*) held behind each formation, and the elephants were stationed with their protective armour and saddles. He further ordered a simultaneous blowing of trumpets and beating of kettle drums, barrel-shaped drums and large drums. The elephants' backs were draped with plates, elephant ornaments and white shells (i.e. for jangling); conches were blown, and drums and *b.ḥūr* (?)[64] beaten. Without exception every individual present was almost stricken deaf by such a din, men lost their senses, and all those persons from Turkestan and Transoxania present in that encampment were terrified (lit. 'their gall bladders almost split').[65]

The Meeting of Yūsuf Qadïr Khān and Sultan Maḥmūd, God's Mercy upon Them Both!

When Qadïr Khān, who was the leading figure in all Turkestan and the Great Khan, received news of Yamīn al-Dawla's crossing the Oxus, he set out from Kashghar with the aim of arranging an encounter with Amir Maḥmūd, so that he might then go and meet with him face to face and renew their previous agreement. Leaving Kashghar, he came to Samarqand and travelled on from there, with peaceful and amicable intentions, until he came within a parasang of Amir Maḥmūd's army and encamped there. He ordered a camp enclosure to be erected, and he sent envoys to acquaint Amir Maḥmūd [M 271] with his arrival and to express his keen desire for a meeting with him. Amir Maḥmūd sent back a correspondingly enthusiastic reply and named a place for their meeting. Then the Amir and Qadïr Khān, both accompanied by detachments of cavalry, [N 83] went to this place. When they came into view of each other, they both dismounted. Amir Maḥmūd had previously given a jewel of high value, wrapped up in a cloth, to his treasurer, instructing him to place it in Qadïr Khān's hands. Qadïr Khān had similarly brought with him a jewel, but through the fear and agitation which had come over him had forgotten it. Only after he had left Maḥmūd's presence did he remember it, so he sent it with one of his retainers, sought forgiveness (i.e. for his negligence) and returned to his camp. The next day, Amir Maḥmūd gave orders for a large tent of embroidered brocade to be erected and for an entertainment to be prepared, and he sent an envoy to Qadïr Khān inviting him as his guest.

A Description of the Celebration and the Feast

When Qadïr Khān arrived, Maḥmūd ordered trays of food to be set out as splendidly as possible, and the two monarchs sat down and ate at the same table. When they had finished the feast, they moved on to the place where music and other festive entertainments had been prepared. This had been magnificently decorated with rare and unusual sweet-smelling plants, luscious fruits and precious jewels. The hall had goblets of gold and crystal, remarkable mirrors and various rare objects so that Qadïr Khān remained in the midst of all this dazzled. They remained seated there for a good length of time. Qadïr Khān did not drink wine, since it was not customary for the monarchs of Transoxania, and especially the Turkish ones of them, to drink wine. They listened to music and singing for a while and then they arose.

Amir Maḥmūd then ordered a display of presents on a scale worthy of the occasion, to be brought in: gold and silver drinking vessels; costly jewels; unusual specialities imported from Baghdad; fine clothes; expensive arms; valuable horses with gold accoutrements and with goads studded with jewels; [M 272] ten female elephants with gold trappings and goads set with jewels; mules from Bardhaʿa with golden bells; litters for mules with girths, moon-like ornaments of gold and silver [N 84] and bells for their necks; litters covered with embroidered brocade and woven patterns; valuable carpets, including those from Armenia with raised patterns (*maḥfūrī-hā*) and *uwaysī* and particoloured rugs; pieces of woven and embroidered cloth; lengths of rose-coloured cloth from Ṭabaristān[66] with designs on them; Indian swords; aloes wood from Khmer; yellow-tinged[67] sandalwood; grey-flecked amber; she-asses; skins of Barbary panthers; hunting dogs; falcons and eagles trained to a high pitch for hunting down cranes; and gazelles and other game animals. He sent Qadïr Khān back homewards with great honour and magnificence, heaping favours on him and asking to be excused (i.e. for the inadequacy of the reception and the presents). [H 189]

When Qadïr Khān got back to his encampment and he saw that immense amount of precious objects, furnishings and carpets, weapons and wealth, he was filled with astonishment and did not know how he could requite Maḥmūd for them. He ordered his treasurer to open up the treasury door. He took out a great amount of wealth and sent it to Amir Maḥmūd, together with various items which were specialities of Turkestan, including fine horses with precious trappings and accoutrements of gold; Turkish slave boys with golden belts and quivers; falcons and hawks; pelts of sable (*samūr*), grey squirrel (*sinjāb*), ermine (*qāqum*) and fox (*rūbāh*); vessels made from leather skins; narwhal or walrus horn (? *danīsha-yi khutuww*);[68] delicate cloth and Chinese brocade; Chinese *dārkhāshāk*;[69] and suchlike.[70] The two monarchs parted from each other completely satisfied and in peace and benevolence.

When ʿAlītegin got news of this meeting, he fled into the desert. Amir Maḥmūd posted intelligence officers for the direction ʿAlītegin had taken. Then information arrived that [Arslān] Isrāʾīl b. Seljuq had moved to a secret location. Yamīn al-Dawla despatched troops to ferret him out from there, and he sent him to Ghaznīn and thence to India, where he remained till the end of his life (i.e. in captivity).[71]

The news came that ʿAlītegin's family and baggage were about to follow him into the desert. Amir Maḥmūd [N 85] sent the Ḥājib Bilgetegin in pursuit of them. Bilgetegin [M 273] set out and used various stratagems to capture ʿAlītegin's wives, daughters and baggage, and forwarded them to Amir Maḥmūd. This was in the year 416 [/1025–6].

The Beginnings of the Seljuq Turks

At this time when Amir Maḥmūd was in Transoxania, a group of persons, comprising the military chiefs and leading men of Turkestan, came into his presence complaining of the tyranny exercised over them by their amirs and of the injurious treatment they were enduring at their hands. They said,

> We number 4,000 families. If the lord were to issue a command and allow us to cross the Oxus and settle in Khurasan, he would be relieved of worrying about us [H 190] and there would be plenty of space for us in his realm, since we are steppe people and have extensive herds of sheep. Moreover, we would provide additional manpower for his army.[72]

Amir Maḥmūd looked favourably on this request for them to cross the Oxus. He gave them encouragement and hopes of a good outcome, and ordered that they should be allowed to cross the Oxus. In accordance with his command, 4,000 families of them, men, women and children, and their baggage and their sheep, camels, horses and beasts of burden, crossed the river in their entirety, and they installed themselves in the desert of Sarakhs and the desert of Farāwa and Bāward, pitched their tents and made their home permanently there.

When Amir Maḥmūd crossed back from over the Oxus, the Amir of Ṭūs, Abu 'l-Ḥārith Arslān al-Jādhib,[73] came to him saying, 'Why did you bring these Turkmens into your realm? You committed an error here! But now that you have admitted them, either kill them all or [at least] allow me to cut off their thumbs so that they won't be able to shoot arrows.' Amir Maḥmūd was astonished and accused him of being a pitiless and hard-hearted man. The Amir of Ṭūs replied, 'If you don't do it, you'll much regret it!' It happened exactly thus, and even to this present time, [N 79] there has been no satisfactory outcome of the problem.[74]

Amir Maḥmūd came from Balkh to Ghaznīn and spent the summer there. When [M 274] winter began, he led a raiding expedition into India, as was his usual custom. A story had been related to him that there was a great city on the shores of the All-Encompassing Sea (sc. the Indian Ocean) called Somnath (Sūmnāt, Somanātha) which was venerated by the Indians just as the Muslims venerate Mecca. It contained numerous idols of gold and silver, and the idol Manāt, which had been transported from the Kaʿba by way of Aden in the time of the Lord of the World (i.e. Muḥammad), was there. It had been adorned with gold and set with jewels, and a vast amount of wealth had been laid up in the treasuries of that idol temple. However, the route to it was difficult and full of danger, containing many fearful places and extremely arduous.

When Amir Maḥmūd heard this account, he became gripped by the idea of marching against that city and destroying those idols and of embarking on a raiding expedition. He left northern India (Hindūstān) for Somnath by the route through Nahrawāla. When he reached the latter town, it had been completely evacuated and all its inhabitants had fled. He gave orders for his army to carry off food and fodder from there, and set out for Somnath.[75] When he drew near to the city, and the Shamanān[76] and Brahmans saw that army, they all busied themselves with worshipping and invoking the idols. The military commander of the city came forth, and then got into a boat with his family and baggage, and launched out across the sea. The boat hove to at an island, and all of them remained there as long as the army of Islam remained in that region, not budging from the island.

When the army of Islam approached the city, the inhabitants all retreated into the fortress and engaged in battle. It was not very long before the fortress was conquered, and Amir Maḥmūd's troops poured into it and inflicted the most frightful slaughter, and large numbers of the infidels were killed. [H 191] Amir Maḥmūd gave orders, and the muezzin climbed to the top of the shrine (*d.y.h.ra*)[77] and gave the call to prayer. All the idols were smashed up, burnt and destroyed. The stone embodying Manāt was wrenched from its base and [N 87] smashed to pieces. Some of these pieces were loaded on to the backs of mules and brought to Ghaznīn, and to this day have been dumped by the gate of the mosque of Ghaznīn.

There was a treasure hoard beneath the idols, which they carried off. [M 275] The Amir acquired a vast amount of wealth from there, made up of silver idols and their jewels on one hand and of treasure plundered from other sources on the other. Then he returned home. The reason for this decision was that Bhīmdeva (*b.h.y.m dīv*), the king of the Indians, was blocking the way. Amir Maḥmūd said, 'No stroke of ill fortune must mar this mighty victory!' He did not take the direct route [homewards], but took a guide for the other route, and set off for Multan via the road to Manṣūra and the banks of the Indus river (Sayḥūn).[78] In the course of the journey, the troops suffered great tribulations, both on account of the parched desert conditions and also on account of the Jhats[79] of Sind and of every other sort of disaster. Great numbers of the troops of the army of Islam perished on that journey back, including the major part of the beasts of burden. They finally reached Multan and from there set out for Ghaznīn. Amir Maḥmūd entered Ghaznīn with his army in the year 417 [/1026].[80]

During this same year, envoys arrived from Qitā Khān and Yughur Khān. They brought for Amir Maḥmūd messages couched in cordial terms and they performed the rites of obeisance before him. They came seeking a marriage alliance between the two sides. Amir Maḥmūd ordered that they should be fittingly lodged and entertained, but then sent a message in reply to them, 'We are Muslims and you are unbelievers, and it would be inappropriate for us to offer you our sisters or daughters. But if you become Muslims, that can be arranged,' and he sent the envoys back with an honourable provision.[81]

In Shawwāl of the year 417 [/November–December 1026], a letter came from al-Qādir bi'llāh with an investiture diploma and standard for Khurasan, India, Nīmrūz and Khwarazm, and there were honorific titles for Amir Maḥmūd, his sons and his brothers. For Amir Maḥmūd there was that of *Kahf al-Dawla wa 'l-Islām* ('Refuge of the State and of Islam'); for Amir Mas'ūd, those of *Shihāb al-Dawla wa-Jamāl al-Milla* ('Shooting Star of the State and Adornment of the Religious Community'); for Amir Muḥammad, those of *Jalāl al-Dawla* [N 88] *wa-Jamāl al-Milla* ('Eminence of the State and Adornment of the Religious Community'); and for Amir Yūsuf, those of *'Aḍud al-Dawla wa-Mu'ayyid al-Milla* ('Upper Arm of the State and Strengthener of the Religious Community'). A letter had also been written that said, 'Appoint as your designated heir whomsoever you wish, and we will agree to your choice!' [M 276] Qādir expressed his profuse thanks to Amir Maḥmūd for the raids and expeditions he had led and heaped many praises on him. This investiture diploma, and the standard and honorific titles, arrived at Balkh.[82]

Amir Maḥmūd had an intense feeling of anger in his heart against the Jhats of Multan and Bhatinda (Bhātiya) on the Indus banks because of the harassment they had kept up when he was on the way back from Somnath, and he wished to retaliate for it and inflict punishment on them. So at the beginning of the year 418 [/February 1027], as the twelfth episode [of his campaigns into Hindustan],[83] he assembled the army and set out for Multan. When he arrived there, he gave orders for 1,400 boats[84] to be constructed in a stout fashion. He further ordered that each boat should be fitted with three strong, sharpened iron spikes, one projecting forward from the prow and two from each side of the boat. Each spike was to be extremely strongly made and sharp-pointed so that, whatever place the spike might strike, even if it were against something strong, it would rend, smash [H 192] and destroy that thing. He gave orders for the 1,400 boats to be launched on the banks of the Indus and that each boat should contain twenty soldiers with arrows and quivers, containers for hurling naphtha and the naphtha for them, and shields. When the Jhats heard about Amir Maḥmūd's approach, they transported their baggage and families to distant islands in the river, and came just with their weapons, unencumbered by them. They launched 4,000 boats – some say 8,000 – each with a numerous complement of men, fully armed, and they prepared to fight. When the two forces came together and clashed, the army of Islam's archers let fly a hail of arrows and the naphtha-throwers hurled containers of fire. Whenever [N 89] one of the boats of Maḥmūd's fleet engaged closely one of the Jhats' boats, the projecting spike would strike the Jhats' boat and disable it, and it would be smashed to pieces and sink. The fighting continued in this manner until the Jhats' boats were smashed up or sunk or were put to flight. Cavalry, infantry and elephants had been stationed on the Indus banks so that anyone who managed to scramble out of the river, those cavalrymen and infantrymen seized and killed him. From that point, the troops moved along the Indus banks in the same fashion [M 277] till they came upon the Jhats' baggage and families; they plundered these and took many captives as slaves. From there, they set out back to Ghaznīn victorious and favoured by fortune.[85]

When the year 4[1]8 approached its end [/January 1028], the people of Nasā, Bāward and Farāwa came to the court complaining about the Turkmens' violent behaviour and the tyrannical acts they were continually perpetrating in those regions. Amir Maḥmūd ordered a letter to be written to the governor of Ṭūs, Abu 'l-Ḥārith Arslān al-Jādhib, instructing him to inflict punishment on those Turkmens and put a stop to their acts of tyranny against the subjects. In accordance with the instruction, the Amir of Ṭūs led an attack on the Turkmens, who had meanwhile grown in numbers. The Turkmens moved towards him and engaged in fighting, killing many people and wounding many others. The Amir of Ṭūs launched several attacks on them but could achieve nothing, and those complaints of oppression and cries for help sent to Amir Maḥmūd's court were in no way halted. Amir Maḥmūd sent a further letter to the Amir of Ṭūs blaming him and imputing to him weakness. The Amir of Ṭūs wrote back in reply,

> The Turkmens have become extremely strong, and the only way to suppress this mischief of theirs is through the exalted banner and stirrup (i.e. the Sultan's personal presence). Unless the lord himself comes to repair this damage, they will become stronger and dealing with the problem will be even more difficult.

When Amir Maḥmūd read this letter, he became anxious and distressed. He lingered no longer but mobilised his army, and in the year 419 [/1028] left Ghaznīn and headed for Bust, and thence went to Ṭūs. The Amir of Ṭūs [N 90] came out to meet him and escort him back and rendered service. When Amir Maḥmūd asked him about the situation, he gave him a true and exact relation of what the Turkmens were up to. Amir Maḥmūd issued orders that a numerous military force, with several senior commanders, should accompany the Amir of Ṭūs and attack the Turkmens. When the Ghaznavid army reached the *ribāṭ* of Farāwa, the two sides confronted each other, the Turkmens having grown audacious and confident. Battle was joined. When the Ghaznavid forces showed themselves strong and resolute and vanquished the Turkmens, they put the Turkmens to the sword, killing 4,000 of their crack horsemen and [M 278] taking large numbers captive. The remnants fled to Balkhān [Kūh] and Dihistān, and their depredations in that region became less.[86] [H 193]

When Amir Maḥmūd felt happier in mind about the matter of the Turkmens, he led an expedition against Ray. He set out for Gurgān and reached it by taking the road through the defile of Dīnārzārī.[87] From there, he proceeded against Ray. A trusted authority informed me that Amir Maḥmūd sent from Nishapur against Ray the Ḥājib Īkūtegin[88] with a force of 2,000 cavalry but with no specific orders. When Īkūtegin had travelled two stages, the Amir sent him a message telling him to halt until the Ḥājib Ghāzī should catch up with him bringing a further 2,000 cavalry. He likewise gave Ghāzī no specific orders. When the two commanders had travelled onwards for five stages, the Amir sent them a message to halt till the Ḥājib ʿAlī should come up with them. He gave the Ḥājib ʿAlī orders and despatched him with 4,000 cavalry. When the Ḥājib reached that place (i.e. of rendezvous), he held a review of the army. He placed Īkūtegin over the right wing and the Ḥājib Ghāzī over the left wing whilst he himself took command of the centre. They proceeded onwards in that formation up to the gates of Ray.

When the news reached the Amir of Ray, the Shāhanshāh Majd al-Dawla Abū Ṭālib Rustam b. Fakhr al-Dawla, he thought that Amir Maḥmūd had come in person. He went forth (i.e. to greet him) with a force of a hundred cavalrymen drawn from his personal guard, retainers and attendants [N 91] and a numerous body of infantrymen, comprising those who ran alongside the horses, shield-bearers, lance/javelin bearers and suchlike. When the Ḥājib ʿAlī saw him, he sent a messenger with the instructions, 'You must dismount whilst I deliver the message which I bear.' Majd al-Dawla straightway came forward, and the Ghaznavid forces erected tents and a marquee and encamped there. The Ḥājib ʿAlī gave orders, and the gates of the city were seized and no-one allowed to leave. They did not permit anybody to go out from or to enter the city. Meanwhile, what had happened to Majd al-Dawla was kept quiet.

The Ḥājib ʿAlī kept Majd al-Dawla in that tent under arrest, and all the weapons that had been brought with him he confiscated. Abū Ṭālib was held captive in that tent for four days. The Ḥājib ʿAlī [M 279] wrote to Amir Yamīn al-Dawla giving news about the situation. A reply came back, and Abū Ṭālib and six other persons were then set on the backs of camels and despatched to Amir Maḥmūd. The latter ordered that Abū Ṭālib should be conveyed to Ghaznīn, and he remained there for the rest of his life. Amir Yamīn al-Dawla came to Ray and occupied the city unopposed and without any difficulty. The Buyids' treasuries, which had been laid up there from a long time back, he carried off in their entirety. He found there wealth that seemed beyond any counting and limitless.

Information was brought to Amir Maḥmūd that there were large numbers of adherents of the Bāṭiniyya and Carmathians within the city of Ray and its environs. He gave orders that anybody suspected of holding that belief should be brought out and stoned to death. He killed large numbers of adherents of that belief, and some of them he placed in bonds and sent to Khurasan, where they were held in captivity in his castles and prisons till they died. He remained at Ray for some time until he had set in order all that kingdom's affairs. He appointed officials, and he entrusted the governorship of Ray and Isfahan to Amir Mas'ūd and himself returned to Ghaznīn. The conquest of Ray was in Jumādā I of the year 420 [/May–June 1029].[89] [N 92]

Amir Maḥmūd showed symptoms of the malady of consumption. It had been appearing over some considerable time, but it grew worse and every day he kept becoming weaker from it and at the same time suffering pain. He managed, with great effort and the use of various expedients, ostensibly to retain his strength, and he gave out to people that he had no sickness or pain. In this condition, he came to Khurasan. He went to Balkh and spent the winter there. When [H 194] spring came round, his illness became much worse. He set out for Ghaznīn and was there for several days. He tried many remedies but could not secure any relief for his condition. He became extremely weak, and death approached. He could not manage to sleep lying down on a bed but could only sit up, and in that state he yielded up the ghost, may God's mercy be upon him and may He illuminate his tomb! Amir Maḥmūd's passing was on Thursday, 23 Rabī' II [M 280] of the year 421 [/30 April 1030].[90] With his death, a whole world was brought to destruction; the vile became elevated and the great were brought low.

The Rule of Amir Jalāl al-Dawla wa-Jamāl al-Milla Abū Aḥmad Muḥammad b. Yamīn al-Dawla, God Most High's Mercy upon Them Both!

When Amir Maḥmūd passed away, Amir Mas'ūd was in Isfahan and Amir Muḥammad was in Gūzgānān. At that point, the Ḥājib 'Alī [N 93] b. Il Arslān, who was Amir Maḥmūd's kinsman, got a firm grip on affairs of state. He brought stability to the monarchy and did not allow anyone to use excessive measures against another person. The town of Ghaznīn became such that the wolf and the sheep lived peaceably side by side.

The Ḥājib 'Alī sent an emissary and he brought back Amir Muḥammad, and he ascended the throne in his father's place. The first thing Muḥammad did was to preside over sessions for hearing complaints of injustice and tyranny (*maẓālim*); he listened to the petitioners and arranged just settlements between the parties concerned. Then he ordered the registers and tax assessment books for the various regions to be brought out for examination. In regard to every place which had become laid waste and whose proprietors were excessively burdened because of the land-tax on it, he looked into that tax burden carefully and he looked after the interests of the subjects. He ordered the doors of the treasury to be thrown open, and he awarded robes of honour and presents of money for all the court troops and other soldiers, whether of lowly or exalted status, obscure or in the public eye. He appointed his paternal uncle Abū Yaʿqūb Yūsuf b. Nāṣir al-Dīn as commander-in-chief of the army, and gave him a splendid robe of honour and handsome financial rewards. He appointed Khʷāja Abū Sahl Aḥmad b. al-Ḥasan al-Ḥamdawī as his vizier and followed his counsel in the running of affairs. The state of the kingdom became flourishing and expansive, and daily life became good for the populace. The level of prices was low, and the troops and the bazaar traders became universally contented. When news of Ghaznīn's prosperity and ampleness of life reached other cities, merchants flocked to it from distant parts, bringing every conceivable variety of merchandise, textiles, etc., for trading. The level of prices became low and goods became cheap. [M 281]

Despite all this prosperity which Amir Muḥammad brought about for the mass of subjects and the soldiery alike, the troops and the subjects inclined to the side of Amir Shihāb al-Dawla Abū Saʿīd Masʿūd b. Yamīn al-Dawla and sought after him.

Fifty days after Amir Maḥmūd's death, Amir Ayāz[91] conspired with the [royal] ghulāms and took from them a sworn pledge for going over to Amir Masʿūd's side; they all agreed to this and swore an oath over it. He sent an envoy to Abu 'l-Ḥasan ʿAlī b. ʿAbdallāh, who was known as ʿAlī Dāya,[92] [N 94] and ʿAlī Dāya agreed to approach those troops. Next day, the palace ghulāms came out and went to the stables, brought forth horses and mounted them with a full array of arms. They rode out of the palace gates openly, and in this wise went along boldly and ready for action, heading for Bust. [H 195]

When Amir Muḥammad heard about this, he sent an army in pursuit of them. These troops included Suvendharāy, commander of the Indian division,[93] who went after them with a numerous force of cavalrymen. He caught up with them and attacked them. The ghulāms fought back and killed many of the Indians, including Suvendharāy. A large number of the palace ghulāms were also killed and their heads brought before Amir Muḥammad.

Abu 'l-Najm Ayāz b. Aymaq and ʿAlī Dāya, together with a numerous force of ghulāms, travelled along swiftly until they all reached Nishapur and appeared before Amir Masʿūd. When they saw the Amir, all of them made obeisance and rendered service, hailing him as king. He accepted their submission, spoke encouraging words to them, sought excuses [from them] and asked about their journey, giving them hopes of future favour.

Amir Muḥammad remained there in Ghaznīn, indulging in listening to music and singing, merry-making and busying himself with wine drinking, to the point that his close retainers told him,

> All this you're doing is a mistake. The mass of people have begun talking about you unfavourably and are blaming you for what you're doing just now, saying that 'Your enemy has come from Western Persia ('Irāq [-i ʿAjam]) and has mounted an attack upon you, yet you pay no heed to him [M 282] and have

devoted yourself to wine drinking and self-satisfied behaviour.' Unless you march out against him, this royal power will slip away from you.

When four months of his reign had elapsed, Amir Muḥammad made plans to march forth. He gave orders and the tented encampment was transported to the vicinity of Bust and set up. He handed out donatives to the troops and then marched out of Ghaznīn with a well-equipped and powerful army. But when he reached Tegīnābād, all the leading figures and army commanders came together in a conclave and sent a message to Amir Muḥammad,

> You are leading us against an enemy [N 95] who has the entire population as his supporters and followers. We know for certain that you won't be able to stand up to him. The wisest course is that you should remain here in this place so that we may go to him, seek pardon for our actions and convey your words [to him]. In this way, he might relent towards us and in the same way become favourably disposed to you and summon you to his presence, and both you and ourselves will thereby be in a secure relationship with him.

When Amir Muḥammad saw that the whole of his army had changed its allegiance, he realised that there was no means of retrieving the situation and that submission was the only remedy. He immediately acceded to their demands, and they brought him to the fortress of Rukhkhaj[94] and held him captive there. Amir Yūsuf, the Ḥājib ʿAlī and the leading figures and commanders seized the treasuries and the armoury, got the army moving in the direction of Amir Masʿūd and proceeded to Herat.[95] [H 196]

The Rule of Amir Nāṣir Dīn Allāh Ḥāfiẓ ʿIbād Allāh wa-Ẓahīr Khalīfat Allāh Abū Saʿīd Masʿūd b. Yamīn al-Dawla [Walī] Amīr al-Mu'minīn, God's Mercy upon Them Both!

When Ayāz b. Aymāq and ʿAlī Dāya reached Nishapur, Amir Masʿūd became much heartened. He held a court and presided over *maẓālim* sessions, listening to the subjects' complaints and meting out justice between contending parties. When several days had passed, the investiture diploma and standard sent by the Commander of the Faithful al-Qādir bi'llāh were brought in; Abū Sahl Mursil b. Manṣūr b. Aflaḥ Gardīzī [N 96] had fetched these (i.e. from Baghdad). Amir Masʿūd commended Mursil [M 283] and gave him hopes of future favour. He remained at Nishapur for a while and then from there came to Herat. When Amir Masʿūd had been at Herat for some days, the Ḥājib ʿAlī came into his presence. He took his hand in greeting and asked about his journey. ʿAlī's brother Mengütirek had come to Amir Masʿūd before ʿAlī's arrival. The Amir had bestowed on him the rank of Ḥājib and was treating him with great respect and consideration. When the Ḥājib ʿAlī came back from attendance on the Amir at court, he was borne along to a prison cell. Mengütirek put his hand to has sword hilt, but the Ḥājib ʿAlī expostulated with him, saying that Masʿūd was his lord, and the son of his lord, and that whatever he might ordain the two of them had to show obedience. Thereafter, no-one ever saw those two brothers again.[96]

When the body of troops and the treasuries reached Amir Mas'ūd, he set out from Herat for Balkh and spent the winter there. He brought a firm hand to the administration of the realm. His reign began in Shawwāl of the year 421 [/October 1030]. He made his first concern the appointment of a vizier, with a consideration of those who were the most suitable persons for the post. There was no-one more proficient in his job, more learned in *adab* and with a greater fund of knowledge than Khwāja Abu 'l-Qāsim Aḥmad b. Ḥasan Maymandī.[97] Khwāja Aḥmad had been held prisoner in the fortress of Jankī in India.[98] Amir Mas'ūd now despatched someone, and he was brought back from that fortress. He appointed him as his vizier, giving him a fine robe of honour and entrusting to him all affairs relating to the organisation of the army.

Ḥasan b. Muḥammad al-Mikālī[99] had been arrested. The Amir gave orders that he was to be made forcibly to disgorge his gains, and wealth was obtained from him. Then the Amir ordered that he should be killed and gibbeted at Balkh. The reason for this was that Amir Ḥasanak had sought permission from Amir Maḥmūd [H 197] and had gone off on the Pilgrimage. He had returned from this by way of the Syrian route because the road across the [Arabian] desert [M 284] was disturbed. From Syria he had travelled to Egypt and had accepted a robe of honour from the ruler of Egypt.[100] [N 97] Suspicion had thereby been thrown on him that he was favourably disposed towards the ruler of Egypt and was thus liable to the penalty of stoning. Amir Mas'ūd commanded that a helmet should be placed on Ḥasanak's head and that he should be placed on the gallows platform and stoned. Afterwards his head was borne away and sent to Qādir in Baghdad.[101]

Every person who had opposed Amir Mas'ūd or who had conspired with his enemies, he arrested and without exception inflicted punishment on them and brought them to destruction. He seized the treasurer Aḥmad [b.] Yïnāltegin, who had filled this office under Maḥmūd, and forced him to disgorge his gains, ordering a great amount of wealth to be exacted from him. When Aḥmad handed over the money, the Amir sent him to India and appointed him commander of the army there, despatching him thither in place of the Ḥājib Eryārūq.[102] All that show of anger, the forcible confiscations, the ill-treatment and humiliations inflicted on Aḥmad [b.] Yïnāltegin remained lodged in his heart, and when he reached India he threw off obedience and rebelled.[103]

Amir Nāṣir Dīn Allāh gave orders for Abū Ṭālib Rustam Majd al-Dawla to be brought back from India.[104] He summoned Majd al-Dawla to his court session and spoke with him in a cordial manner. He ordered a residence to be built for him in Ghaznīn and gave instructions that Majd al-Dawla should on all occasions be admitted to the court to offer his service. He remained in Ghaznīn till the end of his life.

At this time, the Amir of Makrān, Ḥusayn b. Ma'dān, came to the court and made complaint about his brother Abu 'l-'Askar, asserting that the latter had appropriated the royal power for himself, had deprived Ḥusayn of his rights and had refused to give him his due. So Amir Nāṣir Dīn Allāh issued orders for Tāsh Farrāsh to go back with Ḥusayn to Makrān, secure restitution from Abu 'l-'Askar for his brother and set Ḥusayn on the throne there as ruler.[105] [N 98]

Amir Mas'ūd then left Balkh for Ghaznīn. When the people of Ghaznīn heard this news, they set about organising festivities. Everyone became busy preparing merry-making and rejoicings, the markets were decorated, and musicians and singers were stationed in positions outside the town. They were there for several days, with rejoicings going on continuously day and night, [M 285] in anticipation of Nāṣir Dīn Allāh's arrival. The notables, prominent figures and community leaders of the town all went out to greet him, offering up their service, and laid on festivities and merry-making. When the Amir reached Ghaznīn, the townspeople scattered dirhams and dinars as a sign of rejoicing. Next day, the Amir sat down in state and held court. People came along continuously and were bringing presents, according to the accepted custom. Amir Mas'ūd likewise showed his benevolence to everyone, speaking encouraging words and raising people's hopes of future beneficence. All the people of Ghaznīn spontaneously and with one accord broke out in voice, addressed profuse praises to him, offered up prayers for divine favour and besought God, He is Exalted and Magnified, to grant him a long reign, made their obeisances and returned homewards.

Once the Amir had finished with affairs at Ghaznīn, he formed the intention of taking action regarding Āmul, Isfahan and Ray, and set out for those places. When he reached Herat, people from Sarakhs and Bāvard came with cries for help, complaining about the Turkmens. So Amir Mas'ūd designated a commander with a large military force, and sent to accompany him Abū Sa'd 'Abdūs b. 'Abd al-'Azīz as adjutant and administrator (*kadkhudā*) and quartermaster for that army; this was in [H 198] the year 422 [/1031]. When the army made contact with the Turkmens at Farāwa, they launched an assault on them and engaged in battle. Many men were killed. The Turkmens removed their baggage and their families to Balkhān [Kūh], and their cavalrymen were then able to fight unencumbered by these impedimenta and dependents. Each day detachment after detachment kept coming on, and the fighting was continuous. After being thus engaged for a certain period of time, these warriors (i.e. the Ghaznavid forces) returned to base.[106]

At the beginning of the year 423 [/December 1031–January 1032], Khʷāja Aḥmad b. al-Ḥasan [N 99] passed away. The Martyr Amir took counsel with his advisers concerning a new vizier, and the names of various persons were passed in review. The decision fell on Khʷāja Abū Naṣr Aḥmad b. Muḥammad b. 'Abd al-Ṣamad, who was a man of good character and a shrewd person, possessing a high degree of wisdom, perspicacious judgement and ability successfully to direct affairs. He had exercised the function of vizier in Khwarazm for a considerable time and had, through his clear-sighted exercise of authority and unerring judgement made that province flourishing and populous. The Martyr Amir wrote a letter summoning him back from Khwarazm. [M 286] He conferred on Khʷāja Aḥmad the post of directing state affairs and awarded him a robe of honour appropriate to that position.[107] He then set out for Ghaznīn and returned to the seat of his power.

In the year 424 [/1033], he led an expedition into India. There was a fortress called Sarastī in the pass leading into Kashmir. He proceeded there and laid siege to it. Its defenders fought back vigorously. In the end, he captured it, and the [Ghaznavid] army acquired from the fortress a great booty of wealth and slaves. When it was spring, he set off back to Ghaznīn.[108]

In the year 425 [/1034], he led an expedition to Āmul and Sārī. He mobilised his troops and proceeded there with a well-armed and fully equipped army. News of his approach had reached those lands, and all the people there had got ready for war. A large army of town-dwellers, mountain folk, Jīlīs and Daylamīs had been assembled and had taken up a position on the road, with detachments placed at intervals in ambushes in the thick forests and narrow places.[109] When the Ghaznavid army arrived there, the enemy poured forth from very direction and were engaging in fighting. The Martyr Amir was mounted on an elephant. Shahrākīm b. Sūriyal, the Amir of Astarābād, confronted him, armed to the teeth. An elephant was coming on; Shahrākīm made a spear thrust,[110] [N 100] and the elephant was wounded in the side and fell down. When the Martyr Amir looked down from the back of his elephant and saw that, he hurled a javelin (*zūbīn*) which struck Shahrākīm's face and felled him. The [Ghaznavid] troops came up and made him captive. Shahrākīm's men had also entered the fray, and they engaged in fighting at Sārī. In the end, they were put to flight and the Martyr Amir captured the town. Impulsive elements of the troops plundered part of the town. The townspeople came forward and complained, saying that 'We are traders, pious and God-fearing, and your troops are treating us with violence.' He gave orders to the troops to desist from plundering and spoliation.

He had his tented enclosure erected at the gates of Āmul. Bā Kālījār, the Amir of Ṭabaristān,[111] sent messengers. [M 287] Representatives from both sides met together [H 199] and a peace agreement was made on the basis that Bā Kālījār should immediately convey 300,000 dinars as tribute, hand over taxation annually, make the *khuṭba* throughout Ṭabaristān in Amir Mas'ūd's name and give hostages for good behaviour. Bā Kālījār brought in this stipulated payment and delivered it to the Martyr Amir, and he sent his own son and the son of his brother Shahrū[ī] b. Surkhāb as hostages.[112]

When Āmul, Sārī and Ṭabaristān had passed under the Martyr Amir's control, he departed from there heading for Ghaznīn. When he reached Nishapur, victims of oppression and wrongdoing came into his presence, complaining about the Turkmens. The Martyr Amir took counsel with his viziers, boon-companions and military commanders regarding the problem of the Turkmens, stating that their violent behaviour had become acute. All those present considered the matter and put forward their views. The Ḥājib Begtughdï said, 'These acts of destruction arise from the fact of many commanders having been involved.[113] If you send a single person with responsibility for dealing with this matter, he will necessarily give it his whole-hearted attention and will deal with the problem successfully.' The Martyr Amir told Begtughdï, 'You must go and undertake the task, and Ḥusayn b. 'Alī b. Mīkā'īl is to accompany you (i.e. as *kadkhudā*).'[114] He then despatched them with a numerous army comprising Indians, Kurds, Arabs and Turks, and with them troops from every other ethnic group, and he also sent high-quality war elephants.

They set out from Nishapur [N 101] and came to Ṭūs. From there they went on to Nasā. When they arrived at a place called S.p.n.dānqān (?),[115] envoys came from the

Turkmens. Their verbal message was communicated to Begtughdï, it being couched in these terms: 'We are slaves and are obedient. If you accept our presence and make available for us pasture grounds, we'll stop our depredations and no-one will suffer any harm from us.' Begtughdï expostulated violently with the envoy and used many rough words to him. He told the Turkmens, 'Between me and you is the sword. If you are really obedient and carry out our commands, send an envoy of yours to King Mas'ūd and seek to make your excuses to him. Bring back to us a letter (i.e. from the Amir) and we will turn away from confronting you in war; but if you don't do this, we shall in no circumstances turn back.' [M 288]

Begtughdï then sent the envoy back and deployed his army for battle. He appointed the treasurer Qut-tegin (?; text, *'.f.t.k.y.n*) over the right, the Ḥājib Böri (text, *p.y.r*) over the left, and he himself took charge of the centre. He sent forward the Arab contingent[116] as scouts together with 500 cavalrymen who formed the mounted element of the Arab contingent. When the contingent reached Mār.r.n.y (?), it gained a victory over the Turkmens' advance troops; large numbers of them were killed and the Turkmens took to flight. Begtughdï's army pursued them till his troops came upon the Turkmens' baggage. They seized all of this as plunder and gained an immense amount of booty. They brought away the beasts and goods and returned to their army camp since that place was a constricted one.

At this period, the greater part of Begtughdï's army was away, either engaged in attacking the enemy or else plundering. When Dāwūd (i.e. Chaghrï Beg), the Turkmen leader, got news of this, he and a strong military force emerged from the defiles and narrow places of the mountain, took up positions directly facing the Ghaznavid army and formed themselves into battle lines. The fighting continued for two days and nights, with the Turkmens gaining the upper hand. Begtughdï then said to Ḥusayn b. 'Alī [b.] Mīkā'īl, [N 102] 'There's no possibility of holding our ground.' The *ra'īs* Ḥusayn answered, 'In no circumstances will I go back to the Amir as one who has fled the field; I'll either emerge victorious or be killed.'

Begtughdï turned and fled, but Ḥusayn stood his ground and kept on fighting until all his troops took to flight and he was left there a lone figure. The Turkmens poured in, surrounded his elephant and forced him to dismount from it. They were about to kill him when Dāwūd got news of this and sent someone with instructions not to kill Ḥusayn. [H 200] They brought him into Dāwūd's presence, bound him hand and foot and kept him captive in a tent, with several Turkmens detailed to guard him. Ḥusayn has remained there amongst the Turkmens until this present time. Begtughdï went back and entered the Martyr Amir's presence. The Amir was in depair. Because of the fact that the Daylamī hostages and captives were with him,[117] he was unable to remain there and went back to Ghaznīn, bringing the prisoners, who were sent to various fortresses and towns, in the month of Ramaḍān 426 [/July–August 1035].[118] [M 289]

Reports were continuously arriving from India that Aḥmad [b. Yïnāltegin] was behaving oppressively within his Indian governorship, had arrested and imprisoned the tax-collecting officials, and was treacherously appropriating the money. The Martyr Amir sent Bānha b. Muḥammad b. M.l.l.y, the commander (*sālār*) of the Indians,[119] with a large army. When the two opposing sides met, they clashed together and engaged in battle. Large numbers of troops from both sides were killed. Bānha was killed in the course of the fighting and his troops all put to flight. Aḥmad Yïnāltegin's power thus became strong.

When the Martyr Amir heard the news of this, he despatched Tilak b. Jahlan,[120] the supreme commander (*sipahsālār*) of the Indian contingent [within the Ghaznavid army], and Tilak set off with a large army of Indian troops. He engaged in warfare with Aḥmad [b.] Yïnāltegin, and there were several clashes and battles between the two sides. Tilak was victorious on all these occasions. Aḥmad [b.] Yïnāltegin took to flight and his army was completely destroyed. All those soldiers of Aḥmad's, the traders who had attached themselves to Aḥmad's camp and were adherents of his, whom Tilak captured, he cut off one hand and their noses, [N 103] thus inflicting exemplary punishment, until he had dealt with a large number of persons in this way.

Aḥmad [b.] Yïnāltegin fled, and headed for Manṣūra and Sind. He tried to cross the Indus river, but unfortunately for him, a flood swept down and carried him away, and he suffered death by drowning. When the waters bore along his mutilated body, they threw it up at a certain spot. One of his soldiers and doughty warriors found his body and recognised it. He cut off the head and it was brought before Tilak. Tilak sent it to Balkh, and Amir Masʿūd gave orders for a column to be erected and the head to be set on it.[121]

At this time, i.e. in the year 427 [/1035–6], the New Palace at Ghaznīn was completed, together with the golden throne set with jewels that had been specially made for the palace. The Martyr Amir gave orders for that golden throne to be installed in the palace. A golden crown, which weighed seventy *man*s and was set with jewels, had been made, and this was suspended above the throne by golden chains. Amir Masʿūd then sat down on the throne and placed the suspended crown on his head, and he held a court session for his guards and retainers and the masses of people.[122] [Also in this same year, the Amir awarded his son Mawdūd][123] a ceremonial drum and standard and sent him [M 290] to Balkh.

In Dhu 'l-Qaʿda of the year 427 [/August–September 1036], he mobilised the army for campaigning in India. There was a fortress called Hānsī, considered impregnable, strongly fortified and with a numerous garrison of defenders.[124] The Martyr Amir led an attack on that fortress. When he arrived there, he ordered [H 201] his army to surround it. They launched an attack on it, whilst the defenders were fighting back from the upper parts of the fortress. The defending garrison believed that no-one would ever be able to conquer the fortress because of the strength of its defences. After six days of fighting, one wall of the fortress was demolished and it became exposed to attack (lit. 'exposed to ravishment', *ʿawrat shūd*).[125] The army of Islam poured in and sacked the fortress. They acquired a vast amount of wealth and plunder [N 104] and numerous captives.

From there they marched towards the fortress of Sūnīpat, the seat of Daypāl Hariyāna. When the latter learnt of their approach, he fled into the open plains and the forests, abandoning that fortress with all its wealth and goods. When the army of Islam arrived there, the Martyr Amir gave orders for the fortress to be sacked. They burnt down the idol temples and carried off as spoils all the gold and silver, the food stores and furnishings that they could find. Spies then arrived and brought the news that Daypāl Hariyāna was to be found in a certain stretch of forest. The Martyr Amir proceeded there until he drew near to Daypāl Hariyāna's army. When Daypāl received information about this, he immediately fled, abandoning his army. The army of Islam fell upon the army of infidels, slew a great number of them, took many captives and seized innumerable slaves.

They went back from there and marched towards the seat[126] of Rām. When Rām heard of their approach, he despatched an emissary to the Martyr Amir seeking pardon (i.e. offering submission), saying, 'I am an aged man, and have no strength to come and render service in person,' but he sent a great sum of money by the hand of one of his retainers. The Martyr Amir accepted his submission and his offering. He went back from there and headed for Ghaznīn. Then he gave the governorship of Lahore to Amir Majdūd b. Mas'ūd. [M 291] He awarded him a ceremonial drum and standard, and despatched him to Lahore with an army and his personal retainers, whilst he himself came back to Ghaznīn. The conquest of Hānsī was in the year 428 [/1036–7].[127]

Once the Amir had established himself at Ghaznīn there was a continuous stream of petitioners and persons arriving from Khurasan crying for help and complaining about the Turkmens, and the intelligence agents and postmasters were continually sending letters with the information that the violence and evildoing of the Turkmens had gone beyond all measure.[128] Then, at the end of the year 428 [/October 1037], the Amir set out for Balkh with the plan of setting aright the affairs of Khurasan and of putting an end to the Turkmens' violence and evildoing. When [N 105] he reached Balkh, a group of Turkmens who were in that vicinity moved away from their camping places, and the province of Balkh became free of them.

News was brought to the Martyr Amir that a disturbed situation had arisen in the Transoxanian region, caused by Böritegin and his troops, who were continually oppressing the local people.[129] The Martyr Amir decided to lead an expedition and suppress this evildoing. [It had all arisen] because the Great Khān Qadïr Khān had died and the local people had been put in fear of Böritegin. The Amir thought that he might be able to seize the opportunity and gain control of Transoxania for himself. So he commanded that a bridge should be thrown across the Oxus. He conveyed the army across the river and set off into Transoxania. All the magnates and leaders of Transoxania abandoned their seats of power and departed, and no-one came to join the Amir. When they had been in Transoxania for several days, a letter reached the Martyr Amir from the Vizier Kh^{w}āja Aḥmad b. Muḥammad b. 'Abd al-Ṣamad in Balkh with the news that the Turkmen leader Dāwūd, with all [H 202] his host, was planning to attack Balkh and that he himself lacked adequate soldiers, auxiliary troops and matériel to withstand them; unless the Amir returned, a disaster would occur. Amir Mas'ūd returned fom Transoxania immediately and came to the Katar steppe.[130] He deployed his army for battle and got it ready to engage the Turkmens. On receiving information about the Amir's crossing back over the river, the Turkmen chief Dāwūd straightway got his forces ready to move and left for Merv.[131]

When the Martyr Amir [M 292] heard about Dāwūd's departure, he came to Balkh and then went on to Gūzgānān. Several people from that region came before him and laid complaints about the oppressive activities of ʿAlī Quhandizī. This ʿAlī Quhandizī was an *ayyār* and evildoer, and had been guilty of many tyrannical acts in these regions. The Martyr Amir issued orders for someone to be sent to this ʿAlī and that he should be summoned to the court. [N 106] When the envoy reached him he refused to come. In that region there was a fortress where he now sought refuge, moving his family and his belongings into it and fortifying it against a siege. The Martyr Amir gave commands for that fortress to be taken and laid waste. ʿAlī Quhandizī was brought down from it. When he was brought before the Martyr Amir, the latter forthwith ordered him to be executed. This happened in the year 429 [/1038].[132]

When the Turkmens learnt about the Martyr Amir's march towards Merv, they were filled with fear. They straightway sent an envoy to him, saying,

> We are slaves and obedient to his commands. If the Amir will now admit us into his territories and allot us pasture lands, we will transfer our beasts and our baggage to those pasture lands and will devote ourselves exclusively to the Exalted Stirrup's service, if the Amir should see his way to do this.

The Martyr Amir sent back a messenger, and the requisite formal agreement was made with Yabghu.[133] The latter was made to swear that he would not again be refractory, would remain fully obedient, would restrain his family and retainers and the whole tribe from these oppressive acts, and would opt for those pasture lands allotted to them by the Martyr Amir. They solemnly subscribed to all these conditions, pledged themselves to them and swore oaths. All the chiefs and commanders of the Turkmens agreed to that solemn agreement and gave guarantees that they would observe all its conditions.

The Martyr Amir set out from there towards Herat, but a Turkmen force attacked the baggage train of the Martyr Amir's army en route for Herat, carried off much equipment and possessions, killed several persons and inflicted wounds on others. The Martyr Amir issued orders, and the army went in pursuit of the Turkmens. The army attacked them, killed a large number of them and took numerous prisoners. The captives, together with the heads of the slain, were brought before the Martyr Amir. He commanded that those heads should be loaded on [M 293] asses and delivered to Yabghu, with an accompanying message that, whoever broke his solemn agreement would, as his reward, suffer the same fate. When Yabghu [N 107] saw those heads, he sought pardon and heaped reproaches on the perpetrators of that attack. He gave the reply that 'We knew nothing about this action; we only wish to do whatever the Amir himself is doing.'[134]

The Martyr Amir spent several days in Herat and then set out for Nishapur. When he reached Ṭūs, a detachment of the Turkmen forces advanced towards him. Battle was given and a large number of Turkmens were killed. From there [H 203] he made for Nasā and Bāward, but those regions proved to be completely free of Turkmens.

Information then reached the Martyr Amir that the people of Bāward had handed over their citadel to the Turkmens and had entered into friendly relations with them. He immediately marched to Bāward, and very soon afterwards the men garrisoning the citadel were brought before the Amir. He gave orders that the greater part of them should be put to death. His mind was relieved of that matter, and he came to Nishapur, where he spent the winter. This was in the year 430 [/1038–9].[135]

When spring came round, he left Nishapur[136] and headed for Bāward, having received reports that the Turkmen chief Ṭoghrïl was there. When Ṭoghrïl heard of the Martyr Amir's approach, he withdrew to N.z.n (?) of Bāward and avoided all contact with Amir Masʿūd. When the Martyr Amir found no trace of him,[137] he went to Sarakhs via the Mayhana road. The people of Sarakhs refused to hand over any taxation and fortified themselves within the town. The Amir gave orders, and the garrison was brought down from the citadel and the citadel itself demolished. Some of the defenders of the citadel were put to death whilst others had their hands cut off.[138]

From there he went to L.stāna (?) and stayed in that place for a while, and then he set out from there for Dandānqān. When he arrived there, the army encamped. When morning dawned, the Turkmens had seized control of all the steppe lands and mountains and had blocked the ways for the army of Ghazna. When the Martyr Amir saw the situation, he gave orders that the troops should get ready for battle. The army took up its battle formation and the troops formed up into unbroken lines (*ṣaff-hā*). [M 294] The Turkmens also set about preparing for battle and followed their usual practice in forming up for battle, since they fight in separate compact groups (*kurdūs kurdūs*), and they all deployed themselves thus. The two sides were engaged in fighting [N 108] and the Ghaznavid army gained the upper hand, but then a section of it turned away and went over to the enemy.[139] The Martyr Amir personally stood firm and felled to the ground a good number of battle-hardened warriors, some with his spear, some with his sword and some with his mace. He fought more fiercely on that day than any previous monarch had ever personally done. He sent a message to his army commanders ordering them to fight on, but they gave up the fight, turned away and took to flight. He himself kept on fighting in that fashion described above until there was hardly anyone left at his side. When he realised that the battle had ended in disaster, he turned and abandoned the field; however, none of the Turkmens dared to go after him because they had seen his prowess in the fray. This battle at Dandānqān was on Friday, 8 Ramaḍān of the year 431 [/23 May 1040].[140]

The Martyr Amir set out from Dandānqān for Marw al-Rūd, and various stragglers from the army came to join him. From Marw [al-Rūd] he set off for Ghaznīn, travelling via the Ghūr road and reaching Ghaznīn. The first thing he did there was to take action against those three commanders who had disobeyed orders during the battle and had been negligent,[141] such as the Commander-in-Chief ʿAlī Dāya, the Great Ḥājib Sübashï and also the Ḥājib Begtughdï. He had them seized and bound, he confiscated their wealth and property, and he consigned them to fortresses in India, where on the same day all three died.[142] [H 204]

The Martyr Amir then formulated a plan how that situation might be retrieved. It was agreed that he should go to India, collect there a mighty army, come back and restore the position.[143] He appointed Amir Mawdūd governor of Balkh and despatched the Vizier Khʷāja [Aḥmad b.] Muḥammad b. ʿAbd al-Ṣamad to Balkh to accompany him (i.e. as his *kadkhudā*). He also appointed as military commander for Mawdūd the Ḥājib Ertegin, [N 109] sending with him 4,000 cavalry. Mawdūd proceeded towards Balkh. [M 295] When Amir Mawdūd reached Hupyān, he took up his position there.[144] The Martyr Amir sent Amir Majdūd to Multan with 2,000 cavalry and Amir Īzad-yār to the mountain fringes (*kūh-pāya*) around Ghaznīn where there were Afghans and other rebellious elements, instructing him, 'Keep a firm grip on that region lest any adverse situation arise there.'[145]

He then gave orders for all the treasuries and stores of precious objects that Amir Maḥmūd had deposited in fortresses and at various places, such as the fortresses of Dīdī-Rū, Mandīsh, Nāy-Lāmān, Maranj and B.nāmad–Kōt (?),[146] should all be brought to Ghaznīn. Then all the wealth in the shape of jewels, gold, silver, clothing, carpets and hangings, and vessels, were loaded on to the backs of camels. He mobilised the army and set out for India with that treasury, his womenfolk and baggage. When en route, he sent an emissary with instructions that his brother Amir Muḥammad should be fetched from the fortress of Barghund[147] to the army camp.[148]

When he drew near to the *ribāṭ* of Mārīkala,[149] the treasury was being borne along before him. A number of indisciplined royal ghulāms and soldiers, heedless of all consequences, came up with the treasury. They saw an immense string of camels and other beasts of burden all loaded with jewels, gold and silver. They fell upon them and carried off a quantity of them. The army became mutinous, and in one fell swoop carried away and pillaged all the treasuries. When they had acted in this mutinous manner, they realised that they would not get away with it except by raising to power a new amir. It happened that Amir Muḥammad came along at that moment, and a group of the criminals then came forward and hailed him as king.

When the Martyr Amir saw what had happened, and discerned no hope of punishing the rebels or of combatting them, he went and shut himself up in the *ribāṭ* of Mārīkala, remaining there that night. Next morning, he came forth and made strenuous efforts (i.e. to regain his authority), but the decree of Fate had come down and he could achieve nothing. [N 110, H 205] He went back inside the *ribāṭ* and fortified himself within it. But the army, comprising troops and elephants, surrounded it. A detachment of troops broke into it and brought out Amir Masʿūd. He was put in bonds and taken from there to the fortress of Gīrī. He remained there until [M 296] 11 Jumādā I of the year 432 [/17 January 1041]. Finally, that same group who had brought about his deposition conspired together in a plot. They sent an envoy to the castellan of Gīrī with a message purporting to come expressly from Amir Muḥammad; in fact, the latter knew nothing about it. [Acting on the message,] the castellan killed Masʿūd, and cut off his head and sent it to Amir Muḥammad. Amir Muḥammad wept copiously and heaped reproaches on those who had plotted Masʿūd's death.[150]

The Rule of Amir Shihāb al-Dīn wa 'l-Dawla wa-Quṭb al-Milla Abu 'l-Fatḥ Mawdūd b. Nāṣir Dīn Allāh Mas'ūd b. Maḥmūd, God's Mercy upon Them Both!

When news of the events at Mārīkala and the death of the Martyr Amir reached Amir Mawdūd, he turned back to Hupyān with the intention of travelling to that place (i.e Mārīkala), dealing with the situation and seeking vengeance for his father. However, Abū Naṣr Aḥmad b. Muḥammad b. 'Abd al-Ṣamad dissuaded him from this course of action, saying, 'The soundest plan is that we should go to Ghaznīn in the first place and take possession of it. Once we have secured control of Ghaznīn, the army there will speedily rally to us.'

From Hupyān, Amir Mawdūd came to Ghaznīn with his army. The populace of Ghaznīn all flocked to him and expressed their grief and condolences. He fulfilled the requisite mourning ceremonies. When he had completed these, all the people of Ghaznīn came forward and offered their services. Amir Mawdūd [N 111] spoke encouraging words to them.

He spent the whole winter involved in preparations for war and in making plans. When spring came round, he mobilised his forces and set off to confront his uncle in battle. When he reached Dunpūr,[151] Amir Muḥammad's army had already arrived there. The lines of battle were drawn up, both armies assumed their fighting formations and battle was joined. [H 206] Fighting raged all through the day, until at nightfall the armies disengaged.

When Amir Mawdūd returned to his encampment, he summoned the Vizier and the army commanders for advice and consultations. Then he secretly sent an envoy to the Most Exalted Amir Sayyid Abū Manṣūr 'Abd al-Rashīd b. [M 297] Yamīn al-Dawla, may God prolong his royal power,[152] and conveyed to him the spoken message,

> I know that you cannot straightway turn round and come to me, but if you can remain where you are and not get involved in any fighting until I can engage the enemy in battle and seek my vengeance on him, that would be a great act of favour on your part towards me. If I achieve my aim, I shall have the fame and glory for the victory, but you will have all the control of affairs and issuing of commands, and I will carry out your commands whenever you issue them.

He accordingly took firmly guaranteed oaths and gave solemn pledges that he would never try to misinterpret or evade them. The point was also raised that 'There exists a covenanted agreement between you and my father the Martyr Amir that you will never do any harm to his sons.'

When the message reached the Most Exalted Amir (sc. 'Abd al-Rashīd) and he saw the firm assurances, he became favourably disposed towards Amir Mawdūd, and he announced that 'I will not engage in war nor draw my sword, but will remain where I am until this affair reaches a decisive conclusion.' The next day, the armies drew up their lines of battle and set in place their right and left bodies of troops, their centres and their wings. The champions from each side were continuously engaged in single combat until late morning. The Most Exalted Amir 'Abd al-Rashīd stood aside and took no part in the fighting.[153]

When Amir Mawdūd saw what the situation was, he personally led an attack on the opposing army's right. Many of the troops on this right fell. His own right attacked the enemy's left, and his left the enemy's centre, and with a single assault he put that army, despite its great size, [N 112] to flight. The Ḥājib Ertegin and the palace ghulāms rode into the enemy's rear, killing, striking and taking captives, until large numbers of the enemy troops were either killed or taken prisoner. Amir Muḥammad was captured, together with his son Aḥmad, Sulaymān b. Yūsuf and a group of highly born members of the dynasty (*dawlat*). Amir Mawdūd ordered that the whole lot should be executed: some were killed by arrows shot at them, and some were tied to the tails of savage, refractory horses.[154]

NOTES

Introduction

1 For general surveys of Gardīzī and his work, see C.E. Bosworth, 'Early sources for the history of the first four Ghaznavid sultans (977–1041)', *IQ* VII (1963), pp. 8–10; *EIr* art. 'Gardīzī' (C.E. Bosworth).

2 Ḥabībī's text, p. 252.

3 V. Minorsky, 'Gardīzī on India', *BSOAS* XII (1947–9), p. 625 and n. 3. However, in his chapter 19 'On the sciences and tenets (*ma'ārif*) of the Indians', Gardīzī's expressly acknowledged source is the Samanid author Abū 'Abdallāh Jayhānī (presumably Abū 'Abdallāh Muḥ ammad b. Aḥmad b. Naṣr, vizier to the Samanid Amir Naṣr (II) b. Aḥmad (II), see above, Part Three, p. 55 and n. 18), with material going back to the tradition of the mid-third/ninth century geographer Ibn Khurradādhbih. See Minorsky, *op. cit.*, p. 626; Louise Marlow, 'Some classical Muslim views of the Indian caste system', *MW* LXXXV (1995), pp. 16–17.

4 Fragner, 'The concept of regionalism in historical research on Central Asia and Iran (a macro-historical interpretation)', in *Studies on Central Asian History in Honor of Yuri Bregel*, ed. Devin DeWeese (Bloomington, Ind., 2001), pp. 244–7; and cf. Julie S. Meisami, *Persian Historiography to the End of the Twelfth Century* (Edinburgh, 1999), p. 68.

5 See for al-Sallāmī and his work, W. Barthold, *Turkestan down to the Mongol Invasion*, 3rd ed. (London, 1968), pp. 10–11, 21; Fuat Sezgin, *Geschichte des arabischen Schrifttums*, I, Leiden 1967, 352 no. 5; and *EI*[2] art. 'al-Sallāmī' (C.E. Bosworth).

6 Material from al-Sallāmī seems also to have been used in the seventh/thirteenth century by Ibn Khallikān and 'Aṭā'-Malik Juwaynī; see Barthold, *op. cit.*, p. 10.

7 See below, Ḥabībī's text, p. 131, and Barthold, *op. cit.*, p. 7.

8 *Op. cit.*, pp. 69ff.

9 *Ibid.*, pp. 74–5.

10 Ed. Nazim, pp. 61–2, ed. Ḥabībī, pp. 173–4.

11 A.C.S. Peacock, ''Utbī's *al-Yamīnī*: patronage, composition and reception', *Arabica* LIV (2007), pp. 519–20.

12 See for them, C.E. Bosworth, *The Later Ghaznavids: Splendour and Decay. The Dynasty in Afghanistan and Northern India 1040–1186* (Edinburgh, 1977), pp. 25–47.

13 *Ibid.*, pp. 41–7.

14 On Gardīzī as a source for Khurasanian history, see Barthold, *Turkestan*, pp. 20–1, and as one for Ghaznavid history specifically, see Bosworth, 'Early sources for the history of the first four Ghaznavid sultans', *loc. cit.* Gardīzī's place in the historical writing of the time is penetratingly discussed by Meisami in *op. cit.*, pp. 66–79.

15 See C.A. Storey, *Persian Literature. A Bio-bibliographical Survey* (London, 1927–53), Vol. I/2, pp. 65–7.

16 *Ibid.*, p. 72 n. 5.

17 Cf. Minorsky, 'Gardīzī on India', pp. 625–6. Attempts at elucidating the Turkish names in Bayhaqī have been made by Bosworth in his 'Notes on some Turkish names in Abu 'l-Faḍl Bayhaqī's Tārīkh-i Mas'ūdī', *Oriens* XXXVI (2001), pp. 299–313, and his 'Further notes on the Turkish names in Abu 'l-Faḍl Bayhaqī's *Tārīkh-i Mas'ūdī*', to appear in a Festschrift for Dr Farhad Daftary.

18 Bahār, *Sabk-shināsī yā tārīkh-i taṭawwur-i nathr-i fārsī* (Tehran, 1337/1958), Vol. 2, p. 50.

19 G. Lazard, *La langue des plus anciens monuments de la prose persane* (Paris, 1963), pp. 71–3.

20 See e.g. Ḥabībī's text, p. 133, regarding Hārūn al-Rashīd's death.

21 In the present translation, these are in any case usually omitted.

22 Ḥabībī's text, p. 131.

23 Cf. Bosworth, *The History of Beyhaqi* (see above, pp. 9–10), Vol. 1, Introduction, pp. 59–60, 72.

24 I am grateful to Mr Mel Dadswell for providing me with an English translation of Barthold's introduction to his section of this work on Gardīzī.

25 For surveys of the printed editions of Gardīzī's work, see Storey, *op. cit.*, Vol. I, pp. 66, 1229 (who could at the time only list the edition of Nazim and a Tehran one of the mid-1930s), supplemented and updated by Yuri E. Bregel, *Persidskaya literatura, bio-bibliograficheskii obzor* (Moscow, 1972), Vol. I, pp. 288–9, noting subsequent Tehran prints up to and including that of Ḥabībī. There is also much information in Lazard, *loc. cit.* Concerning the most recent edition by Riḍāzāda Malik, see below and n. 27.

26 Czeglédy, 'Gardīzī on the history of Central Asia', *AOHung*, XXXVII (1973), 257–8; Martinez, 'Gardīzī's two chapters on the Turks', *AEMAe* II (1982), pp. 109–12. It may be noted that, as well as Martinez's English translation, facsimile texts of the relevant parts of the manuscripts and discussion of Gardīzī's two sections on the Turks, there is now a German translation of and commentary on these passages by H. Cöckenjan and I. Zimonyi in their *Orientalische Berichte über die Völker Osteuropas und Zentralasiens im Mittlealter. Die Ǧayhānī-Tradition*, Veröffentlichungen der Societas Uralo-Altaica, Bd. 54 (Wiesbaden, 2001), pp. 95–190 (I am grateful to Dr Pavel B. Lurye for this reference).

27 This became known to me only from a review article by Muḥammad Gulbun in *Āyīna-yi Mirāth/Mirror of Heritage*, NS V/1–2 (Tehran, Spring-Summer, 2007), pp. 367–75. However, work on this present translation and its commentary was virtually complete when Dr Farhad Daftary kindly procured for me from Tehran, after some difficulty, a copy of Riḍāzāda Malik's book, and in the short time available a thoroughgoing comparison of Ḥabībī's and Riḍāzāda Malik's two texts has not been possible.

28 It is Riḍāzāda Malik's restored numbering of the component chapters, and their headings, which is followed in the translation below.

29 Storey, *op. cit.*, Vol. I, p. 66.

30 I am most grateful to M. Étienne de la Vaissière for bringing Arends's work to my notice in the first place and for providing me with a photocopy of it, and also grateful to Mr Mel Dadswell and his expertise in Russian bibliography for help with tracing the book's history up to its publication in 1991.

31 Hodivala, *Studies in Indo-Muslim History. A Critical Commentary on Elliot and Dowson's History of India as Told by its Own Historians*, 2 vols. (Bombay, 1937–57); Ahmad, 'A critical examination of Bayhaqī's narration of the Indian expeditions during the reign of Mas'ud of Ghazna', in *Yād-nāma-yi Abu 'l-Faḍl-i Bayhaqī*, ed. Mashhad University Faculty of Letters and Human Sciences (Mashhad, 1350/1971), English section, pp. 34–83.

Part One: The Arab Governors

1 On this division of the Sasanid realm into 'quadrants', see C. Brunner, ch. 'Geographical and administrative divisions: settlements and economy', in *CHIr*, Vol. 3/2, *The Seleucid, Parthian and Sasanian Periods*, ed. Ehsan Yarshater (Cambridge, 1983), pp. 747ff.

2 As noted by Gardīzī, above, p. 14, this southerly route was the normal one to Sistan

and Khurasan at this early period, since what became the more usual, northerly route along the southern rim of the Elburz chain was menaced by the un-Islamised mountain peoples, Daylamīs, Jīlīs, etc. to the north. See C.E. Bosworth, *Sīstān under the Arabs, from the Islamic Conquest to the Rise of the Ṣaffārids (30–250/651–864)* (Rome, 1968), pp. 13–15.

3 See on this outstanding warrior, H.A.R. Gibb, *The Arab Conquests in Central Asia* (London, 1923), pp. 15–16; J. Walker, *A Catalogue of the Muhammadan Coins in the British Museum. Volume I. A Catalogue of the Arab-Sassanian Coins (Umaiyad Governors in the East, Arab-Ephthalites, 'Abbāsid Governors in Ṭabaristān and Bukhārā)* (London, 1941), pp. xlvi–xlvii; M.A. Shaban, *The 'Abbāsid Revolution* (Cambridge, 1970), pp. 16–25; EI^2 art. "Abd Allāh b. 'Āmir' (H.A.R. Gibb); *EIr* art. "Abdallāh b. 'Āmer' (J. Lassner). Al-Ya'qūbī, *Kitāb al-Buldān*, French tr. G. Wiet, *Les pays* (Cairo, 1937), begins his list of the governors of Khurasan (pp. 114–38) with Ibn 'Āmir and goes up to the last Tahirid governor in Khurasan, Muḥammad b. Ṭāhir. Ḥamza al-Iṣfahānī, *Ta'rīkh Sinī mulūk al-arḍ wa 'l-anbiyā'* (Beirut, 1961), pp. 160–72, who dismisses the governors of Khurasan in the Umayyad period as contemptible tyrants, begins essentially with Abū Muslim and has a fair amount of detail on the governors of the early 'Abbasids, the Tahirids and Saffarids, but does little more than to list the names of the earlier Samanids, ending with 'Abd al-Malik (I) b. Nūḥ (I), the author's contemporary.

4 See on this Inner Asian people, foes of the Sasanids and Arabs alike, EI^2 art. 'Hayāṭila' (A.D.H. Bivar); *EIr* art. 'Hephthalites' (A.D.H. Bivar).

5 G. Le Strange, *The Lands of the Eastern Caliphate* (Cambridge, 1905), p. 405.

6 Riḍāzāda Malik's reading of *sipanj* for an unclear consonant ductus seems better than Ḥabībī's *basīj* 'arms, gear, equipment'.

7 According to al-Balādhurī, *Futūḥ al-buldān*, ed. M.J. de Goeje (Leiden, 1866), pp. 409–10, Umayr was the first to settle Arabs at Merv and thereby begin the process whereby the Arabs acquired taxable land in the Merv oasis, settling down and intermarrying with the Persian population. There thus began a process of assimilation there very different from elsewhere, in which the Arabs kept themselves apart from the indigenous population by keeping within fortified garrison cities and encampments. Gardīzī, however, attributes this programme of Arab settlement in the Merv oasis to Mu'āwiya's governor Sa'īd b. 'Uthmān (see above, p. 18), and this seems more likely. Cf. EI^2 art. 'Marw al-Shāhidjān' (A.Yu. Yakubovskii and C.E. Bosworth).

8 Conjecture of Ḥabībī of a possible reading for the text's *b.s.tām.*

9 For this invasion of Sistan in 31/651–2, see Bosworth, *Sīstān under the Arabs*, pp. 16–17.

10 For these places along the Pilgrimage route from Iraq to Medina and Mecca, see Yāqūt, *Mu'jam al-buldān* (Beirut, 1374–6/1955–7), Vol. 1, p. 414, Vol. 2, p. 111, Vol. 5, pp. 255–6, 278–9; Abdullah Al-Wohaibi, *The Northern Hijaz in the Writings of the Arab Geographers 800–1150* (Beirut, 1973), pp. 102–12 (for Juḥfa).

11 In early Islamic times, *kharāj* seems to have been the land-tax paid by the non-Muslim *dhimmīs* in conquered lands, whilst the Muslims there paid *'ushr* on their land. The subjects who were to pay the *kharāj* in the Merv oasis were obviously, at this time, substantially the Persian, non-Muslim population. Only in 'Abbasid times does *kharāj* become the general, official term for land-tax. See F. Løkkegaard, *Islamic Taxation in the Classic Period, with Special Reference to Circumstances in Iraq* (Copenhagen, 1950), pp. 72ff.

12 Lit. 'he turned their heads', *sar-īshān bar gardānīd*, unless one should read *sirr-īshān* . . ., with a meaning like 'he revealed their secrets'.

13 In pre-Islamic Bedouin society, *fay'* (meaning something like 'what is brought back', i.e. to God and the Muslim community) was a general term for 'booty, plunder'. In early Islamic times it took on the specialised meaning of 'income from the conquered lands whose revenue went to the state, which then paid back a proportion of it to the Arab warriors' (see Løkkegaard, *op. cit.*, pp. 32ff.; EI^2 art. 'Fay'' (Løkkegaard). However, apart from this instance where the words of al-Ḥasan are quoted, Gardīzī uses *fay'* with the older, general meaning of 'plunder', hence as a synonym for *ghanīma.*

14 *Sūrat al-Anbiyā'*, XXI, vol. 111.
15 Following Riḍāzāda Malik's reading *sarmā* rather than Ḥabībī's *ānjā*.
16 There may be some confusion here with the Arab historians' mention of Mujāshiʿ's pursuit of the fugitive Sasanid emperor Yazdagird III; see Bosworth, *Sīstān under the Arabs*, pp. 15–16.
17 For Ziyād in the East, see J. Wellhausen, *The Arab Kingdom and Its Fall*, English tr. Margaret G. Weir (Calcutta, 1927), pp. 119–30; Gibb, *The Arab Conquests in Central Asia*, pp. 16–17; Walker, *A Catalogue of the Muhammadan Coins in the British Museum*, I, pp. xlii–xlv; Bosworth, *Sīstān under the Arabs*, pp. 20–1; Shaban, *The 'Abbāsid Revolution*, pp. 29–34; *EI*[2] art. 'Ziyād b. Abīhi' (I. Hasson).
18 For Muhallab, see *EI*[2] art. 'al-Muhallab b. Abī Ṣufra' (P. Crone).
19 Ḥabībī, p. 105 n. 9, thinks that this may refer to the Oxus.
20 See on him, Walker, *op. cit.*, pp. xlvii–xlix; Bosworth, *op. cit.*, pp. 42–4; *EI*[2] art. ''Ubayd Allāh b. Ziyād' (C.F. Robinson).
21 This seems the best translation here, given that Muhallab's opponents here were Sogdians rather than Persians.
22 Gibb, *op. cit.*, pp. 17–19.
23 See on Saʿīd, Shaban, *The 'Abbāsid Revolution*, pp. 37–8.
24 Gibb, *op. cit.*, pp. 17–19; Shaban, *op. cit.*, pp. 38–9. See also above, p. 15 and n. 7.
25 Thus in Nafīsī's text (*chand sāl*) for the reading of the mss.' *ṣad sāl* 'a hundred years' adopted by Ḥabībī and Riḍāzāda Malik. Al-Yaʿqūbī, *Buldān*, tr. Wiet, p. 148, says that ʿAbd al-Raḥmān functioned in Khurasan for four months only, and was then dismissed for his feebleness and supine attitude.
26 See on him, Gibb, *op. cit.*, pp. 21–2; Walker, *op. cit.*, pp. xlix–li; Bosworth, *Sīstān under the Arabs*, pp. 44–5, 48–9; Shaban, *op. cit.*, pp. 39–41; *EI*[2] art. 'Salm b. Ziyād b. Abīhi' (C.E. Bosworth).
27 This was the Queen-Mother (*khātūn* = 'lady', Sogdian *γwt'ynh*) acting as regent for the infant son of the ruler of Bukhara, the subsequent Bukhār-Khudāh Ṭughshāda. See Gibb, *op. cit.*, pp. 17–22; Narshakhī, *Tārīkh-i Bukhārā*, English tr. R.N. Frye, *The History of Bukhara* (Cambridge, Mass., 1954), pp. 9–10.
28 A *mawlā* of this Arab governor was Ruzayq, progenitor of the Tahirid governors of Khurasan in the third/ninth century, see above, pp. 42ff.
29 On Ṭalḥa in Sistan, see Walker, *op. cit.*, p. liv; Bosworth, *Sīstān under the Arabs*, p. 45.
30 For ʿAbdallāh's lengthy governorship, during which he, as a Sulamī, headed the Qaysī ascendancy in Khurasan and struck both dirhams and dinars in his own name, see al-Yaʿqūbī, *Buldān*, tr. Wiet, pp. 120–1; Barthold, *Turkestan*, p. 184; Wellhausen, *The Arab Kingdom*, pp. 416–21; Walker, *op. cit.*, pp. lii–liii and index at p. 221; *EI*[2] art. ''Abd Allāh b. al-Khāzim' (H.A.R. Gibb).
31 Words added here by Nafīsī to complete the sense.
32 Phrase supplied here from al-Yaʿqūbī, *Buldān*. The *Khurāsāniyān* mentioned here are, of course, the Arab troops and settlers in Khurasan rather than the population at large, as are likewise the *ahl-i Khurāsān* that Gardīzī often mentions below in various relationships with the governors and caliphs, becoming after the ʿAbbasid Revolution one of the mainstays of the regime. See on them Farouk Omar, 'The composition of ʿAbbāsid support in the early ʿAbbāsid period', in his *'Abbāsiyyāt. Studies in the History of the Early 'Abbāsids* (Baghdad, 1976), pp. 42–5.
33 Various words supplied here to complete the sense.
34 On the roles of these two tribal leaders in Khurasan, Baḥīr b. Warqā' and Bukayr b. Wishāḥ, and their involvement with ʿAbdallāh b. Khāzim, see Wellhausen, *The Arab Kingdom*, pp. 418ff.
35 There is some uncertainty in the sources concerning the exact form of his name; he is not mentioned in al-Yaʿqūbī's list of the governors.
36 Baḥīr was from Ṣarīm, a sub-clan of Saʿd of Tamīm; see Wellhausen, *op. cit.*, p. 421.

37 See on him al-Yaʿqūbī, *Buldān*, tr. Wiet, p. 121; Wellhausen, *op. cit.*, pp. 421–2, 426; Walker, *op. cit.*, pp. lvii–lviii; Bosworth, *Sīstān under the Arabs*, pp. 49–50; Shaban, *The 'Abbāsid Revolution*, pp. 44–6.

38 For al-Ḥajjāj's policy in the East, see Wellhausen, *op. cit.*, pp. 426ff.; Shaban, *op. cit.*, pp. 53–75; *EI*[2] art. 'al-Ḥadjdjādj b. Yūsuf' (A. Dietrich).

39 For the sons of al-Muhallab, see *EI*[2] art. 'Muhallabids' (P. Crone).

40 Ratbīl or Rutbīl or Zunbīl was more properly the title of the indigenous rulers of Zamīndāwar and Zābulistān, to the southeast of Kabul; see on them below, Part Two, n. 18.

41 For `Ibn al-Ashʿath and his rebellion, see Bosworth, *Sīstān under the Arabs*, pp. 55–63; *EI*[2] art, 'Ibn al-Ashʿath' (L. Veccia Vaglieri).

42 Ḥabībī reads an undotted consonant ductus as *bakhtiyān*, 'Bactrian camels'. But Riḍāzāda interprets it with greater plausibility as *najībān* 'camels of noble breed', hence 'swift-running', supported by the fact that al-Yaʿqūbī, in his History, when recounting this incident, speaks of *najā'ib*; this translation is accordingly followed here.

43 On Qutayba's governorship, see in general Barthold, *Turkestan*, pp. 184–7; Wellhausen, *The Arab Kingdom*, pp. 429–44; Gibb, *The Arab Conquests in Central Asia*, pp. 29–56; Shaban, *The 'Abbāsid Revolution*, pp. 63–75; *EI*[2] art. 'Ḳutayba b. Muslim' (C.E. Bosworth).

44 See for this place below, Part Four, n. 15.

45 *tāzagī*. *Tāzig* was the Middle Persian term for 'Arab'; see D.N. MacKenzie, *A Concise Pahlavi Dictionary* (Oxford, 1990), p. 83.

46 On the fall of Qutayba, see Wellhausen, *op. cit.*, pp. 439–43; R. Eisener, *Zwischen Faktum und Fiktion. Eine Studie zum Umayyadenkalifen Sulaimān b. 'Abdalmalik und seinem Bild in den Quellen* (Wiesbaden, 1987), pp. 91–7.

47 On Wakīʿ's tenure of power, see Wellhausen, *op. cit.*, pp. 442, 444–6; Eisener, *op. cit.*, pp. 97–8. His governorship does not appear as such in al-Yaʿqūbī's list, and seems to have been a provisional one; this historian in fact says (*Buldān*, tr. Wiet, p. 123) that Wakīʿ expected to be made governor, but the new caliph Yazīd b. ʿAbd al-Malik preferred to give the post to Yazīd b. Muhallab, thus temporarily restoring the ascendancy of the Yemenis in Khurasan.

48 i.e. that laid down in the Qur'ān; see *EI*[2] art. 'Ḥadd' (B. Carra de Vaux, J. Schacht).

49 On this second governorship of Yazīd, see al-Yaʿqūbī, *Buldān*, tr. Wiet, pp. 123–4; Wellhausen, *op. cit.*, pp. 445–8; Shaban, *The 'Abbāsid Revolution*, pp. 77–83.

50 *dar-i āhanīn*. This must refer to the narrow valley and gorge connecting the upland plain of Arghiyān and Juwayn in northern Khurasan with the Caspian lowlands of Gurgān, in which flows the Gurgān river; the valley is called in the *Ḥudūd al-'ālam*, English tr. V. Minorsky, 2nd ed. (London, 1970), p. 64, comm. p. 200, the Dīnār-zārī, now the Dahana-yi Gurgān.

51 This is the 'Ṣūl the Turk' of al-Ṭabarī, *Ta'rīkh al-Rusul wa 'l-mulūk*, ed. M.J. De Goeje *et al.* (Leiden, 1879–1901), Secunda series, p. 1323, English tr. D.S. Powers, *The History of al-Ṭabarī. Vol. XXIV. The Empire in Transition* (Albany, 1989), p. 48, located by him in Dihistān, to the north of Gurgān in the steppelands on the eastern shore of the Caspian Sea. The Turks in question were possibly Oghuz who had infiltrated southwards from the steppes to the north of the Aral Sea. See Barthold, *A History of the Turkmen People*, in *Four Studies on the History of Central Asia*, English tr. V. and T. Minorsky (Leiden, 1962), Vol. 3, pp. 87–8. Members of the family of Ṣūl, now Islamised, were to have a career in ʿAbbasid service and to produce a celebrated literary figure of the fourth/tenth century, Abū Bakr Muḥammad al-Ṣūlī. On the name Ṣūl/Sol and its possible meaning, see L. Rásonyi and I. Baski, *Onomasticon turcicum. Turkic Personal Names as Collected by László Rásonyi* (Bloomington, Ind., 2007), Vol. 2, pp. 665–6.

52 For Yazīd's military operations in Gurgān, see Eisener, *op. cit.*, pp. 100–1.

53 See on his term of office, al-Yaʿqūbī, *Buldān*, tr. Wiet, p. 124; Barthold, *Turkestan*, p. 188; Wellhausen, *The Arab Kingdom*, pp. 450–2; Shaban, *The 'Abbāsid Revolution*, pp. 86–7; *EI*[2]

art. 'al-Djarrāḥ b. 'Abd Allāh' (D.M. Dunlop). Jarrāḥ has a claim to fame in the history of Arabic palaeography and diplomatic as the addressee of the only Arabic document from the Eastern Islamic world extant from this early period, sc. a letter found at Mount Mugh in what is now the Tajik Republic. See Geoffrey Khan, *Studies in the Khalili Collection. Volume V. Arabic Documents* (London, 2007), p. 15 (Khan here edits and translates a cache of Arabic documents from the mid-eighth century AD, apparently emanating from northern Afghanistan; these have greatly swelled the previously very exiguous extant corpus of early Arabic documents from the East).

54 i.e. the great-grandson of the Prophet's uncle al-'Abbās. Gardīzī is here registering the beginning of the 'Abbasid *da'wa* in Kufa when Muḥammad b. 'Alī took over the claims of Abū Hāshim, son of 'Alī's son Muḥammad b. al-Ḥanafiyya. See Shaban, *op. cit.*, pp. 150–1.

55 For Sa'īd, an Umayyad from the Abu 'l-'Āṣ branch of the clan, and nicknamed Khudhayna 'Little Lady' by the Khurasanian troops, who regarded his mildness as misplaced, see Barthold, *op. cit.*, pp. 188–9; Wellhausen, *op. cit.*, pp. 451–2; Shaban, *op. cit.*, pp. 99–101.

56 Following Nafīsī's reading, *mujāmalat.*

57 'Umar was indeed governor for Yazīd, but was replaced by Hishām on his accession in 105/724. See EI^2 art. 'Ibn Hubayra' (J.-C. Vadet).

58 Khālid was governor of Iraq and the East for the greater part of Hishām's twenty-years' caliphate, with his brother Asad as governor in Khurasan for almost as long, dying in 120/738. See Wellhausen, *The Arab Kingdom*, pp. 455–6; Gibb, *The Arab Conquests in Central Asia*, pp. 67–89; Shaban, *The 'Abbāsid Revolution*, pp. 106–27; EI^2 art. 'Asad b. 'Abd Allāh' (H.A.R. Gibb); EI^2 art. 'Khālid b. 'Abd Allāh al-Ḳasrī' (G.R. Hawting).

59 Ḥabībī interprets the text here as *shumā hamī irjāf afgandīd.*

60 See on him Barthold, *Turkestan*, pp. 189–90; Wellhausen, *op. cit.*, pp. 456–9; Shaban, *op. cit.*, pp. 109–12.

61 This is apparently the Abū Muzāḥim of Arabic historical sources, the Qaghan of the Türgesh or Western Turk empire at this time, whose actual name is only known from its form in the Chinese annals, Su-lu. See Barthold, *op. cit.*, pp. 190–1; Gibb, *The Arab Conquests in Central Asia*, pp. 73ff.

62 *khārijī*, not, however, to be taken here in the sectarian sense of 'Khārijite'. Al-Ḥārith seems to have been in theology a Murji'ite and, in practice, an ascetic calling for just rule according to the Qur'ān and Sunna, as noted by Gardīzī below, and for allegiance to one acceptable to the whole Muslim community (*al-riḍā*). His anti-government activity in Khurasan continued till his death in 128/746. See Wellhausen, *The Arab Kingdom*, pp. 459–98; Barthold, *Turkestan*, pp. 190–3; EI^2 art. 'al-Ḥārith b. Suraydj' (M.J. Kister).

63 See on him Barthold, *op. cit.*, p. 191; Wellhausen, *op. cit.*, pp. 461–2, 466–7; Shaban, *op. cit.*, pp. 118–21.

64 On this second spell of office for Khalid and Asad as his deputy, see Barthold, *loc. cit.*, Wellhausen, *op. cit.*, pp. 467–74; Shaban, *The 'Abbāsid Revolution*, pp. 121–7.

65 This lay in the westernmost part of Khurasan, to the west of Nishapur and adjoining the province of Qūmis; see Le Strange, *The Lands of the Eastern Caliphate*, p. 430.

66 i.e. for a hostel or caravanserai.

67 See on him Barthold, *op. cit.*, pp. 192–4; Wellhausen, *op. cit.*, pp. 474–91, 523–40; Gibb, *op. cit.*, pp. 89–93; Shaban, *op. cit.*, pp. 127–37, 159–61; E.L. Daniel, *The Political and Social History of Khurasan under Abbasid Rule, 747–820* (Minneapolis and Chicago, 1979), pp. 44–5, 54–8; Moshe Sharon, *Black Banners from the East II. Revolt. The Social and Military Aspects of the 'Abbāsid Revolution* (Jerusalem, 1990), pp. 34–7, 42–7, 63, 107ff., 147ff.; EI^2 art. 'Naṣr b. Sayyār' (C.E. Bosworth).

68 Naṣr introduced significant financial reforms in Khurasan in 121/739 aimed at redressing the grievances of the Arab settlers in the Merv oasis (Gardīzī's *ahl-i Khurāsān* here) against the local Persian *dihqān*s who had been collecting taxation from the oasis. See D.C. Dennett, *Conversion and the Poll Tax in Early Islam* (Cambridge, Mass, 1950), pp. 124–8; Shaban, *op. cit.*, pp. 129–30.

69 See on this 'Alid, a descendant on his mother's side of Muḥammad b. al-Ḥanafiyya, Daniel, *op. cit.*, pp. 38–9; Sharon, *Black Banners from the East. The Establishment of the 'Abbāsid State – Incubation of a Revolt* (Jerusalem/Leiden, 1983), pp. 175–9, 181; *EI*[2] art. 'Yaḥyā b. Zayd' (W. Madelung).

70 See on these agents, Shaban, *The 'Abbāsid Revolution*, pp. 151–2; Sharon, *Black Banners from the East*, pp. 188–97; Sharon, *Revolt. The Social and Military Aspects of the 'Abbāsid Revolution*, pp. 20–1; *EI*[2] art. 'Naḳīb. I. In Early Islamic History' (C.E. Bosworth).

71 As Ḥabībī remarks, n. 11, copyists seem to have split the name of the fifth *naqīb* into two separate persons, with the two brothers given as the twelfth one making up the full number.

72 Text, *z.r.y.q.* This is the first appearance in Gardīzī's pages of a family – probably of *mawlā* origin in Basra, and of unknown ethnic affiliation – which was to have a glorious future in both Iraq and Khurasan. Both Ṭalḥa and his brother Muṣ'ab were, as appears here, involved with the 'Abbasid *da'wa*, and the patronage of the new caliphal dynasty subsequently favoured the family's rise, with Muṣ'ab's grandson Ṭāhir Dhu 'l-Yamīnayn becoming al-Ma'mūn's commander during the civil war with al-Amīn (see above, pp. 40–1) and founding the line of Tahirid governors of Khurasan. See Mongi Kaabi, 'Les origines ṭāhirides dans la *da'wa* 'abbāside', *Arabica*, XIX (1972), pp. 145–64; Kaabi, *Les Ṭāhirides au Ḫurāsān et en Iraq (III*[ème] *H./IX*[ème] *J.-C.)* (Tunis, 1983), Vol. 1, pp. 62–3.

73 Text, *'.n.y.sū*; cf. Ḥabībī's n. 5 and *EI*[2] art. 'Yaḥyā b. Zayd' (W. Madelung).

74 This explanation, and the more usual (and plausible) one that Marwān was called al-Ḥimār because of the wild ass's proverbial hardihood and endurance, are given by al-Tha'ālibī in his *Laṭā'if al-ma'ārif*, English tr. C.E. Bosworth, *The Book of Curious and Entertaining Information* (Edinburgh, 1968), p. 61.

75 See on Jahm and his doctrines, W. Montgomery Watt, *The Formative Period of Islamic Thought* (Edinburgh, 1973), pp. 145–8; *EI*[2] arts. 'Dj̲ahm b. Ṣafwān' and 'Dj̲ahmiyya' (Montgomery Watt).

76 Shaybān b. Salama had been an adherent of the Khārijite rebel in Iraq and al-Jazīra, al-Ḍaḥḥāk b. Qays, and had fled from there to Khurasan, where he became an associate of Juday' al-Kirmānī until he was killed by Abū Muslim in 130/748. See Daniel, *The Political and Social History of Khurasan*, pp. 78–9.

77 This was presumably the first protective ditch constructed at Mākhān or Mākhwān (see below, n. 80) by Abū Muslim as a defence against possible attack by Naṣr, see Daniel, *op. cit.*, pp. 52–3. He then had a second ditch made at Gīrang or Kīrang, which lay on the Murghāb river, presumably to disrupt communication between Naṣr and his supporters in Marw al-Rūd; see Le Strange, *The Lands of the Eastern Caliphate*, p. 400, and *Ḥudūd al-'ālam*, tr. Minorsky, p. 105, comm. p. 328.

78 The origins of Abū Muslim are in fact very obscure, making him an enigmatic figure in Islamic history; see Sharon, *Black Banners from the East*, pp. 203–7. It is not clear whether he was a free man or a *mawlā*, or of Persian ethnos, as is usually assumed.

79 For Qaḥṭaba, the second most important person of the 'Abbasid *da'wa* in Khurasan after Abū Muslim, and one of the *nuqabā'* (see above, pp. 27–8), see P. Crone, *Slaves on Horses. The Evolution of the Islamic Polity* (Cambridge, 1980), p. 188; *EI*[2] art. 'Ḳaḥṭaba' (M. Sharon).

80 This is described by Yāqūt as a village three parasangs from Merv. Various traditions make Abū Muslim's father, as Abū Muslim himself, a native of Mākhān. See Irène Mélikoff, *Abū Muslim, le <<Porte-Hache>> du Khorasan, dans la tradition épique turco-iranienne* (Paris, 1962), p. 93 n. 5.

81 On the apocalyptic and prophetic sayings which seem to have been put into circulation by what Sharon has called the "Abbasid official propaganda machine', see his *Black Banners from the East*, pp. 87ff.

82 In Bīrūnī's original (see next note), *ṣalāt*.

83 This passage about Bihāfarīd is clearly taken from al-Bīrūnī's *al-Āthār al-bāqiya 'an al-qurūn al-khāliya*, ed. E. Sachau (Leipzig, 1878), English tr. E. Sachau, *The Chronology of Ancient*

Nations (London, 1879). See on this Zoroastrian reformer, Gh.H. Sadighi, *Les mouvements religieux iraniens au IIe et au IIIe siècle de l'Hégire* (Paris, 1938), pp. 111–31; B. Scarcia Amoretti, ch. 'Sects and heresies', in *CHIr*, Vol. 4, *The Period from the Arab Invasion to the Saljuqs*, ed. R.N. Frye (Cambridge, 1975), pp. 489–90; *EI*[2] art. 'Bih'āfrīd b. Farwardīn' (D. Sourdel). Meisami, *Persian Historiography*, pp. 74–5, noted Gardīzī's concern – as shown also by other historians in medieval Islam – with the movements of various pseudo-prophets and religious reformers, the implication being that it is the ruler's duty to eradicate such dissidence and to support the true faith.

84 Actually at Ushmūnayn in Upper Egypt; see *EI*[2] art. 'Marwān II' (G.R. Hawting).

85 On this pro-ʿAlid revolt of Sharīk b. Shaykh al-Mahrī, centred on Bukhara, see Barthold, *Turkestan*, pp. 194–5.

86 The background to this is explained by al-Ṭabarī, *Ta'rīkh*, Secunda series, p. 1891, English tr. J.A. Williams, *The History of al-Ṭabarī. Vol.* XXVII. *The ʿAbbāsid Revolution* (Albany, 1985), p. 211: that al-Saffāḥ had been fearful of an army of several thousand Khurasanian troops descending on Iraq and, on the plea that the Pilgrimage Road across the Arabian desert of Najd could not feed and supply such a throng, instructed Abū Muslim to bring 1,000 troops only. See also H. Kennedy, *The Early Abbasid Caliphate. A Political History* (London and Totowa, N.J., 1981), p. 54.

87 On ʿAbdallāh b. ʿAlī's revolt with the support of the Syrian army, see J. Lassner, *The Shaping of ʿAbbāsid Rule* (Princeton, 1980), pp. 35–8; Kennedy, *op. cit.*, pp. 58–60.

88 Reading thus, following Nafīsī's text rather than the completely implausible *Ḥarra* of Ḥabībī and Riḍāzāda Malik, Ḥīra being an ancient centre of Christianity in central Iraq, where this *tarsā'ī* was presumably a monk or anchorite.

89 This seems to be a reference to the dispute over the plunder captured from ʿAbdallāh b. ʿAlī's army when Abū Muslim defeated it at Nisibīn. According to al-Ṭabarī, *Ta'rīkh*, Tertia series, pp. 102–3, English tr. Jane D. McAuliffe, *The History of al-Ṭabarī. Vol.* XXVIII. *ʿAbbāsid Authority Affirmed* (Albany, 1995), p. 23, for the distribution of this booty, the caliph sent his own agent, the *mawlā* Abū Khaṣīb (on whom see Crone, *Slaves on Horses*, p. 190), with Abū Muslim protesting that the caliph was only entitled to a fifth (*khums*) of captured spoils. See also Kennedy, *op. cit.*, p. 61.

90 Abū Mujrim, punning on Abū Muslim's name.

91 Salama, Manṣūr's mother, being a Berber slave.

92 The detailed Arabic historical sources (e.g. al-Yaʿqūbī, al-Ṭabarī) list further petty accusations hurled at Abū Muslim by the caliph.

93 *sar-i kas*; Nafīsī's text has *sarhang* 'senior officer'; al-Ṭabarī has *ṣāḥib al-ḥaras*. See on ʿUthmān b. Nahīk, Crone, *Slaves on Horses*, p. 189.

94 Meisami, *Persian Historiography*, pp. 70–1, partially translates these exchanges between al-Manṣūr and Abū Muslim, noting the apocalyptic and prophetic overtones in this story of the unfolding of the ʿAbbasid Revolution and its consequences for a protagonist like Abū Muslim.

95 Abū Dāwūd had been one of the original twelve *naqīb*s (see above, p. 26) and one of Abū Muslim's most trusted lieutenants. See on him al-Yaʿqūbī, *Buldān*, tr. Wiet, p. 129; Daniel, *The Political and Social History of Khurasan*, pp. 86, 132, 158–9.

96 There are, however, in the sources differing accounts of his death, including one which makes Abū Dāwūd an object of suspicion, because of his previous closeness to Abū Muslim, for al-Manṣūr, who accordingly had him murdered. See Daniel, *op. cit.*, pp. 158–9, who makes the point that the killing of Abū Muslim ushered in a period of sharp factional strife in Khurasan between the erstwhile supporters of Abū Muslim and the partisans of al-Manṣūr and the ʿAbbasids.

The 'Wearers of White' (in Arabic contexts appearing as the *Mubayyiḍa*) mentioned here by Gardīzī must have been a *ghulāt* group, one of several who claimed to be avenging the death of Abū Muslim and whose activity in Khurasan antedated that of the rebel al-Muqannaʿ ("The Veiled One") of some twenty years later (see above, p. 34). This Saʿīd

Jawlāh (?) does not seem to be mentioned in other sources, but there was at this time *ghulāt* agitation in Khurasan led by one Isḥāq al-Turk (the latter component of his name does not seem necessarily to imply Turkish ethnicity, but that he had worked among the Turks on the fringes of Transoxania); see concerning Isḥāq, Sadighi, *Les mouvements religieux iraniens*, pp. 150–4; Scarcia Amoretti, ch. 'Sects and heresies', pp. 496–7; and Daniel, *op. cit.*, p. 132.

97 Ḥamza al-Iṣfahānī, *Ta'rīkh Sinī mulūk al-arḍ wa 'l-anbiyā'*, p. 162, mentions here with some diffidence ('He [sc. God] knows best the truth of matters') that the commander of the police guard, one Abū 'Iṣām 'Abd al-Raḥmān b. Salīm, functioned as governor for a year and a month after Abu Dāwūd's death.

98 See on him and his subsequent revolt, Ya'qūbī, *Buldān*, tr. Wiet, pp. 129–30; Daniel, *The Political and Social History of Khurasan*, pp. 159–61; Crone, *Slaves on Horses*, pp. 173–4.

99 Ibrāhīm and his brother Muḥammad were grandsons of al-Ḥasan b. 'Alī b. Abī Ṭālib. In 145/762 the two of them led an unsuccessful revolt in Basra against al-Manṣūr, being killed in the attempt. See Lassner, *The Shaping of 'Abbāsid Rule*, pp. 72, 74, 76–7, 81–4.

100 This agitator may have carried on the work of the Isḥāq the Turk mentioned above; see Daniel, *op. cit.*, pp. 132–3.

101 Zam(m) was a crossing-point on the Oxus, on the left bank roughly midway between Āmul and Tirmidh. See Le Strange, *The Lands of the Eastern Caliphate*, pp. 403–4.

102 On this episode of 'Abd al-Jabbār's rebellion against the caliph – for whatever reason – see Daniel, *op. cit.*, pp. 159–62, who stresses, as one element at work here, the tension between governors and other officials who represented Khurasanian Arab interests, and the centralising policies of the 'Abbasids.

103 Much obscurity surrounds Ustādsīs and his revolt. He was, according to some sources, a local ruler (*malik*) in the Bādghīs region, and he may originally have assisted the 'Abbasid *da'wa*; others connect him with the Khārijites of neighbouring Sistan; less probable, given his obvious links with Muslim groups, even if somewhat heterodox ones like the Khārijites, is that, like Bihāfarīd, his movement had elements of a reformed version of Zoroastrianism. See Sadighi, *Les mouvements religieux iraniens*, pp. 155–62; Scarcia Amoretti, ch. 'Sects and heresies', pp. 497–8; Daniel, *op. cit.*, pp. 133–7; *EI*[2] art. 'Ustā<u>dh</u>sīs' (W. Madelung).

104 *taqdīrī kun*, perhaps, in the light of what follows, with the implication 'allot us a share in captured booty!'

105 Thus Ḥabībī, *chīzī ba-dād*; Riḍāzāda Malik has the opposite, *chīzī na-dād*, 'he gave them nothing'.

106 On Marājil, Hārūn's slave concubine, see Nabia Abbott, *Two Queens of Baghdad. Mother and Wife of Hārūn al-Rashīd* (Chicago, 1946), pp. 110, 141; according to Ibn Shākir al-Kutubī, she died in childbirth, having borne al-Ma'mūn. Daniel, *op. cit.*, p. 136, suggests that this putative connection between al-Ma'mūn and Ustādsīs may have been put into circulation by pro-Arab, anti-Persian partisans during the Shu'ūbiyya controversies in order to cast aspersions on al-Ma'mūn and his alleged pro-Iranian proclivities.

107 Ḥabībī, n. 6, observes that none of the standard chroniclers, such as al-Ya'qūbī, al-Ṭabarī and Ḥamza al-Iṣfahānī, mentions this ephemeral governor.

108 Ḥumayd had been one of the *nuẓarā'*, i.e. stand-ins or deputies for the twelve *nuqabā'*, in the 'Abbasid *da'wa*. See Crone, *Slaves on Horses*, p. 188; Sharon, *Black Banners from the East*, p. 195.

109 Al-Muqanna''s rebellion probably began *ca.* 160/777, and constitutes the most important of the anti-'Abbasid social and religious movements in the Islamic East during this period. See on this heresiarch, E.G. Browne, *A Literary History of Persia* (London and Cambridge, 1908–24), Vol. 1, pp. 318–23; Barthold, *Turkestan*, pp. 198–200; Sadighi, *op. cit.*, pp. 163–86; Scarcia Amoretti, *op. cit.*, pp. 498–500; Farouk Omar, 'A point of view on the nature of the Iranian revolts in the early Abbasid period', in *'Abbāsiyyāt. Studies in the History of the Early 'Abbāsids*, pp. 81–3; Daniel, *op. cit.*, pp. 137–47; *EI*[2]

art. 'al-Muḳanna'' (ed.). The adoption of a white banner, and the white garments of his followers, *sapīd-jāmagān* or *mubayyiḍa*, were conscious repudiations of ʿAbbasid authority, with its characteristic colour of black for banners, uniforms, etc.; see Omar, 'The significance of the colours of banners in the early ʿAbbāsid period', in *ʿAbbāsiyyāt*, pp. 148–54.

110 This idea of 'transmigration' (*tanāsukh*) involves the transference, or the immanence (*ḥulūl*), of a divine element from one prophet, spiritual leader or (in the case of the Shīʿa) imam to another. In early Islam, the concept was especially characteristic of the Kaysāniyya, partisans of the claims of ʿAlī's son Muḥammad b. al-Ḥanafiyya, and of other subsequent *ghulāt* sects. See *EI*² art. 'Tanāsukh' (D. Gimaret). Here in Central Asia, where there was a ferment of religious ideas and beliefs, it is likely, as Daniel suggests (*The Political and Social History of Khurasan*, pp. 139, 144) that Muqannaʿ's movement drew in adherents of other heterodox currents. Adoption of the name Hāshim would obviously connect al-Muqannaʿ, whatever his real name was, with messianic currents in the original ʿAbbasid *daʿwa*, although his own movement was distinctly hostile to the political authority of the ʿAbbasids.

111 This may refer to Turks settled on the fringes of Transoxania (cf. below, Part Four, n. 10), or those Oghuz which Ibn al-Athīr, obviously utilising older sources, mentions as coming at this time from the farthest fringes of Inner Asia; see P.B. Golden, *An Introduction to the History of the Turkic Peoples. Ethnogenesis and State-Formation in Medieval and Early Modern Eurasia and the Middle East* (Wiesbaden, 1992), pp. 206–7. This mention by Gardīzī is nevertheless interesting in showing that al-Muqannaʿ was able to attract a wide spread of support from all the local peoples of Transoxania, especially those in rural areas; and it is further worthy of note that Narshakhī, *Tārīkh-i Bukhārā*, tr. Frye, p. 72, states that Muqannaʿ had a commander in Bukhara with the name, redolent of the first Turkish empire on the Orkhon, of Kül Er Tegin; see Frye's nos. 66, 259.

112 The readings and sense of the mss. here are unclear. Nafīsī and Ḥabībī read *kūy-hā*, but the latter, n. 6, suggests a possible meaning for the *kūs-hā* ('drums') of the mss.: that important towns had drums that were beaten at the government headquarters as a manifestation of sovereignty, citing the historian of the Delhi Sultanate period Minhāj al-Dīn Jūzjānī, who states that up to 617/1220 and the coming of Chingiz Khān the 'fanfare of drums (*nawbat*) of Abū Muslim' were beaten at Merv (*Ṭabaqāt-i nāṣirī*, ed. Ḥabībī [Kabul, 1342–3/1963–4], Vol. 1, p. 107). The meaning here would accordingly be 'and they beat the ceremonial drums'.

113 This obviously lay in the Bukhara region; Yāqūt, *Muʿjam al-buldān*, Vol. 5, p. 309, reads the name as Nuwajkath but does not pinpoint its exact location.

114 This is the obvious sense of *Ṣughdiyān*, *pace* Frye, *op. cit.*, p. 71, followed by Daniel, *The Political and Social History of Khurasan*, p. 142, both taking it, improbably, as a personal name.

115 This is the revolt of Yūsuf al-Barm. Whether he was a Khārijite or was simply a rebel representing local interests in eastern Khurasan against the ʿAbbasid state apparatus is unclear. See Daniel, *op. cit.*, pp. 166–7.

116 Muʿādh was a *mawlā* of Rabīʿa or of Dhuhl of Bakr. See on him al-Yaʿqūbī, *Buldān*, tr. Wiet, pp. 131–2; Daniel, *op. cit.*, pp. 142–3; Crone, *Slaves on Horses*, pp. 183–4.

117 Ṭawāwīs ('The Peacocks', so-called, says Narshakhī, because the invading Arabs first encountered peacocks there) was one or two days, journey from Bukhara. See *Ḥudūd al-ʿālam*, tr. Minorsky, p. 113; Barthold, *Turkestan*, pp. 98–9; Le Strange, *The Lands of the Eastern Caliphate*, p. 462.

118 This appears to be a personal name, although nothing further is known of the man. It is a not uncommon name in medieval Arabic onomastic, as has been pointed out to me by Professor Van Gelder, citing e.g. the many Khārijas in the index to Caskel and Strenziok-Ibn al-Kalbī's *Ǧamharat an-nasab*. An emendation of the text to *khārijī* 'a Khārijite', seems nevertheless not impossible, since although al-Muqannaʿ himself was not a Khārijite, as observed above, nos. 108–9, he attracted many heterodox elements to his standard.

119 Musayyab was a *mawlā* of Ḍabba who had been a *naẓīr* in the ʿAbbasid *da'wa.* see Daniel, *op. cit.*, p. 168; Crone, *op. cit.*, p. 181.

120 Since the story of al-Muqannaʿ seems early to have attracted fantastic, semi-legendary accretions, there are in the sources various accounts of his death, including self-immolation as well as mass poisoning (this last reminiscent of the mass suicide of Jim Jones and the adherents of his 'The People's Temple Full Gospel Church' at Jonestown, Guyana, in 1978).

121 The author of the *Ḥudūd al-ʿālam*, writing two centuries after al-Muqannaʿ's time, states (tr. Minorsky, p. 117, comm. p. 356) that the people of Īlāq on the middle Syr Darya mostly professed the creed of the *sapīd-jāmagān.*

122 Barthold, *Turkestan*, p. 205, read the second component of this name as *d.h.da/Dahda*, admitting that no governor of that name is mentioned in the sources but suggesting that he was an Arab financial official in Transoxania.

123 Concerning these alloy coins, introduced, so Narshakhī says (*Tārīkh-i Bukhārā*, tr. Frye, pp. 35–7, 129), for local circulation when the price of silver had become excessively high in Khwarazm and Transoxania, see Barthold, *op. cit.*, pp. 204–7.

124 Both Barthold, *op. cit.*, p. 202, and Daniel, *The Political and Social History of Khurasan*, p. 168, note that the governorships of Abu 'l-ʿAbbās and then of the Barmakid al-Faḍl b. Yaḥyā were ones in which beneficial policies for the people of the East were pursued.

125 Khwārazmī defines *bast* (lit. 'something which is bound up, blocked', hence a barrier) as a measurement used at Merv for distributing irrigation water, essentially a board with a hole in it of determined size. See Bosworth, 'Abū ʿAbdallāh al-Khwārazmī on the technical terms of the secretary's art. A contribution to the administrative history of mediaeval Islam', *JESHO* XII (1969), p. 152.

126 Presumably this was a *ribāṭ* for travellers crossing the Qara Qum. It is unmentioned by the geographers, and may have had only an ephemeral existence.

127 This was on 15 Rabīʿ 170/14 September 786.

128 This dating is clearly erroneous, since Ghiṭrīf was governor in this year (see below). We know from other sources that ʿAbbās's raid against Buddhist shrines at Kabul and Shābahār (the latter place to be distinguished from the homonymous place outside Ghazna mentioned in Ghaznavid history) actually took place in 171/787–8; see Bosworth, *Sīstān under the Arabs*, pp. 85–6. Riḍāzāda Malik has the date Muḥarram 170 [/July 786], but this is clearly too early.

129 In 173/789–90. Ḥamza al-Iṣfahānī, *Ta'rīkh Sinī mulūk al-arḍ wa 'l-anbiyā'*, p. 164, has, as governor between Jaʿfar and Ghiṭrīf, Ḥasan b. Qaḥṭaba, but again with the disclaimer 'God knows best'.

130 In 175/791–2. Ghiṭrīf was Hārūn's maternal uncle, the brother of the caliph's mother Khayzurān, wife of al-Mahdī. See Abbott, *Two Queens of Baghdad*, p. 29.

131 This Jabūya/Jabghūya must have been a Turkish chief from some tribal group like the Qarluq, Yabghu being an ancient Turkish princely title. See *EIr* art. 'Jabḡuya. ii. In Islamic sources' (C.E. Bosworth).

132 See above, p. 36. Narshakhī relates that Ghiṭrīf's debased coinage placed a heavy burden on the people of Bukhara (and doubtless elsewhere in the East) because taxes had now to be paid at rates always manipulated in favour of the administration and to the detriment of the taxpayers; see his *Tārīkh-i Bukhārā*, tr. Frye, pp. 36–7. It is clear from various sources that Ghiṭrīf's governorship was regarded as oppressive.

133 Ḥuḍayn seems, from the parallel source of the *Tārīkh-i Sīstān*, to be the correct form of the name rather than the text's Ḥuṣayn. See on his revolt, Bosworth, *Sīstān under the Arabs*, p. 85.

134 al-Yaʿqūbī, *Buldān*, tr. Wiet, p. 133, and Ḥamza al-Iṣfahānī, *op. cit.*, p. 165, record Ḥamza b. Mālik b. Haytham al-Khuzāʿī as Ghiṭrīf's brief successor as governor in 176/792–3 or at the beginning of the next year.

135 For Faḍl's governorship, regarded in the historical sources and in the *adab* literature as a

benevolent, even idyllic one, see Barthold, *Turkestan*, p. 203; Daniel, *The Political and Social History of Khurasan*, p. 169.

136 For the etymology of the name of this Iranian magnate, see F. Justi, *Iranisches Namenbuch* (Marburg, 1895), p. 170: 'Felsen-hahn (Tetraogallus)'. He is mentioned in al-Ṭabarī as the father of Kāwūs, father of the Afshīn Khaydhar or Ḥaydar, who was prominent in al-Muʿtaṣim's caliphate as the vanquisher of Bābak Khurramī (see above, p. 43 and Part Two, n. 5). These princes of Ushrūsana held the title of Afshīn, for which see C.E. Bosworth and Sir Gerard Clauson, 'Al-Xwārazmī on the peoples of Central Asia', *JRAS* (1965), pp. 7–8.

137 Nafīsī has in his text 'to Shahrazūr, and from there to Asadābād, and there'.

138 ʿUmar b. Jamīl did not, so far as we know from historical literature, found a line in Chaghāniyān of any significance, but the history of this province is particularly obscure until the emergence of the Muḥtājids in the early fourth/tenth century; see Bosworth, 'The rulers of Chaghāniyān in early Islamic times', *Iran JBIPS* XIX (1981), p. 3.

139 The story of Hārūn and his breach of faith with the Barmakids, who had been loyal servants of the ʿAbbasids, has been already given by Gardīzī in his section on the caliphs, ed. Ḥabībī, pp. 69–70, ed. Riḍāzāda Malik, pp. 128–9, with an emphasis on the whole episode as a phase in ʿAbbasid decline; cf. Meisami, *Persian Historiography*, p. 73.

140 Manṣūr was thus, like Ghiṭrīf, a maternal relative of the ʿAbbasid royal family, through the brother of al-Manṣūr's Ḥimyarite wife. See Crone, *Slaves on Horses*, pp. 255–6 n. 580.

141 If the referent in *wa bāz gasht* is Manṣūr, then presumably he returned to Iraq; if it is Ḥamza, then he would have gone back to his native province of Sistan. Ḥamza's revolt was the most protracted and serious Khārijite outbreak in the East, beginning in Sistan *ca.* 179/795–6, engulfing neighbouring provinces like Khurasan and Kirman, and only ending thirty years later with Ḥamza's death in 213/828. See Sadighi, *Les mouvements religieux iraniens*, pp. 54–6; Bosworth, *Sīstān under the Arabs*, pp. 91–4; *EIr* art. 'Ḥamza b. Ādarak' (C.E. Bosworth).

Other historians (e.g. al-Ṭabarī, *Taʾrīkh*, Tertia series, p. 644, English tr. C.E. Bosworth, *The History of al-Ṭabarī. Vol. XXX. The ʿAbbāsid Caliphate in Equilibrium* [Albany, 1989], p. 162; Ḥamza al-Iṣfahānī, *Taʾrīkh Sinī mulūk al-arḍ*, p. 165) record that Jaʿfar b. Yaḥyā al-Barmakī was briefly appointed to Khurasan after his successful campaignings in Syria, but he does not seem ever to have gone there personally.

142 On ʿAlī's governorship, regarded in all the sources as repressive and exploitative, see Barthold, *Turkestan*, p. 203; Daniel, *The Political and Social History of Khurasan*, pp. 170–4; *EI*² art. "Alī b. ʿĪsā' (Ch. Pellat). His family was of *mawlā* origin, and had been prominent in the ʿAbbasid *daʿwa*; see Crone, *op. cit.*, pp. 178–9.

143 Nothing is known of this work.

144 Following the reading of Nafīsī given in Ḥabībī's n. 13, *ba-shikast.*

145 i.e. Ṭāhir b. al-Ḥusayn b. Muṣʿab b. Ruzayq, whose family power base was in Pūshang.

146 The affluent stream of the Oxus, on whose banks Balkh stood, is called by Ibn Ḥawqal a century-and-a-half later, Dih Ās '[that which drives] ten mills'; see Le Strange, *The Lands of the Eastern Caliphate*, p. 420.

147 Harthama was of Khurasanian *mawlā* origin, who had risen high in caliphal favour. See on him Crone, *op. cit.*, pp. 75, 177; *EI*² art. 'Harthama b. Aʿyan' (Ch. Pellat).

148 Rāfiʿ's revolt probably reflected popular discontent in Transoxania with ʿAlī b. ʿĪsā's misgovernment there, but it spread also to Khurasan, where ʿAlī's policies were equally rapacious. See Barthold, *Turkestan*, pp. 200–1; Daniel, *The Political and Social History of Khurasan*, pp. 172–5; *EI*² art. 'Rāfiʿ b. al-Layth b. Naṣr b. Sayyār' (C.E. Bosworth).

149 This section on Harthama's governorship is apparently considerably confused in the mss., with an inconsequential chronology of events. This is unnoted by Ḥabībī, but has been put right by Riḍāzāda Malik, and the latter's rearrangement of the entry is followed here.

150 Thus the suggestion of Ḥabībī in his n. 16 for the term *niwishta*, although one would not

expect volunteers like these to be entitled to regular stipends on the *dīwān al-jaysh* rolls; such volunteers normally brought their own arms, equipment and mounts but shared in captured plunder.

151 On the confusion in the sources about the manner and place of Ḥamza's death, and the briefness of Abū Isḥāq Ibrāhīm's headship of the Khārijites of Sistan, see Bosworth, *Sīstān under the Arabs*, pp. 103–4.

152 The sources are likewise confused about the events surrounding the end of Rāfiʿ's uprising. Some state that he accepted a pardon from al-Ma'mūn, after which he drops out of historical mention; see Daniel, *op. cit.*, pp. 174–5.

153 Following here Riḍāzāda Malik's *ba-dādand.*

154 This man is presumably the ancestor of the petty dynasty of the Bānījūrids or Abū Dāwūdids, apparently originally from Farghāna but ruling in Balkh and Ṭukhāristān in the later third/ninth century and possibly in the fourth/tenth one. See C.E. Bosworth, *The New Islamic Dynasties. A Chronological and Genealogical Manual* (Edinburgh, 1996), p. 174 n. 85; *EI*[2] Suppl. art 'Bānīdjūrids' (C.E. Bosworth).

155 According to the anonymous (or conceivably by one Ibn Shādī of the Hamadān region?) *Mujmal al-tawārīkh*, ed. Malik al-Shuʿarā' Bahār (Tehran, 1318/1939), p. 349, the astrologer Dūbān had been sent to al-Ma'mūn by the king of Kabul. Kabul was at this time very much within the Indian cultural world, and India was famed as a home of magical and astrological lore.

156 *qaḍīb*, text *q.ṣ.b.* This and the other two items were insignia of kingship traditionally handed down from caliph to caliph.

157 Amongst a considerable literature on the succession struggle between the two brothers, see the exhaustive study by F. Gabrieli, 'La successione di Hārūn al-Rašīd e la guerra fra al-Amīn e al-Ma'mūn', *RSO* XI (1926–8), pp. 341–97.

158 See on al-Ma'mūn's personal rule in Khurasan, Roy Mottahedeh, ch. 'The ʿAbbāsid caliphate in Iran', in *CHIr*, Vol. 4, pp. 72–4; Daniel, *The Political and Social History of Khurasan*, pp. 175–82.

159 al-Yaʿqūbī, *Buldān*, tr. Wiet, p. 136, and Ḥamza al-Iṣfahānī, *Ta'rīkh Sinī mulūk al-arḍ wa 'l-anbiyā'*, p. 167, record that al-Ma'mūn in 203/818–19 briefly appointed Faḍl b. Sahl's kinsman Rajā' b. Abi 'l-Ḍaḥḥāk to the governorship before Ghassān.

160 Ibn Khallikān, *Wafayāt al-aʿyān*, ed. Iḥsān ʿAbbās (Beirut, 1968–72), Vol. 4, p. 44, has for this name the much more plausible one of 'Ghālib [al-Masʿūdī al-Aswad]'. On the very doubtful connection of this person with the heresiarch Ustādsīs, see above, n. 106.

161 On Ghassān's governorship, see Bosworth, *Sīstān under the Arabs*, pp. 101–2; Daniel, *op. cit.*, p. 181; and on Faḍl b. Sahl, *EIr* art. 'Fazl b. Sahl' (C.E. Bosworth).

Part Two: The Tahirids and Saffarids

1 Thus correctly in Ḥabībī for Nazim's *Shabīb.* For Naṣr's raising of the Qays or North Arabs of Jazīra in rebellion against al-Amīn and then al-Ma'mūn, apparently a movement with anti-Persianising currents within it, see *EI*[2] art. 'Naṣr b. Shabath' (C.E. Bosworth).

2 On Ṭāhir's appointment to Khurasan and his death soon afterwards, see D. Sourdel, 'Les circonstances de la mort de Ṭāhir Ier au Ḥurāsān en 207/822', *Arabica* V (1958), pp. 66–9; Daniel, *op. cit.*, pp. 181–2; Bosworth, ch. 'The Ṭāhirids and Ṣaffārids', in *CHIr*, Vol. 4, p. 95; Mongi Kaabi, *Les Ṭāhirides au Ḫurāsān et en Iraq (III*[ème] *H./IX*[ème] *J.-C.)*, (Tunis, 1983), Vol. 1, pp. 139–86.

3 See above, pp. 38–9.

4 On Ṭalḥa's governorship, see Bosworth, *op. cit.*, pp. 95–6; Kaabi, *op. cit.*, pp. 186–90.

5 On Bābak's movement and the Khurramiyya or Khurramdīnān, see Sadighi, *Les mouvements religieux iraniens*, pp. 187–280; Scarcia Amoretti, ch. 'Sects and heresies', pp. 503–9; G.-H. Yusofi, *EIr* art. 'Bābak Ḵorramī'.

6 On ʿAbdallāh's governorship in general, see Bosworth, ch. 'The Ṭāhirids and Ṣaffārids', pp. 97–101; Kaabi, *op. cit.*, pp. 236–58; *EIr* art. "Abdallāh b. Ṭāher' (Bosworth); and on the Khārijites in Khurasan and the revolt of Ḥamza b. Ādharak specifically, above, Part One, n. 141.

7 The towel was presumably poisoned.

8 Cf. on ʿAbdallāh's circumspection, Barthold, *Turkestan*, p. 209.

9 The text here re-arranged in chronological order by Riḍāzāda Malik.

10 On Māzyār's revolt, see Sadighi, *Les mouvements religieux iraniens*, pp. 290–303; Kaabi, *op. cit.*, pp. 253–5; *EI*² art. 'Ḳārinids' (M. Rekaya).

11 Following here Ḥabībī's *qunī wa q.n.yāt*, there being presumably some difference between the two terms not apparent to us today.

12 Unidentified, but presumably an *adīb* or boon-companion.

13 On his governorship, see Bosworth, ch. 'The Ṭāhirids and Ṣaffārids', pp. 101–2; Kaabi, *op. cit.*, pp. 293–5.

14 Gardīzī omits in his listing al-Muʿtazz, who reigned for three years (252–55/866–69) between al-Mustaʿīn and al-Muhtadī.

15 See on his governorship and his subsequent history, Bosworth, *op. cit.*, pp. 102–3, 114–15; Kaabi, *op. cit.*, pp. 299–311.

16 On the career of Yaʿqūb in general, see Bosworth, *Sīstān under the Arabs*, pp. 112–21, and Bosworth, *The History of the Saffarids of Sistan and the Maliks of Nimruz* (Costa Mesa and New York, 1994), pp. 67–180; *EI*² art. 'Yaʿḳūb b. al-Layth' (Bosworth).

17 For a recent reinterpretation of Yaʿqūb's role as an *ʿayyār* leader, see Deborah G. Tor, *Violent Order: Religious Warfare, Chivalry, and the* ʿAyyār *Phenomenon in the Medieval Islamic World* (Würzburg, 2007), pp. 85ff.

18 On Yaʿqūb and his contacts with the Ratbīls/Zunbīls, see Bosworth, *The History of the Saffarids of Sistan*, pp. 76, 85ff. The correct form of the name or title of this ruler in Zābulistān, Zamīndāwar and Rukhwad/Rukhūd/al-Rukhkhaj, whom the first Arab raiders to Bust and beyond encountered in the later seventh century AD (see above, n. 40), and who was probably one of the southern Hephthalites, has long been enigmatic. On account of the ruler's association in the sources with the local god Zūn or Zhūn and its cult, Josef Marquart in a classic article (J. Marquart and J.J.M. de Groot, 'Das Reich Zābul und der Gott Žūn vom 6–9 Jahrhundert', in *Festschrift Eduard Sachau zum siebigsten Geburtstage von Freunden und Schülern gewidmet*, ed. G. Weil [Berlin, 1915], pp. 248–92) read the first part of the name as *zun*, although the second element *–bīl* was never satisfactorily explained. The Arabic sources, both historical and poetical, generally have Ratbīl, and it now seems fairly certain that this is the most likely form, derived from the Old Turkic title used for a tribal ruler subordinate to the Great Qaghan, *élteber* (concerning which see A. Bombaci, 'On the ancient Turkic title Eltäbär', in *Proceedings of the IXth Meeting of the Permanent International Altaistic Conference* [Naples, 1966], pp. 1–66; Sir Gerard Clauson, *An Etymological Dictionary of Pre-Thirteenth Century Turkish* [Oxford, 1972], p. 134). Forms related to it are known from various parts of northwestern India and what is now northern and eastern Afghanistan, including the *uilotobēr* = *hilitiber* of the recently discovered documents in the Eastern Middle Iranian language of Bactrian. See N. Sims-Williams, 'Ancient Afghanistan and its invaders. Linguistic evidence from the Bactrian documents and inscriptions', in N. Sims-Williams (ed.), *Indo-Iranian Languages and Peoples* (Oxford, 2002), p. 235; Bosworth, 'The appearance and establishment of Islam in Afghanistan', in *Islamisation de l'Asie centrale. Processus locaux d'acculturation du VII*ᵉ *au XI*ᵉ *siècle*, ed. E. de la Vaissière (Paris, 2008), pp. 97–114.

19 See Bosworth, 'Notes on the pre-Ghaznavid history of eastern Afghanistan', *IQ* IX (1965), pp. 18, 20, 22.

20 The text has *Māhjūr* for the last element of this name. See on Dāwūd b. al-ʿAbbās's line, above, Part One, n. 154.

21 Fīrūz b. K.b.k or K.b.r is mentioned in the sources variously as the son of the Ratbīl/Zunbīl (see above, n. 18) and as 'the ruler of Zābulistān'. See Bosworth, *The History of the Saffarids of Sistan*, pp. 99–100.

22 This place in Bādghīs was an enduring centre of the Khārijites. See Le Strange, *The Lands of the Eastern Caliphate*, p. 410; *EI*[2] art. 'Karūkh' (ed.).

23 Thus restored in the text of Ḥabībī, p. 140 n. 6. Farhādhān or Farhādgird, a place on the road between Herat and Nishapur, in the district of Nishapur called Asfand, for the *F.r.hād* of the mss. See Le Strange, *op. cit.*, p. 388.

24 On this annexation of Nishapur and Khurasan by Yaʿqūb (short-lived, as it proved), see Bosworth, *The History of the Saffarids of Sistan*, pp. 109–21; Bosworth, ch. 'The Ṭāhirids and Ṣaffārids', pp. 114–15. The episode is noted in an anecdote of Bayhaqī; see Bosworth, *The History of Beyhaqi (The History of Sultan Mas'ud of Ghazna, 1030–1041)* (New York, 2009), Vol. 1, pp. 352–3.

25 This place is frequently mentioned in the chronicles of the Caspian coast region; see, e.g., Ibn Isfandiyār, English tr. E.G. Browne, *An Abridged Translation of the History of Ṭabaristán Compiled about AH 613 (AD 1216)* (Leiden and London, 1905), p. 182.

26 See Bosworth, *The History of the Saffarids of Sistan*, pp. 110, 123–7; and for the background of the Ḥasanid *da'wa* in Gurgān and Ṭabaristān, W. Madelung, ch. 'The minor dynasties of Northern Iran', in *CHIr*, Vol. 4, pp. 206–12.

27 Nazim has, apparently erroneously, Ḍallālī for this name, whilst Ḥabībī has Ḍallābī; it is most probably the Ṣallābī of Riḍāzāda Malik which is correct. The *nisba* in fact remains mysterious; G.C. Miles, *The Numismatic History of Rayy* (New York, 1938), p. 129, registers *al-Ṣalānī*; Al-Samʿānī in his *Kitāb al-Ansāb* does not record it.

28 Thus, *du barādar*, whereas a plurality of brothers, ʿAbdallāh and an unspecified number, are mentioned previously.

29 Reading, with Ḥabībī and Riḍāzāda Malik, *manfadh* rather than Nazim's *m.n.q.d* (? *munqadd*). An ancient canal, the Nahr al-Malik, running from Fallūja on the Euphrates, joined the Tigris just above Dayr al-ʿĀqūl; see Le Strange, *The Lands of the Eastern Caliphate*, p. 68.

30 For Yaʿqūb's defeat at the hands of the caliphal army and its aftermath, see Bosworth, ch. 'The Ṭāhirids and Ṣaffārids', p. 113; Bosworth, *The History of the Saffarids of Sistan*, pp. 158ff. Gardīzī telescopes these events after the Dayr al-ʿĀqūl battle. During the two years before his death, Yaʿqūb was in Khuzistan and involved in a three-way struggle with ʿAbbasid forces and the Zanj rebels; see *ibid.*, pp. 162–8.

31 Following Ḥabībī's text for these two names, see his n. 3.

32 I.e. because of the ending of the threat to Sistan (this phrase only in Ḥabībī). On Yaʿqūb's and ʿAmr's prolonged struggles with this ambitious rival commander, Aḥmad Khujistānī, for control of Khurasan, see Bosworth, *The History of the Saffarids of Sistan*, pp. 127–33, 194–201.

33 Otherwise *gazīt* in early New Persian (= Arabic *jizya*); see F. de Blois, 'A Persian poem lamenting the Arab conquest', in *Studies in Honour of Clifford Edmund Bosworth. II. The Sultan's Turret: Studies in Persian and Turkish Culture*, ed. Carole Hillenbrand (Leiden, 2000), p. 87 and n. 20.

34 *sabal*, thus suggested by Habibi, n. 4, for an uncertain reading of the mss. For this unusual word, said to be from the name of a celebrated mare in ancient Arabian times, see Lane, *Lexicon*, p. 1301c.

35 On ʿAmr's administrative and financial system, see Barthold, *Turkestan*, pp. 220–1; Bosworth, *The History of the Saffarids of Sistan*, pp. 358–9.

36 On his organisation of the army, see Bosworth, 'The armies of the Ṣaffārids', *BSOAS*, XXXI (1968), pp. 545, 549–51; *idem*, *The History of the Saffarids of Sistan*, pp. 351–4. This description of the *'arḍ*, with inspection of everyone's military preparedness, from the Amir himself downwards, is also given in the lengthy biography of Yaʿqūb and his brother in Ibn Khallikān's *Wafayāt al-a'yān*, at Vol. 6, pp. 421–2, English tr. McG. de Slane, Vol. 4, p. 322, both accounts being obviously derived from the common source of al-Sallāmī's *Ta'rīkh Wulāt Khurāsān* (see above, Introduction, p. 2). Ibn Khallikān has the

further detail of a comparison of the *'arḍ* under 'Amr with that of the Sasanid emperor Khusraw Anūshīrwān; Barthold, who in *Turkestan*, p. 221, also gives an account of this Saffarid *'arḍ*, remarked that the resemblance between the two military procedures, though separated by some three centuries, could hardly be coincidental.

37 On the diplomatic exchanges between 'Amr and the caliph, leading up to 'Amr's ill-fated decision to march against the Samanids, see Bosworth, *The History of the Saffarids of Sistan*, pp. 223–8.

38 For 'Amr's attack on Ismā'īl b. Aḥmad, his defeat and his imprisonment and consequent death see Bosworth, ch. 'The Ṭāhirids and Ṣaffārids', p. 121; Bosworth, *The History of the Saffarids of Sistan*, pp. 229–35.

Part Three: The Samanids

1 Much of this elaborate genealogy, with over fifty generations between Sāmān Khudāh and Kayūmarth, is unintelligible, doubtless at least in part through corrupt transmission. Al-Bīrūnī, in his *al-Āthār al-bāqiya*, tr. Sachau, p. 48, merely traces Sāmān Khudāh's great-grandson Ismā'īl b. Aḥmad back through four more generations to the father of the emperor of Sasanid times, Bahrām VI Chūbīn (r. 590–1), sc. Bahrām Gushnāsp. The late sixth-early seventh/late twelfth-early thirteenth century author Ibn Ẓāfir, citing the fifth/sixth century 'Abbasid historian Ghars al-Ni'ma Hilāl al-Ṣābi', takes the genealogy five generations beyond Bahrām Chūbīn's father to Yazdagird II (r. 399–420) (Luke Treadwell, 'The account of the Samanid dynasty in Ibn Ẓāfir al-Azdī's *Akhbār al-duwal al-munqaṭi'a*', *Iran JBIPS* XLIII [2005], pp. 136, 152). It is clear that Gardīzī was far less informed about the pre-Islamic Persian kings than e.g. his predecessor by about a century, Ḥamza al-Iṣfahānī, in the first chapter of the latter's *Ta'rīkh Sinī mulūk al-arḍ wa 'l-anbiyā'*. Mr de Blois has observed to me that none of the unintelligible names in Gardīzī's genealogy here has any obvious connection with Bactrian or Sogdian onomastic.

2 Narshakhī, *Tārīkh-i Bukhārā*, tr. Frye, pp. 76–7; Barthold, *Turkestan*, p. 209–10; Frye, ch. 'The Sāmānids', in *CHIr*, Vol. 4, p. 136; Frye, *Bukhara, the Medieval Achievement*, 2nd ed. (Costa Mesa, 1996), p. 35.

3 Narshakhi, *op. cit.*, tr. Frye, pp. 82–6; Barthold, *op. cit.*, pp. 209–10; Frye, ch. 'The Sāmānids', pp. 136–7.

4 The name of this rebel Samanid commander is rendered unintelligibly in Nazim, but Ḥabībī has the correct *Ūk.r.t.m.sh*, Turkish *ögretmish* 'he taught, instructed'. See Clauson, *An Etymological Dictionary of Pre-Thirteenth Century Turkish*, p. 114; Faruk Sümer, ed. Turan Yazgan, *Türk devletleri tarihinde şahis adlari* (Istanbul, 1995), Vol. 2, pp. 493–4; Rásonyi and Baski, *Onomasticon turcicum*, Vol. 2, p. 591.

5 I.e. the Daylamī lord Justān (III) b. Wahsūdān, involved at this time in the confused struggles of the 'Abbasids, the Zaydī Imāms of Gurgān and Ṭabaristān and the Samanids for control of northern upland Iran and the Caspian coastlands. See Madelung, ch. 'The minor dynasties of northern Iran', pp. 208–9; Bosworth, *The New Islamic Dynasties*, p. 145 no. 69.

6 Text, *Pārs*, i.e. Turkish *bars* 'leopard', also used for other large felines; see Clauson, *op. cit.*, p. 368; Sümer, *op. cit.*, Vol. 2, s.v.

7 See on Ismā'īl's reign, Narshakhī, *Tārīkh-i Bukhārā*, tr. Frye, pp. 86–94; Frye, ch. 'The Sāmānids', pp. 138–41; Frye, *Bukhara, the Medieval Achievement*, pp. 38–49; Treadwell, 'The account of the Samanid dynasty in Ibn Ẓāfir al-Azdī's *Akhbār al-duwal al-munqaṭi'a*', p. 153. Concerning the title *Amir-i Māḍī*, with the epithet conventionally translated by the common meaning of the word *māḍī* as 'late, one who has passed away', Treadwell has recently cited Van Gelder's opinion that a better rendering in this context would be 'incisive, penetrating, efficacious', referring to Ismā'īl's numerous military successes (see *op. cit.*, p. 153 n. 20). Since the epithets applied posthumously to the succeeding Samanid amirs all refer to such kingly qualities as good fortune, piety, righteousness, justice, divine guidance, etc., this suggestion seems a sound one.

8 I.e. Khurasan in its widest sense, all the lands east of Ray and Qūmis, including Transoxania.

9 The investiture diploma sent by the caliph in 298/910–11 included a renewal of the grant of governorship over Sistan and its dependencies which al-Muʿtaḍid had given Ismāʿīl b. Aḥmad ten years previously; see Bosworth, *The History of the Saffarids of Sistan*, p. 263. This grant now became the legal justification for Samanid attempts to annex Sistan to their lands; a policy ultimately unsuccessful, however, given the distance of Sistan from the Samanid centre of power in Transoxania, as the events recorded below show.

10 Muʿaddal and his brother Muḥammad, sons of a brother of Yaʿqūb and ʿAmr, had succeeded to power in the truncated Saffarid dominions in the confused years after ʿAmr b. Layth's capture; see Bosworth, *op. cit.*, pp. 260–6.

11 On this superannuated former soldier of the Samanids, Muḥammad b. Hurmuz, see Bosworth, 'The armies of the Ṣaffārids', p. 539, and Bosworth, *The History of the Saffarids of Sistan*, pp. 269–71.

12 Sīmjūr Dawātī was a Turkish ghulām commander of the Samanids whose family was to play a notable role in the warfare of the Samanids with their rivals in northern Persia, at times acting as governors of Khurasan and acquiring estates in Quhistān. See Bosworth, *The New Islamic Dynasties*, p. 175 no. 86, and *EI*² art. 'Sīmd̲j̲ūrids' (Bosworth).

13 For the episode of Samanid intervention in Sistan, followed by an abortive attempt by al-Muqtadir to recover the province for the caliphate, see Bosworth, *The History of the Saffarids of Sistan*, pp. 263–75.

14 Firabr lay just north of the right bank of the Oxus, opposite Āmul-i Shaṭṭ, and on the road to Bukhara. See Le Strange, *The Lands of the Eastern Caliphate*, p. 443.

15 This ʿAlid made firm the Zaydī imāmate which had been established in Ṭabaristān in the latter half of the third/ninth century, and ruled there till his death in 304/917; the Samanid army sent against him under Muḥammad b. Ṣuʿlūk was disastrously defeated by Ḥasan just before Amir Aḥmad's murder. See *EI*² art. 'Ḥasan al-Uṭrūs̲h̲' (R. Strothmann) and Madelung, ch. 'The minor dynasties of northern Iran', pp. 208–10.

16 See on Aḥmad's reign, Frye, ch. 'The Sāmānids', p. 141, and specifically for his murder, Treadwell, 'Ibn Ẓāfir al-Azdī's account of the murder of Aḥmad b. Ismāʿīl al-Sāmānī and the succession of his son Naṣr', in *Studies in Honour of Clifford Edmund Bosworth. II. The Sultan's Turret. Studies in Persian and Turkish Culture*, pp. 397–419. Treadwell notes (pp. 414ff.) that this account seems to be independent of that of al-Sallāmī or a source of his, and was probably written by a contemporary of the events in question. Some of the sources state that the Amir was murdered by his guard because of his excessive favour to scholars and the religious classes, and possibly because he had favoured the use of Arabic at court over Persian; see Barthold, *Turkestan*, p. 240.

17 See the references in the previous note, with once again an especially detailed account in Ibn Ẓāfir *apud* Treadwell, pp. 405–13. Naṣr was clearly intended to be the puppet of the elements who had conspired to kill his father.

18 There is much confusion over the members of the Jayhānī family, at least three of whom served the Samanids as viziers in the course of the fourth/tenth century, in particular, over the exact forms of their names (Muḥammad and Aḥmad being especially liable to be mixed up with each other). The one mentioned here by Gardīzī was apparently the first Jayhānī, serving Amir Naṣr till *ca.* 310/922 and being then replaced by Abu 'l-Faḍl Muḥammad b. ʿUbaydallāh Balʿāmī (see above, p. 57), who was in turn replaced, at the end of Naṣr's thirty years' reign, by the second Jayhānī, Abū ʿAlī Muḥammad b. Muḥammad, very probably the son of the first Jayhānī. Gardīzī expatiates here on Jayhānī's great learning and intellectual curiosity, and this is confirmed by the geographer al-Maqdisī's description of Abū ʿAbdallāh as skilled in philosophy and astronomy and as one who sought out persons from all the the world in order to get information on their homelands, their specialities and characteristics (partial Fr. tr. André Miquel, *Aḥsan at-taqāsīm fī maʿrifat al-aqālīm (La meilleure répartition pour la connaissance des provinces)* [Damascus,

1963], pp. 12–14 §§ 10–11). There seems to have been a taint of Ismāʿīlism, perhaps more of that faith's philosophical aspect than of it as a radical, politically activist creed, surrounding the three main members of the family involved in political life during Samanid times (see Patricia Crone and Luke Treadwell, 'A new text on Ismailism at the Samanid court', in Chase F. Robinson (ed.), *Texts, Documents and Artefacts. Islamic Studies in Honour of D.S. Richards* [Leiden, 2003], pp. 54–5). Ch. Pellat suggested that the celebrated, lost geographical work attributed to a Jayhānī, a *Kitāb al-Mamālik wa 'l-masālik*, was not the work of a single person but was added to or remodelled by more than one member of the family, a process not unknown in Arabic literature. See Frye, ch. 'The Sāmānids', pp. 142–3; *EI*[2] Suppl. art. 'al-Djayhānī' (Pellat).

19 This seems to be the correct reading for this place name. According to Yāqūt, *Muʿjam al-buldān*, Vol. 2, p. 365, it was three parasangs from Samarqand and famed as the site of the great traditionist Muḥammad b. Ismāʿīl al-Bukhārī's tomb; see also Barthold, *Turkestan*, p. 126.

20 Thus in both mss.; later sources have varying forms for this doubtful name.

21 Thus in the surmise of Ḥabībī, p. 151 n. 8 for the *ẓ.rāh* of the mss.

22 I.e. of Yazdagird III (r. 632–51), the last Sasanid emperor.

23 Ḥabībī, p. 151 n. 10, identifies this with Kīrang, which he says was a well-known place in Mongol times.

24 Text, *s.b.k.r.y.* Sebük-eri (this could be, in Turkish, something like 'beloved man', but the etymology remains far from sure) was to play a dominant role within the Saffarid state after the capture of ʿAmr and the succession in the capital Zarang of his weaker grandson Ṭāhir b. Muḥammad b. ʿAmr in 287/900. See Bosworth, *The History of the Saffarids of Sistan*, pp. 243ff.

25 This is Qarategin al-Isfījābī (d. 317/929), who towards the end of his career in the service of the Samanids withdrew to Bust and al-Rukhkhaj on the far southern fringes of the Samanid amirate and established there a virtually independent line of Turkish ghulāms who held power until the Ghaznavid founder Sebüktegin expanded into that region in 367/977–8. His son Manṣūr later appears as commander-in-chief in Khurasan for the Samanids, see above, p. 60, and also his grandson Aḥmad b. Manṣūr, see above, p. 67.

26 Ḥabībī, p. 152 n. 10, points out that this place, defectively written in the mss., is mentioned by the geographers as being a district of Marw al-Rūd (which would accord with the mention here of a river; in this case, the river would be the Murghāb).

27 Naṣr's youth obviously allowed these rebels and rival claimants to the throne to rear their heads. See Narshakhī, *Tārīkh-i Bukhārā*, tr. Frye, pp. 95–6; Barthold, *Turkestan*, p. 241; Frye, ch. 'The Sāmānids', p. 141; Treadwell, 'The account of the Samanid dynasty', pp. 155–7.

28 I.e. the Amir's vizier, see below, n. 37.

29 See Barthold, *op. cit.*, p. 242, who notes that Abū Bakr al-Khabbāz must have had a charismatic personality and have had a great influence amongst the populace of Bukhara for there to have arisen this story of the miraculous preservation of his body from effects of the flames.

30 Thus the suggested reading in Ḥabībī, cf. p. 153 n. 3, for the manuscripts' *s.n.jāb*.

31 The Muḥtāj family were hereditary lords of the principality of Chaghāniyān on the north bank of the upper Oxus river, probably of Iranian or Iranised Arab descent, and members of them served the Samanids as commanders and governors until the mid-fourth/tenth century, when the family lapsed out of public life and were apparently of significance only in Chaghāniyān itself. See Bosworth, 'The rulers of Chaghāniyān in early Islamic times', pp. 1–10; Bosworth, *The New Islamic Dynasties*, p. 177 n. 88; *EI*[2] art. 'Muḥtādjids' (Bosworth).

32 As Nazim, p. 30 n. 2 notes, there seems to be a lacuna here.

33 Other sources like Masʿūdī, Miskawayh and Ibn al-Athīr confirm that the leading assassin

here was Bajkam, but do not expressly attribute to him, as here, a connection with Mardāwīj's enemy and rival for power in northern Persia and a fellow-Daylamī, Mākān b. Kākī. Nazim does not specify the name Bajkam amongst the assassins but interprets the text here as *ba-ḥukm-i Mākān* 'at the instigation of Mākān'; what Gardīzī originally wrote here is thus unclear.

The name Bajkam was a name well known amongst Turkish slave troops of this time, see Sümer, *Türk devletleri tarihinde şahis adlari*, Vol. 2, pp. 482–3. It is, however, most probably in origin an Iranian word with the sense of 'tassel, fringe or tail of horsehair, etc., tied on to a standard', see G. Doerfer, *Türkische und mongolische Elemente im Neupersischen* (Wiesbaden, 1963–75), Vol. 2, *Türkische Elemente im Neupersischen*, p. 425 n. 840.

34 Once Amir Naṣr had grown to maturity and had mastered the various threats to his throne, he adopted a forward policy in northern Persia, aiming at exerting Samanid authority over the Caspian provinces and securing control of Ray; in the later part of the century, this would bring them into prolonged conflict with the Buyids. As a result of these ambitions, Samanid forces clashed at this time with the Zaydī Imāms and with various Daylamī and Jīlī soldiers of fortune, eager to carve out principalities for themselves. The most notable of these were the commanders mentioned here, Mākān and Mardāwīj, the latter and his son Wushmgīr being the founders of a long-lasting line of amirs in Gurgān and Ṭabaristān. See Madelung, ch. 'The minor dynasties of northern Iran', pp. 208ff.; *EI*[2] arts. 'Mākān b. Kākī'; 'Mardāwīdj'; 'Wushmgīr b. Ziyār' (C.E. Bosworth).

35 See on Naṣr's reign, Narshakhī, *Tārīkh-i Bukhārā*, tr. Frye, pp. 95–6; Barthold, *Turkestan*, pp. 240–6; Frye, ch. 'The Sāmānids', pp. 141ff; Frye, *Bukhara, the Medieval Achievement*, pp. 51ff.; Treadwell, 'The account of the Samanid dynasty', pp. 155–7; *EI*[2] art. 'Naṣr b. Aḥmad b. Ismā'īl' (C.E. Bosworth). A notable feature of Gardīzī's account of this Amir and his reign is the fact that, as with the other strictly historical sources, he has no mention of what seems to have been the temporary, if only limited, success of an Ismā'īlī Shī'ī *da'wa* at the Samanid court, with converts to this heresy (as Sunnīs regarded it), or at least sympathisers towards its philosophical aspects, from the Amir himself downwards. It does appear that the episode has been edited out of the historical sources, since the evidence for its existence comes from the basically *adab* and literary sources of Ibn al-Nadīm, al-Tha'ālibī and Niẓām al-Mulk. This is not the place for discussing what is a complex matter, but amongst recent writing on the topic, mention should be made of Crone and Treadwell, 'A new text on Ismailism at the Samanid court', pp. 37–67, and A.C.S. Peacock, *Mediaeval Islamic Historiography and Political Legitimacy. Bal'amī's Tārīkhnāma* (London and New York, 2007), pp. 25–31.

36 Following the conjecture of Ḥabībī, p. 154, see n. 7: *wa ḥadd wa du gurūhī andar uftād*, for a disturbed text here.

37 For Bal'amī, see *EIr* art. 'Bal'amī, Abu'l-Fażl Moḥammad' (C.E. Bosworth), and for the Jayhānī family, see above n. 18.

38 I.e. Abu 'l-Faḍl Sulamī, noted for his piety and vizier until 335/946, see below.

39 Thus in Ḥabībī, following Ibn al-Athīr's *Ṭughān al-ḥājib* for the incomprehensible *Ṭ.gh.y al-māj.t* of the mss.

40 Following the text in Ḥabībī, *ba-Marw*.

41 The interpretation of Ḥabībī and Riḍāzāda Malik, *ḥīlatī karda būd*, seems better than the *ḥamlatī karda būd* of the mss. and Nazim.

42 Yāqūt, *Mu'jam al-buldān*, Vol. 1, p. 291, says that Ayghān was a village of Panj-dih, which lay on the Murghāb.

43 The Sinj of *ibid.*, Vol. 3, p. 265.

44 In the mss., *r.kh.ta ḥ.m.w.y*, which Ḥabībī, p. 156 n. 3, reads as possibly R.khna, Rukhna being the name of one of the gates of the suburb of Bukhara according to Ibn Ḥawqal, *Kitāb Ṣūrat al-arḍ*, ed. J.H. Kramers (Leiden, 1938–39), Vol. 2, p. 484, French tr. J.H. Kramers and G. Wiet, *Configuration de la terre* (Paris, 1964), Vol. 2, p. 465.

45 Thus in Nazim, but Ḥabībī and Riḍāzāda Malik have Khartang. The first seems

nevertheless correct; see Barthold, *Turkestan*, pp. 248, 259, remarking that this place is not to be confused with the Khartang mentioned above, see n. 19.

46 This seems the most probable rendering, since the name is attested in Turkish onomastic; the mss. have *q.t.gīn*. *Qut* means 'spirit, life, vitality' and 'fortune, success', so that the name could mean 'fortunate prince'. See Rásonyi and Baski, *Onomasticon turcicum*, II, pp. 505–6.

47 Ḥabībī, n. 13, suggests that this *nisba* (appearing thus in the mss.) comes from a place in Zābulistān (presumably the present-day Uruzgan, in the province of the same name in eastern Afghanistan).

48 This was the celebrated gorge, now the Buzgala defile, through which the road from Tirmidh to Kish and Nakhshab in Sogdia passed. See Le Strange, *The Lands of the Eastern Caliphate*, pp. 441–2; Barthold, *Turkestan*, p. 138.

49 Or Rāsht? See *Ḥudūd al-ʿālam*, tr. Minorsky, pp. 63, 120, comm. pp. 361–3. Zhāsht or Rāsht lay in the Buttamān mountains which separated the upper basins of the Oxus and, to their north, the Zarafshān, and was the haunt of the predatory Kumījīs, who were probably the remnants of an earlier Inner Asian people like the Sakas. See Bosworth and Clauson, 'Al-Xwārazmī on the peoples of Central Asia', pp. 8–9.

50 Apparently the Wayshagirt or Bishgird (< *Wēshgird), the modern Fayḍābād, of *Ḥudūd al-ʿālam*, tr. Minorsky, pp. 115, 120, comm. pp. 353–4.

51 Thus correctly in Ḥabībī and Riḍāzāda Malik. See on it *Ḥudūd al-ʿālam*, Barthold's Preface, pp. 38–9, tr. Minorsky, p. 114; Barthold, *Turkestan*, p. 74.

52 Although Gardīzī, in company with other historians, may have deliberately omitted mention of the presence of Ismāʿīlism at the Samanid court in Amir Naṣr b. Aḥmad's reign (see above, n. 18), he clearly had a considerable interest in messianic and millenarian movements, if this was indeed one; and earlier in his history he had taken note of such movements as those of al-Muqannaʿ, Ustādsīs and Bābak. See above, Introduction, pp. 3–4.

53 Nazim, p. 36 n. 1, implausibly suggests that this is the Warduk of al-Maqdisī, *Aḥsan al-taqāsīm*, p. 264, listed there as a dependency of Binkath in the district of Shāsh, i.e. north of the Syr Darya; but this region is a long way from the upper Oxus mountain region, the locale of this episode.

54 I.e. Abū ʿAlī Ḥasan b. Būya, Rukn al-Dawla, the Buyid ruler in Jibāl; see on him EI^2 art. 'Rukn al-Dawla' (H. Bowen and C.E. Bosworth). Gardīzī usually writes his name with the Persian *iḍāfa*, Ḥasan-i Būya, but occasionally with the Arabic *ibn*.

55 See on Nūḥ's reign, Narshakhī, *Tārīkh-i Bukhārā*, tr. Frye, pp. 97–8; Barthold, *op. cit.*, pp. 246–9; Frye, ch. 'The Sāmānids', p. 151; Treadwell, 'The account of the Samanid dynasty', p. 157.

56 The texts have Abu 'l-Fatḥ, confusing the father Abu 'l-Faḍl Muḥammad with his son and successor Abu 'l-Fatḥ ʿAlī, both of whom were viziers to the Buyids and celebrated literary stylists. See EI^2 art. 'Ibn al-ʿAmīd' (Cl. Cahen); J.L. Kraemer, *Humanism in the Renaissance of Islam. The Cultural Revival during the Buyid Age* (Leiden, 1986), pp. 241–59.

57 *mayzad, mīzad*, thus conjectured by Ḥabībī, p. 160 n. 1, for an obscure text here. Riḍāzāda Malik proposes the equally possible reading *mabarrat-hā* 'acts of beneficence'.

58 The Khurasanian family of the ʿUtbīs, of Arab descent, provided two viziers for the later Samanids and a secretary, the famed historian, author of the *Taʾrīkh al-yamīnī*, Abū Naṣr Muḥammad b. ʿAbd al-Jabbār al-ʿUtbī, for Maḥmūd of Ghazna. See EI^2 art. 'al-ʿUtbī' (C.E. Bosworth).

59 Abū Manṣur was a *dihqān* of Ṭūs and from a family that traced itself back to late Sasanid times. As well as his military role in Samanid affairs, he also has fame in Persian literature as the patron of a now lost New Persian prose version, made from the Pahlavi original, of the national epic, the *Shāh-nāma*. See V. Minorsky, 'The older preface to the Shāh-Nāma', in *Studi orientalistici in onore di Giorgio Levi Della Vida* (Rome, 1956), Vol. 2, pp. 162–3; *EIr* art. 'Abū Manṣūr … b. ʿAbd al-Razzāq' (Dj. Khaleghi-Motlagh).

60 Reading here, with Ḥabībī and Riḍāzāda Malik, *liyāqat*.

61 I.e. the son of the Abu 'l-Faḍl Muḥammad Bal'amī who had served Ismā'īl b. Aḥmad and his grandson Naṣr as vizier (see above, p. 57). Abū 'Alī was to achieve lasting literary fame as the author of the Persian translation and remodelling of Ṭabarī's History, the *Tārīkh-i Bal'amī*. See *EIr* art. 'Amīrak Bal'amī' (Dj. Khaleghi-Motlagh); Peacock, *Mediaeval Islamic Historiography and Political Legitimacy*, pp. 31–5. The sources imply that Abū 'Alī was inferior to his father in political wisdom and a better littérateur than statesman.

62 Reading here, with Ḥabībī and Riḍāzāda Malik, *kamtar*.

63 See on 'Abd al-Malik's reign, Narshakhī, *Tārīkh-i Bukhārā*, tr. Frye, p. 98; Treadwell, 'The account of the Samanid dynasty', pp. 157–8 (mentioning that, during his lifetime, this Amir was known as *al-muwaffaq* 'The Divinely-Assisted One'); Barthold, *Turkestan*, pp. 249–50.

64 This sentence not in Ḥabībī's text. The son whose succession Alptegin favoured was, according to the geographer al-Maqdisī, Naṣr, who only held the throne, however, for one day; see Barthold, *op. cit.*, p. 250.

65 The words of a lacuna here have been supplied by Nazim and Ḥabībī.

66 Ḥabībī, n. 3, opines that this otherwise unknown place, obviously lying to the northeast of Nishapur in the direction of Sarakhs, Merv and the Oxus, may be the Ṣāha mentioned by al-Maqdisī, *Aḥsan al-taqāsīm*, p. 351.

67 In Narshakhī, *op. cit.*, p. 99, the general deputed to attack Alptegin is named as Ash'ath b. Muḥammad; in Niẓām al-Mulk's recounting of this episode in his *Siyāsat-nāma*, ch. XXVII, no name is given.

68 Alptegin's withdrawal to Ghazna after the failure of the putsch mounted by him and Abū 'Alī Bal'amī (who apparently made his peace with the new regime, since he continued in office as vizier during the early part at least of Amir Manṣūr's reign) marks the beginning of a line of former Samanid Turkish ghulām commanders in Ghazna, culminating in Sebüktegin's assumption of power in 366/977 and the eventual foundation of the Ghaznavid sultanate. See on these ghulām commanders in Ghazna, Bosworth, 'Notes on the pre-Ghaznavid history of eastern Afghanistan', pp. 16–18.

69 This phrase in Nazim's text but omitted (by inadvertence?) from Ḥabībī's one.

70 al-Maqdisī, *Aḥsan al-taqāsīm*, p. 352, lists N.m.kh.k.n as a stage between Nishapur and Herat.

71 This is the reading of the texts, and would ostensibly refer to the town of Gurgānj in Khwarazm, the region at that time ruled by the Shāhs of the Banū 'Irāq line and in theory tributaries of the Samanids (see M. Fedorov, 'The Khwarazmshahs of the Banū 'Irāq (fourth/tenth century)', *Iran JBIPS* XXXVIII [2000], pp. 71–5); but no other source refers to a raid into Khwarazm at this time.

72 There is some uncertainty over the date of Bal'amī's death, since 'Utbī states that he served briefly as vizier to Nūḥ (II) b. Manṣūr (I) in 382/992 when the latter reoccupied Bukhara on the death of the Qarakhanid Hārūn or Ḥasan Bughrā Khān (see above, p. 72). See Peacock, *Mediaeval Islamic Historiography and Political Legitimacy*, pp. 32–3.

73 This lay in the western part of Ghūr, to the east-south-east of Herat, and still in fact exists today as a small town; see Bosworth, *The History of the Saffarids of Sistan*, p. 409 n. 1252.

74 For the expedition into Ghūr of Abū Ja'far (who came from a prominent family of Bayhaq and had been made governor of that town by Abu 'l-Ḥasan Sīmjūrī, see Bosworth, 'The early Islamic history of Ghūr', *CAJ* VI (1961), p. 122.

75 Khalaf b. Aḥmad, of the so-called 'second line' of Saffarid Amirs of Sistan, had for long been at odds, first with Abu 'l-Ḥusayn Ṭāhir (apparently connected maternally with the Saffarid dynasty) and then with the latter's son Ḥusayn, over control of Sistan. Sources like al-'Utbī state that the Samanids intervened on the side of Ḥusayn because Khalaf had cut off the customary tribute and presents to Bukhara. See Bosworth, *The History of the Saffarids of Sistan*, pp. 302ff.

76 *recte*, in 363/974.

77 The texts have Abu 'l-Faḍl, i.e. the reverse of the confusion of names noted in n. 56 above; the father Abu 'l-Faḍl had in fact died in 360/970.

78 I.e. only five months after Bal'amī's death, if this did indeed take place in Jumādā II 363.

79 See on Manṣūr's reign, Narshakhī, *Tārīkh-i Bukhārā*, tr. Frye, pp. 98–9; Barthold, *Turkestan*, pp. 250–2; Frye, ch. 'The Sāmānids', pp. 152–6; Treadwell, 'The account of the Samanid dynasty', p. 158. Niẓām al-Mulk mentions a recrudescence of Ismā'īlism as occurring during Manṣūr's amirate, but Crone and Treadwell suggest that, rather than being an organised *da'wa* on the scale of that in Naṣr b. Aḥmad's time (see above, n. 35), this was more probably sporadic provincial disturbances by Ismā'īlīs, Khurramīs or other sectaries and not a major outbreak in the Samanid heartland of Sogdia. See their 'A new text on Ismailism at the Samanid court', pp. 48–52.

80 The Farīghūnids, apparently of Iranian stock, were local rulers of the region of Gūzgān in northern Afghanistan and tributaries of the Samanids; when Maḥmūd of Ghazna succeeded to the Samanid heritage in Khurasan, Gūzgān was speedily absorbed into his domains. See Minorsky, *Ḥudūd al-'ālam*, comm., pp. 173–8; *EIr* art. 'Āl-e Farīgūn' (C.E. Bosworth).

81 The Samanids were normally abstemious in their personal use of titles and the granting of them, but from the middle years of the century, the Amirs were often in effect compelled to award grandiloquent *laqab*s to powerful governors and commanders. See Bosworth, 'The titulature of the early Ghaznavids', *Oriens* XV (1962), pp. 214–15.

82 Abu 'l-Ḥasan Sīmjūrī represented, of course, the powerful military commanders' growing ascendancy in the state that Abu 'l-Ḥusayn, like others of his predecessors in the vizierate, could be expected to try and curb.

83 Ḥabībī, p. 165 n. 7 is unable to make sense of this word; the first syllable looks however like the negative particle *na-*. The sense must in fact be something like 'inadvisable'.

84 This is something like a colloquial English equivalent to the text's idiomatic phrase *wallāhi ki man sitāra ba-rūz bad-īshān namāyam*, lit. 'By God, I'll make them see the stars by daylight', i.e. turn their bright day into deep night; cf. Riḍāzāda Malik's *ta'līqa* at pp. 592–3.

85 Member of the influential Nishapur family of Mīkālīs, which seems to have been of Sogdian origin; various of them served the Samanids, then the early Ghaznavids in administrative and secretarial posts, and one of them at least served the Seljuq Ṭoghril Beg. See *EI²* art. 'Mīkālīs' (C.E. Bosworth); *EIr* art. 'Āl-e Mīkāl' (R.W. Bulliet).

86 From 371/981 to 387/997, Qābūs's family patrimony of Gurgān and Ṭabaristān was occupied by the Buyids 'Aḍud al-Dawla, his son Mu'ayyid al-Dawla and then 'Aḍud al-Dawla's brother Fakhr al-Dawla, with Qābūs as an exile in the Samanid lands. See *EI²* arts. 'Ḳābūs b. Wushmagīr b. Ziyār' and 'Ziyārids' (C.E. Bosworth).

87 I.e. to don civilian dress, the garment of secretaries and officials, instead of the garb and panoply of war.

88 In the final phase of his struggle with Ḥusayn b. Ṭāhir, Khalaf b. Aḥmad sought help from Sebüktegin, who had been in control of Bust since *ca.* 367–8/977–9, and received from him a force of the troops formerly in the service of Sebüktegin's predecessor there, Bāytūz. It was presumably these who were now employed against Abū 'Alī. See Bosworth, *The History of the Saffarids of Sistan*, pp. 311–12.

89 The vizier's kinsman, the historian Abū Naṣr al-'Utbī, with justice considered Abu 'l-Ḥusayn to be the last vizier of the Samanids worthy of the name. See Barthold, *Turkestan*, pp. 252–3; *EI²* art. 'al-'Utbī. 2.' (C.E. Bosworth).

90 This seems the most probable interpretation of the text's *'.n.j*; *ïnanch* Turkish 'belief, trust', is wellattested in onomastic from Orkhon Turkish times onwards. See Rásonyi and Baski, *Onomasticon turcicum*, vol. 1, pp. 318–19; Sümer, *Türk devletleri tarihinde şahis adları*, vol. 1, pp. 39, 59.

91 I.e. the son of Sulaymān b. Satuq Bughra Khān. See O. Pritsak, 'Die Karachaniden', *Isl.* XXXI (1953–4), p. 26.

92 See above, n. 19.
93 For these complex operations in Khurasan and Transoxania, now signalling the end of Samanid independent power, see Barthold, *op. cit.*, pp. 252–4.
94 This royal estate just outside Bukhara, with palaces and beautiful gardens, and dating back to the pre-Islamic princes of Sogdia, was a favoured residence of the Samanids. See the description of Narshakhī, *Tārīkh-i Bukhārā*, tr. Frye, pp. 26–9.
95 The Ilig's nomination of ʿAbd al-ʿAzīz to the Samanid throne, such as it was by now, was based on the fact that the latter's father Amir Nūḥ (I) b. Naṣr (II) had nominated ʿAbd al-ʿAzīz as fourth in line of succession, as explained by Gardīzī, above, ed. Nazim, p. 39, ed. Ḥabībī, p. 159, but this son's rights had been usurped by Manṣūr (I) b. Nūḥ (I) when he nominated his own son Nūḥ (II) as his successor. When Amir Nūḥ reoccupied his capital after the Ilig's departure, he took vengeance on his uncle and had him blinded. See Barthold, *Turkestan*, p. 260; Treadwell, 'The account of the Samanid dynasty', p. 160 and n. 78.
96 This place probably lay somewhere in the region of Aulié-Ata, medieval Ṭarāz, modern Dzambul (hence near the northwestern border of modern Kyrgyz Republic with that of the Kazakh Republic), in the surmise of Barthold. See his *Zur Geschichte des Christentums in Mittel-Asien bis zur mongolischen Eroberung* (Tübingen and Leipzig, 1901), p. 35.
97 On this first Qarakhanid invasion of the Samanid lands, see Barthold, *Turkestan*, pp. 257–60; Pritsak, 'Die Karachaniden', p. 26. Bayhaqī has some information on it; see Bosworth, *The History of Beyhaqi*, Vol. 1, pp. 294–5.
98 See *EI*[2] art. 'Sebüktigin' (C.E. Bosworth).
99 Thus in Ḥabībī's text, *yaqīn dārand*; in Nazim's one, *t.ʿy.n dārand.*
100 Dārā presumably shared in his father's exile from the ancestral Buyid lands whilst the Buyids were in occupation of them (see above, n. 86), and obviously became a soldier of fortune in the struggles for control of Khurasan in these last days of Samanid rule there. His later career is somewhat obscure. From the information of sources like al-ʿUtbī, Ibn Isfandiyār and Ibn al-Athīr, he was the rival of his brother Manūchihr for power in the Caspian lands, being sheltered by Sultan Maḥmūd at his court as a check on the loyalty of Manūchihr. Ibn al-Athīr mentions him in connection with Abū Kālījār, the ruler in Gurgān and Ṭabaristān during Masʿūd's reign, but it is strange that neither Gardīzī nor Bayhaqī mention him at this time. See Bosworth, 'On the chronology of the Ziyārids in Gurgān and Ṭabaristān', *Isl.* XL (1964), pp. 32–4.
101 Following the definitions given by H.G. Farmer, in his *EI*[2]art. 'Ṭabl'.
102 See Barthold, *Turkestan*, pp. 261–2.
103 The celebrated vizier of the Buyids Mu'ayyid al-Dawla and Fakhr al-Dawla, called Kāfī al-Kufāt 'The Supremely-Capable One', also famed as a littérateur and Maecenas. See *EI*[2]art. 'Ibn ʿAbbād' (Cl. Cahen and Ch. Pellat); Kraemer, *Humanism in the Renaissance of Islam. The Cultural Revival during the Buyid Age*, pp. 259–72.
104 Thus plausibly surmised by both Nazim and Ḥabībī; the mss. have *turkān-i ṣ.l.ḥ.*, though it would be possible to read this phrase as *turkān-i ṣulḥ* 'Turks in a treaty relationship', such Turks being mentioned on the northern fringes of Transoxania by the *Ḥudūd al-ʿālam*, tr. pp. 118–19, as *turkān-i āshtī.* The Khalaj Turks are known to have nomadised at this time in what is now eastern Afghanistan, possibly brought there some centuries previously as part of the following of the Sakas or Hephthalites, and were utilised as auxiliary troops by Sebüktegin and later by his son Maḥmud. See Bosworth, *The Ghaznavids, Their Empire in Afghanistan and Eastern Iran 994:1040* (Edinburgh, 1963), pp. 35–6, 109; *EI*[2]art. 'Khaladj. i. History' (Bosworth).
105 This Shāh was Abū ʿAbdallāh b. Aḥmad (r. not earlier than 366–7/977 to 385/995), last of the Banū ʿIrāq or ʿArāq line of Kāth. As Gardīzī goes on to relate, Abū ʿAbdallāh was at this point overthrown and killed by the Ma'mūnid line of Gurgānj who were later to fall victims to the aggression and violence of Maḥmud of Ghazna, see above, p. 85–6. See Fedorov, 'The Khwarazmshahs of the Banū ʿIrāq (fourth/tenth century)', pp. 71–5.

106 For these events leading to the capture and eventual death of Abū 'Alī Sīmjūrī, see Barthold, *Turkestan*, pp. 261–3.
107 This victory of Ma'mūn b. Muḥammad of Gurgānj inaugurated a new, but short-lived, line of Khwārazm Shāhs. See Bosworth, *The New Islamic Dynasties*, pp. 178–9 no. 89, and above, p. 74.
108 For this name, see Rásonyi and Baski, vol. 1, p. 139, vol. 2, p. 813; Sümer, *Türk devletleri tarihinde şahis adları*, vol. 1, p. 125, vol. 2, p. 544. *Tüzün* can mean 'smooth, self-controlled, well-behaved', see Clauson, *Etymological Dictionary*, p. 576, but the second element of the name may also, but less probably, reflect the Orkhon Turkish official function of the *todhun*, see *ibid.*, p. 457.
109 The three texts have 13 Rajab for this date, but al-'Utbī, Vol. 1, p. 255, has 14 Rajab, giving the correct correspondence.
110 See on Nūḥ's reign, Narshakhī, *Tārīkh-i Bukhārā*, tr. Frye, p. 99; Barthold, *Turkestan*, pp. 252–64; Frye, ch. 'The Sāmānids', pp. 154, 156–8; Treadwell, 'The account of the Samanid dynasty', pp. 158–60.
111 Text here incomprehensible, with a defectively written word in the text.
112 See below, n. 118.
113 On Maḥmūd's struggle with Ismā'Il l for the succession, see Muḥammad Nāẓim, *The Life and Times of Sulṭān Maḥmūd of Ghazna* pp. 38–41.
114 According to Nazim, text, p. 59 n. 2, there is a lacuna in the text here.
115 Thus making the reading 'al-Jayhānī' of Barthold, *Turkestan*, p. 265, and Nāẓim, text, p. 59, unnecessary.
116 See for it, Yāqūt, *Mu'jam al-buldān*, Vol. 2, p. 391.
117 See on Manṣūr's reign, Barthold, *op. cit.*, pp. 264–6; Frye, ch. 'The Samanids', pp. 158–9; Treadwell, 'The account of the Samanid dynasty', pp. 160–1; and for Bayhaqī's account of these events, Bosworth, *The History of Beyhaqi*, Vol. 2, pp. 339–42.
118 Correctly, Arslān Ilig Abu 'l-Ḥasan Naṣr b. 'Alī of Uzgend or Özkend (Arslān Ilig being the designation of the subordinate Khān in the Qarakhanid hierarchy of rule, in this case, subordinate to his brother the Great Khān Abū Naṣr Aḥmad). He was the nephew of the first Qarakhanid to invade Transoxania, Hārūn or Ḥasan Bughrā Khān. See Pritsak, 'Die Karachaniden', p. 27; Doerfer, *Türkische und Mongolische Elemente im Neupersischen. II. Türkische Elemente im Neupersischen*, pp. 210–13 no. 661.
119 Uzgend in Farghāna, now a mere village in the Andijān district of the Kyrgyz Republic, was at this time the main town of the region and the Ilig's capital, later becoming that of the eastern branch of the Qarakhanid confederation. See EI^2 art. 'Özkend' (C.E. Bosworth); Valentina D. Goriatcheva, 'A propos de deux capitales du kaganat karakhanide', in *Cahiers d'Asie centrale No. 9, Études karakhanides* (Tashkent/Aix-en-Provence, 2001), pp. 104–14.
120 See on 'Abd al-Malik's brief reign, Barthold, *Turkestan*, pp. 266–8; Nāẓim, *Sulṭān Maḥmūd of Ghazna*, pp. 43–5; Frye, ch. 'The Samanids', p. 159; Treadwell, 'The account of the Samanid dynasty', p. 161.

Part Four: The Early Ghaznavids

1 Thus in Riḍāzāda Malik, *kaldāniyān*, for the *kalāniyān* of the mss., followed by Nazim and Ḥabībī but of no obvious meaning.
2 See Barthold, *op. cit.*, p. 271; Bosworth, 'The titulature of the early Ghaznavids', pp. 217–18; Bosworth, 'The imperial policy of the early Ghaznawids', *Islamic Studies, Journal of the Central Institute of Islamic Research, Karachi*, I/3 (1962), pp. 62–3.
3 See Nāẓim, *op. cit.*, p. 67; Bosworth, *The History of the Saffarids of Sistan*, p. 322.
4 It is unclear to what this laconic reference refers.
5 al-'Utbī details the rich presents of the specialities of the Inner Asian steppes and East Asia given to Maḥmūd on this occasion by the Qarakhanid, including *khutuww*. (In this context, probably narwhal or walrus ivory or possibly even fossilised mammoth tusks

from Siberia, but the term is also used for rhinocerus horn; see, on the ambiguity of the term, Minorsky, *Sharaf al-Zamān Ṭāhir on China, the Turks and India* [London, 1942], pp. 82–3, and on this whole episode, Barthold, *op. cit.*, p. 272.)

6 This last of the Samanids was a son of Nūḥ (II) b. Manṣūr (I), hence brother of the two preceeding ephemeral Amirs. See Bosworth, *The New Islamic Dynasties*, pp. 170–1 no. 83.

7 As Ḥabībī, p. 175 n. 4 says, the specific significance of this designation is mysterious, and the parallel sources (al-ʿUtbī, Ibn al-Athīr) throw no light on it; but it presumably points to the presence already of Indian troops, and here an Indian commander, in Maḥmūd's army, already known from their mention at Zarang in 393/1003, according to the *Tārīkh-i Sīstān*. See Bosworth, *The Ghaznavids*, p. 110.

8 Clearly a copyist's error; a reading here like *Kūchān* would make sense geographically.

9 On this Turkish name, *tüz tash*, lit. 'straight, level stone', see Sümer, *Türk devletleri tarihinde şahis adları*, Vol. 2, p. 551.

10 Ibn Ẓāfir's source seems to be the only other one mentioning this aid to Muntaṣir by the Yabghu of the Oghuz, and Ibn Ẓāfir specifically identifies him with Arslān Isrāʾīl b. Seljuq, as Barthold also was inclined to do. See Treadwell, 'The account of the Samanid dynasty', p. 161; Barthold, *Turkestan*, p. 269. However, Pritsak suggested that this person was the original Yabghu of Jand on the lower Syr Darya, whose tenure of this ancient Turkish title, one going back to the succession of the Uyghur to the Orkhon Turkish state in 744, was continued into the time of Sultan Masʿūd of Ghazna, when the then Yabghu, Shāh Malik of Jand (son of the Yabghu who gave aid to Muntaṣir?) conquered Khwarazm as an ally of Masʿūd; this seems more probable. Arslān Isrāʾīl's assumption of the title of Yabghu was done in rivalry with the original Yabghu, there being strong hostility between the two branches of the Oghuz. See Cl. Cahen, 'Le Malik-nâmeh et l'histoire des origines seljukides', *Oriens* II (1949), pp. 46, 53–5; Bosworth, *The Ghaznavids*, pp. 221–2; Golden, *An Introduction to the History of the Turkic Peoples*, pp. 206. 218; and on earlier appearances of the title in Islamic sources, above, Part One, n. 131.

11 Following the reading of Ḥabībī, cf. n. 2, *bar ān kuh*, presumably referring to the previously mentioned Kūhak.

12 This is how Barthold, *Turkestan*, p. 269, interpreted the manuscripts' *wa Ghuzzān wa asīrān burdand.*

13 In both Nazim and Ḥabībī given as *w.rghān*, but this is the well-known town of Darghān on the left bank of the Oxus at the point where one first entered Khwarazmian territory, as noted by the Arab geographers. See Barthold, *op. cit.*, pp. 142–3, 270; Le Strange, *The Lands of the Eastern Caliphate*, pp. 451–2.

14 Cf. Rásonyi and Baski, *Onomasticon turcicum*, Vol. 2, p. 532: *marïs, marïš.*

15 According to the *Ḥudūd al-ʿālam*, tr. Minorsky, p. 105, and other geographers detailed in Le Strange, *op. cit.*, p. 400, Kushmayhan or Kushmīhan was a large village of the northeastern part of the Merv oasis, on the road across the Qara Qum desert to the Oxus and across it to Bukhara.

16 This phrase concerning the accession of strength to Abū Ibrāhīm's forces is supplied by Nazim in his text from parallel sources, cf. Barthold, *Turkestan*, p. 270.

17 Ḥabībī, n. 10, states from al-ʿUtbī's *Yamīnī* that Ibn (*sic*) Surkhāk was a member of the Samanid family.

18 Muntaṣir's Samanid kinsman Ibn Surhak had lured Muntaṣir into returning to Transoxania, whilst at the same time conniving with the Ilig against him. See Barthold, *loc. cit.*

19 See on Muntaṣir and his brave but futile attempt to restore the fortunes of his house, Barthold, *Turkestan*, pp. 269–70; Nāẓim, *Sulṭān Maḥmūd of Ghazna*, pp. 45–6; Frye, ch. 'The Sāmānids', pp. 159–60; Treadwell, 'The account of the Samanid dynasty', pp. 161–2. Gardīzī telescopes events here considerably, with al-ʿUtbī giving more detail of Muntaṣir's actions (he in fact made no fewer than four forays into Transoxania seeking to regain power there before he was finally killed).

20 I.e. of the Hindūshāhī dynasty, whose powerful kingdom in northwestern India was based on Wayhind, modern Und near Attock. See *EI*[2] art. 'Hindū-Shāhīs' (C.E. Bosworth).
21 See Nāẓim, *op. cit.*, pp. 86–7; H.C. Ray, *The Dynastic History of Northern India (Early Mediaeval Period)* (Calcutta, 1931–6), Vol. 1, pp. 85–7.
22 Following the interpretation of the text in Ḥabībī, p. 177 n. 8, *mīrak* to be read as *marg*?
23 A stage on the road between Zarang and Bust, with a caravanserai, according to Ibn Ḥawqal, *Kitāb Ṣūrat al-arḍ*, Vol. 2, p. 422, tr. Kramers and Wiet, *Configuration de la terre*, Vol. 2, pp. 409–10. On this ending of Saffarid power in Sistan, see Bosworth, *The History of the Saffarids of Sistan*, pp. 325–7.
24 On its identification and location of the text's Bhāṭiya with Bhatinda, now in the southern part of the Indian Union's Panjab province, see Nāẓim, *op. cit.*, pp. 200–1, *pace* S.H. Hodivala, *Studies in Indo-Muslim History*, Vol. 1, pp. 138–9, identifying it with Bhera on the Jhelum river. The date of this expedition, unspecified by either al-ʿUtbī or Gardīzī, was probably the winter of 395/1004–5, see Nāẓim, *Sulṭān Maḥmūd of Ghazna*, pp. 202–3.
25 The consonant ductus for the title is confused and seems to be trying to represent both Rāō and Rājah.
26 The correction of Ḥabībī and Riḍāzāda to *āb-i Sind* 'river of Sind', i.e. the Indus, seems unlikely, given the distance of Bhatinda from that river; Nāẓim, *op. cit.*, p. 100 n. 8, suggests that this Sāsind was the old name of a branch of the River Hakra.
27 Thus in the mss. and Nazim; in Ḥabībī, Arg, both being possible, although *ḥiṣār-i arg* sounds tautologous. Ūk would be a variant spelling for the place to the north of Zarang, Ūq, frequently mentioned in the historical and geographical sources for Sistan; see Bosworth, *The History of the Saffarids*, pp. 77–8 and n. 217.
28 See Nāẓim, *op. cit.*, pp. 96–7; Bosworth, *The Ghaznavids*, pp. 52–3. Only five years later, Maḥmūd was to lead a further expedition against Multan, ostensibly because it was a nest of Carmathians but in reality because of the lure of the city's great riches; see above, p. 83.
29 In 390/999, at a time when the Samanids had not yet been totally defeated, Maḥmūd and the Ilig Naṣr had made an agreement to divide up the Samanid lands, with the Ilig having Transoxania and Maḥmūd the lands south of the Oxus (Barthold, *Turkestan*, pp. 266–7, 271–2; Nāẓim, *op. cit.*, pp. 47–8). As is evident, this agreement did not last long.
30 The text is dubious here: Nazim has *s.m.r.w*, and Ḥabībī has *b.m.r.w* : ?*ba-marr-i u.* Riḍāzāda's interpretation *ba-marw* seems improbable.
31 Barthold, *op. cit.*, p. 273 n. 2, observed that the text here is badly mutilated. He translated here '[Maḥmūd's soldiers] sang a Turkish song to a Khotanese melody'. Nazim's text is unintelligible, and the translation here follows Ḥabībī, p. 179, cf. n. 1: *dabdaba-yi tākhtan va āyīna ba-zadand.*
32 Thus according to the reading in Ḥabībī, p. 179, cf. n. 2, but there is obviously a lacuna and/or corruption in the text here. A difficulty about Ḥabībī's reading is that the commander Ghāzī turns up alive and well in Sultan Masʿūd's reign some two decades later as one of the Maḥmūdiyān, men of the former regime whose destruction the new Sultan then engineered, as related by Bayhaqī.
33 Ḥabībī reads here *chashm rasad* where the mss., followed by Nazim, have *ḥasham rasad.* The whole sentence is difficult, and the translation here follows Barthold's interpretation of this passage; he apparently read *jān-rā ba-zadand* for the *khān-rā ba-zadand* of Nazim, Ḥabībī and Riḍāzāda Malik, which last does not easily make sense.
34 The vocalisation of this name as two syllables is indicated in Farrukhī's mention of this victory over the Qarakhanids in *Dīwān*, ed. Muḥammad Dabīr-Siyāqī (Tehran, 1335/1956), p. 71 n. 35, cf. Ḥabībī, p. 179 n. 5. The site of Katar must have lain in Ṭukhāristān between Balkh and the Oxus river.
35 For this campaign, see Barthold, *Turkestan*, pp. 272–4; Nāẓim, *Sulṭān Maḥmūd of Ghazna*, pp. 48–51.

36 Nāẓim, *op. cit.*, p. 98, takes this to be a copyist's mistake for *Kh.w.ra*, Khewra, the common name for the Salt Range in northwestern Panjab.
37 Thus read by Ḥabībī for an unintelligible name in the mss.
38 See Nāẓim, *op. cit.*, pp. 98–9; H.C. Ray, *The Dynastic History of Northern India*, (Calcutta, 1931–6), Vol. 1, pp. 89–91.
39 *Ibid.*, p. 99.
40 *Ibid.*, pp. 103–4,
41 *Ibid.*, pp. 60–2.
42 *Ibid.*, pp. 192–3; Bosworth, 'The imperial policy of the early Ghaznawids', p. 68.
43 Nāẓim, *Sulṭān Maḥmūd of Ghazna*, p. 164; Bosworth, *op. cit.*, p. 60; Heinz Halm, 'Fatimiden und Ghaznawiden', in *Studies in Honour of Clifford Edmund Bosworth. Vol. I. Hunter of the East*, ed. I.R. Netton (Leiden, 2000), pp. 213–15.
44 Nandana or Nārdīn (thus in 'Utbī) lay on a northern spur of the Salt Range, in what is now the Jhelum District of Pakistani Panjab, commanding the route from the region of Attock into the Ganges Do'āb. See Nāẓim, *op. cit.*, p. 91 and n. 4.
45 Nāẓim, *op. cit.*, pp. 91–3; Ray, *The Dynastic History of Northern India*, Vol. 1, pp. 94–101, 136.
46 Nāẓim, *op. cit.*, pp. 104–5; Ray, *op. cit.*, Vol. 1, pp. 136–7.
47 The mss. have Ja'farband, but the geographers situate the town of Jakarband or Jaqarband between Ṭāhiriyya and Darghān; see Le Strange, *The Lands of the Eastern Caliphate*, p. 451.
48 See for his later career, *EIr* art. 'Altuntaš' (C.E. Bosworth).
49 See for Bayhaqī's detailed account of the the Ghaznavid invasion and annexation of Khwarazm (actually derived from al-Bīrūnī), Bosworth, *The History of Beyhaqi*, Vol. 2, pp. 369–400; also E. Sachau, 'Zur Geschichte und Chronologie von Khwârazm', *SBWAW* LXXIV (1873), pp. 292–311; Barthold, *Turkestan*, pp. 275–9; Nāẓim, *Sulṭān Maḥmūd of Ghazna*, pp. 56–60. Gardīzī does not mention that it was Maḥmūd's brutal ultimatum to the Khwarazmians, demanding that they recognise him as first in their *khuṭba*, which precipitated the events giving him a convenient pretext for invading Khwarazm.
50 The modern Bulandshahr, in Uttar Pradesh.
51 See Nāẓim, *op. cit.*, pp. 110–11; Ray, *The Dynastic History of Northern India*, Vol. 1, pp. 598–600; Hodivala, *Studies in Indo-Muslim History*, Vol. 1, pp. 146–8.
52 Ray, however, in *op. cit.*, Vol. 1, p. 606, see also Vol. 2, pp. 690–3, proposed to read *n.n.da* as a corrupt form of Bīdā = the first part of the name Vidyādhara, son and successor of Ganda/Gaṇḍa.
53 The numerals here are confused in the texts, but the figure given here is Riḍāzāda Malik's interpretation.
54 Nāẓim, *Sulṭān Maḥmūd of Ghazna*, pp. 111–13; Ray, *op. cit.*, Vol. 1, pp. 602ff.
55 Nāẓim, *op. cit.* pp. 74–5. These river valleys ran down to the Kabul river, in the regions of Lamghān/Laghmān and Kunar lying to the north of modern Jalālābād. If Islam was indeed permanently implanted in these valleys, it must only have been in their lower reaches, since the highly mountainous, hardly penetrable interior parts of Kāfiristān continued to follow their blend of animism and polytheism till the campaign into Kāfiristān (modern Nūristān) of the Amir of Afghanistan 'Abd al-Raḥmān Khān at the end of the nineteenth century. See *EI²* art. 'Kāfiristān' (C.E. Bosworth).
56 I.e. the sub-Himalayan region of the Panjab west of the Chenab. See Nāẓim, *op. cit.*, p. 105 n. 7, and al-Bīrūnī, *Taḥqīq mā li 'l-Hind*, English tr. E. Sachau, *Alberuni's India* (London, 1910), Vol. 1, p. 208.
57 Nāẓim, *op. cit.*, p. 105; Ray, *op. cit.*, Vol. 1, pp. 137–8.
58 Nāẓim, *op. cit.*, pp. 113–14; Ray, *op. cit.*, Vol. 2, p. 689 n. 3. See also *EI²* art. 'Gwāliyār' (K.A. Nizami).
59 See on the Ghaznavid *'arḍ* or review of troops, Bosworth, *The Ghaznavids*, pp. 122–4; *EI²* art. 'Isti'rāḍ, 'Arḍ' (Bosworth).

60 The ductus of this word is unclear. Ḥabībī, p. 186 n. 3, following a suggestion of Mīrzā Muḥammad Qazwīnī, suggests reading *jast*, and this is followed here in the translation.

61 *arash*, i.e. the breadth between two outstretched arms. The reading here 'two or three . . .' follows Nazim's text.

62 This seems to be how the bridge of boats over the Oxus was constructed, but Barthold confessed, *Turkestan*, p. 282 n. 7, that the technical details here given were not entirely clear to him.

63 Possibly the Muḥtājid prince Abu 'l-Muẓaffar Muḥammad b. Aḥmad, an early patron of the Ghaznavid poet Farrukhī. See Bosworth, 'The rulers of Chaghāniyān in early Islamic times', p. 12.

64 The ductus here without any dots.

65 Barthold, *op. cit.*, pp. 282–3.

66 Reading here, with Ḥabībī, p. 188 n. 8, *ṭabarīhā*.

67 Following the texts' *muṣaffarī*; Barthold, *op. cit.*, p. 284 n. 5, read here *maqāṣīrī* (from Makassar?).

68 The first word in this phrase is obscure, but *khutuww* is a familiar exotic product, see above, n. 5.

69 Barthold, *Turkestan*, p. 284 n. 6, found this term incomprehensible. Ḥabībī, p. 189 n. 5, suggests a possible connection with *khārchīnī*, perhaps an arabisation of the word, said to be a hard substance from which such things as bells, cooking vessels, etc. could be made.

70 Barthold, *op. cit.*, pp. 283–4, translates this passage detailing the gifts that the two sovereigns presented to each other, noting various uncertainties in the texts.

71 For the capture of Arslān Isrā'īl, see Nāẓim, *Sulṭān Maḥmūd of Ghazna*, pp. 63–4; Cahen, 'Le Malik-nâmeh et l'histoire des origines seljukides', p. 52.

72 It seems that these Turkmens, who included the Seljuq family and their followers, had been auxiliaries in the service of the Qarakhanid ʿAlī b. Hārūn or Ḥasan Bughrā Khān, called ʿAlītegin, in the neighbourhood of Bukhara, but were now compelled to move towards the fringes of Khurasan when ʿAlītegin was temporarily driven out of Transoxania by his brother Yūsuf Qadïr Khān; see Bosworth, *The Ghaznavids*, pp. 223–4. The course of the relations between the ʿAlītegin and the Seljuqs is not, however, entirely clear; see the discussion in Cahen, *op. cit.*, pp. 48ff.

73 Thus in all the sources, but Jādhib, from the Arabic root *j-dh-b* 'to drag, pull' gives no sense here, and it is probable that we have here an early misspelling by copyists of the title Ḥājib 'general, commander'.

74 See Nāẓim, *op. cit.*, pp. 64–5; Bosworth, *op. cit.*, p. 224.

75 This short section on the march to Nahrawāla and taking on supplies there is omitted from Nazim's text, perhaps through inadvertence.

76 In an Indian context, the Shamanīs/Sumaniyya often designate the Buddhists, but cf. Minorsky, 'Gardīzī on India', p. 627 n. 3, where H.W. Bailey is quoted as observing that *śramaṇa* means simply 'ascetic'. It is indeed, highly improbable that there were any Buddhists in Kathiawar at this time.

77 Thus written in the text; according to Ḥabībī, p. 191 n. 1, this is a Sanskrit word meaning 'shrine'.

78 Thus in Nazim's text, to be preferred to Ḥabībī's Jayḥūn; the latter has in fact Sayḥūn a few lines below. The name, normally used in Arabic geographical literature for the Jaxartes/Syr Darya, seems to have been used analogically for the Indus because this large river also divided off the Muslim lands from those of the unbelievers; see *EI*[2] art. 'Mihrān' (C.E. Bosworth).

79 This ancient Indo-Aryan people of Sind and the southern Panjabi parts of the Indus valley had been fiercely hostile to the incoming Arabs of Muḥammad b. al-Qāsim at the opening of the eighth century AD, but are little mentioned until now, when they at times barred the advance of Ghaznavid raiders into the Indus valley lands. See *EI*[2] art. 'Djāt' (A.S. Bazmee Ansari).

80 Nāẓim, *Sulṭān Maḥmūd of Ghazna*, pp. 115–21, 209–24.

81 Barthold, *Turkestan*, p. 286; Nāẓim, *op. cit.*, p. 56. It would seem that these two envoys represented Inner Asian potentates from beyond the lands of the Qarakhanids, whose ruling strata, at least, had not by this time become Muslim. If Qitā is a tribal name and not a geographical one, it may refer to the Qitan, who were probably Mongolic in ethnos and language and who occupied the Manchurian-northern China-Mongolian region after earlier Turkic peoples in Mongolia had migrated westwards towards the fringes of the Islamic lands (this last movement may be dimly referred to in Ibn al-Athīr's laconic report, under the year 349/960, that 200,000 tents of the Turks converted to Islam). The Yughur are clearly the Uyghur, who had had a powerful state in Mongolia as successors of the Eastern Turk empire, but who had, after *ca.* 840, fallen into disunity, with new Uyghur political groupings forming in Eastern Turkestan, sc. the Tarim and Turfan basins, and in Kan-chu, the Kansu Corridor leading from eastern Turkestan to China. The faiths of these peoples ranged from animism and Buddhism to Manichaeism and Nestorian Christianity, hence their princes would not be acceptable to Maḥmūd as husbands for his womenfolk. See Golden, *An Introduction to the History of the Turkic Peoples*, pp. 162ff., 183ff.

82 Bosworth, 'The imperial policy of the early Ghaznawids', p. 63; Bosworth, 'The titulature of the early Ghaznavids', p. 219.

83 The campaigns against the heretical Muslims of Multan and against Kashmir not being counted here.

84 Ḥabībī has here 'four and a thousand hundreds', presumably a clerical error since '1,400' is correctly given a few lines below.

85 Nāẓim, *Sulṭān Maḥmūd of Ghazna*, pp. 121–2.

86 Nāẓim, *op. cit.*, pp. 64–6; Cahen, 'Le Malik-nâmeh et l'histoire des origines seljukides', pp. 52, 55–6. Balkhān Kūh was the mountainous refuge region to the east of the Caspian Sea, now in the western part of the Turkmen Republic.

87 See on this *Ḥudūd al-'ālam*, tr. Minorsky, p. 64, comm. p. 200.

88 Of unclear etymology, unless the first element is related to the kinship terms *ekē* 'female relative older than oneself but younger than one's father', or *eke* 'father, uncle, elder brother' (Clauson, *An Etymological Dictionary of Pre-Thirteenth Century Turkish*, p. 100). Sümer, *Türk devletleri tarihinde şahis adları*, Vol. 2, p. 545, merely registers this name as Eygü (?) Tigin without attempting any etymology or meaning for it.

89 Nāẓim, *op. cit.*, pp. 80–3; Bosworth, 'The imperial policy of the early Ghaznawids', pp. 70–2; Bosworth, *The Ghaznavids*, pp. 53–4.

90 Nāẓim, *op. cit.*, pp. 123–4.

91 On Maḥmūd's favourite, his cup-bearer Ayāz, see *EIr* art. 'Ayāz, Abu 'l-Najm Ūymāq' (J. Matīnī), and for his role in later Persian literature, Gertrud Spiess, *Maḥmūd von Ġazna bei Farīdu'dīn 'Aṭṭār* (Basel, 1959).

92 Dāya, presumably cognate with older Turkish *tagāy, dagāy*, Ottoman *dayï* 'maternal uncle' (Clauson, *op. cit.*, p. 474); it may be that 'Alī was connected in some way by marriage with Sultan Maḥmūd.

93 On this Indian commander's name, see Bosworth, *The History of Beyhaqi*, Vol. 2, p. 237 n. 32.

94 The two mss. have *w.l.h*, which Ḥabībī suggested should be amended to Rukhkhaj, the classical Arachosia, the region in which Tegīnābād was situated; from Bayhaqī we learn that Muḥammad's place of incarceration was a fortress called Kūhtīz.

95 On this first sultanate of Muḥammad, see R. Gelpke, *Sulṭān Mas'ūd I. von Ġazna. Die drei ersten Jahre seiner Herrschaft (421/1030–424/1033)* (Munich, 1957), pp. 31–43; Bosworth, *The Ghaznavids*, pp. 228–9; *EI²* art. 'Muḥammad b. Maḥmūd b. Sebüktigin' (Bosworth). It may be noted that Gardīzī's account of the sultanate is not unfavourable to Muḥammad, rather more so than that of Bayhaqī.

96 The arrest and incarceration of these two commanders marks the beginning of a systematic campaign by the new sultan Mas'ūd, extending even to his own uncle Yūsuf

b. Sebüktegin, to remove from positions of power those connected in any way with his brother Muḥammad's sultanate or, indeed, connected at all with the ancien régime of Maḥmūd, these last being stigmatised as the Maḥmūdiyān or Pidariyān. See Gardīzī's own words concerning this vendetta, above, p. 100; Gelpke, *op. cit.*, pp. 48–53; Bosworth, *The Ghaznavids*, pp. 101–2, 230–4.

97 This is the celebrated vizier of Maḥmūd, who was now brought back to serve as Mas'ūd's minister until his death two years later (see above, p. 101). See Nāẓim, *Sultān Maḥmūd of Ghazna*, pp. 130–1, 135–6; Gelpke, *op. cit.*, pp. 59–63; Bosworth, *The Ghaznavids*, pp. 60–1, 71–3; *EI*[2] art. 'Maymandī' (M. Nazim, C.E. Bosworth).

98 See on this governor and castellan, Ray, *The Dynastic History of Northern India*, Vol. 1, pp. 137–8; Hodivala, *Studies in Indo-Muslim History*, Vol. 1, pp. 145–6.

99 See on the Mīkālī family, above, Part Three, n. 85.

100 I.e. from the Fatimid caliph al-Ḥākim.

101 For this episode of Ḥasanak's death, graphically and movingly described by Bayhaqī, see Gelpke, *op. cit.*, pp. 67–71; Bosworth, *The Ghaznavids*, pp. 71, 182–4; Meisami, *Persian Historiography*, pp. 88–94; Halm, 'Fatimiden und Ghaznawiden', pp. 218–19.

102 Text, Il-Yārūq, but the correct form is ascertainable from Bayhaqī, see Bosworth, *The History of Beyhaqi*, Vol. 1, p. 165 etc.

103 See above, pp. 103–4.

104 Earlier, it was stated that Maḥmūd held Majd al-Dawla at Ghazna.

105 For these events in Makrān, see Bosworth, 'Rulers of Makrān and Quṣdār in the early Islamic period', *St.Ir.* XXIII (1994), pp. 206–7.

106 Cahen, 'Le Malik-nâmeh et l'histoire des origines seljukides', p. 56.

107 See on the new vizier, from a family which, like so many of the Ghaznavids' officials, had apparently served the Samanids, Bosworth, *The Ghaznavids*, pp. 58, 61–2, 72.

108 See Nazir Ahmad, 'A critical examination of Bayhaqī's narration of the Indian expeditions during the reign of Mas'ud of Ghazna', pp. 39–44, for a discussion of this expedition and the location of Sarastī.

109 Thus in the texts of Ḥabībī and Riḍāzāda Malik, following the *zāwi-hā* of the mss.; Nazim has *wādī-hā* 'river valleys', and also the Tehran edition (presumably that of 1315/1936–7), according to Ḥabībī.

110 Following Riḍāzāda Malik, *khishtī ba-zad.*

111 Abū Kālījār is here the son of Surkhāb, but is said by the local historian Ibn Isfandiyār to have been the son and successor of Manuchihr b. Qābūs when the latter died in 424/1033, reigning till his own death in 441/1049–50. See Ibn Isfandiyār, tr. Browne, *An Abridged Translation of the History of Ṭabaristán*, p. 235. The history of these later Ziyārids is, however, only sketchily known.

112 Bayhaqī describes Mas'ūd's campaign in the Caspian provinces in considerable detail, but does not conceal the fact that the Sultan's violent and avaricious behaviour created a most unfavourable impression on contemporaries, with complaints being carried as far as the caliph's court in Baghdad and to Mecca. See Bosworth, *The History of Beyhaqi*, Vol. 2, pp. 106–7, 109–23; also Bosworth, *The Ghaznavids*, pp. 74–5, 90–1; Meisami, *Persian Historiography*, pp. 95–8.

113 This seems to be the meaning here of *tabāhī īn az sālār bisyar ast*, i.e. effort has been dissipated by sending several commanders at various times, with no unified plan of campaign.

114 Khwāja Ḥusayn was actually to be captured by the Seljuqs in the course of this ensuing battle (see above, p. 103), and thereafter appears to have entered their service; in the reign of the Great Seljuq Sultan Ṭoghril, successor to the Ghaznavids in Khurasan and Persia, he fulfilled various high offices, possibly as vizier. See H. Bowen, 'Notes on some early Seljuqid viziers', *BSOAS* XX (1957), pp. 105, 107–8.

115 Possibly to be identified, according to Ḥabībī, n. 1, with a place S.w.s.qān or S.w.sn.qān near Merv.

116 This is how Ḥabībī interprets the text's *jāmi'-i 'arabī.*

117 These must have been captives and hostages brought back from the previous Ṭabaristān campaign, see above, p. 102.

118 On Begtughdī's defeat, see Cahen, 'Le Malik-nâmeh et l'histoire des origines seljukides', p. 49; Bosworth, *The Ghaznavids*, pp. 248–9; Meisami, *op. cit.*, pp. 98.

119 I.e. of the Indian division within the main Ghaznavid army, which Suvendharāy had commanded during Muḥammad's brief reign, see above, p. 000.

120 According to Hodivala, *Studies in Indo-Muslim History*, Vol. 1, p. 163, the name of Tilak or Tilaka's father Jahlan/Jalhaṇa/Jahlaṇsi is an old one found in dynastic lists and inscriptions. Presumably Tilak was at his juncture appointed commander of the Indians in Bānha's place.

121 There are some chronological discrepancies in the accounts of Gardīzī and the other two sources describing Aḥmad's revolt, his final vanquishing and his death, sc. Bayhaqī and Ibn al-Athīr. See for a discussion of the whole episode, problems involved with it and identification of the places mentioned in its course, Nazir Ahmad, 'A critical examination of Bayhaqī's narration of the Indian expeditions', pp. 53–6.

122 Bayhaqī has a description of the new Mas'ūdī Palace, which had taken four years to build and for whose construction and decoration a total of fourteen million dirhams had been expended on the wages of craftsmen and payments to forced labour levies. See Bosworth, *The History of Beyhaqi*, Vol. 2, pp. 216–17.

123 This phrase supplied from Bayhaqī and Firishta.

124 Hānsī is situated in the modern Hariyana province of the Indian Union, to the northwest of Delhi. After Mas'ūd's conquest of the fortress from its Chawhān ruler, it became briefly a forward base for Ghaznavid armies launching raids against Delhi, but was recaptured during Mawdūd's reign by the Rājā of Delhi, Mahīpāl, and a coalition of other princes and not regained by the Muslims till Ghurid times. See Nazir Ahmad, *op. cit.*, p. 59; *EI*[2] art. 'Hānsī' (J. Burton-Page).

125 Bayhaqī calls this place 'The Virgin Fortress', *Qal'at al-'Adhrā'*.

126 *dīra*; in the mss., *dara* 'valley'.

127 There are problems arising out of the divergent chronologies of Gardīzī and Bayhaqī for these campaigns of Mas'ūd in India. These are discussed by Nazir Ahmad in his detailed study of the whole episode, in *op. cit.*, pp. 58–66; he opts for the more careful chronology of Bayhaqī, for which see Bosworth, *The History of Beyhaqi*, Vol. 2, pp. 208–9.

128 Gardīzī does not record the fact that, whilst the Amir was campaigning in India, his general Sübashï, ordered to march out from his base at Nishapur, had been defeated by the Turkmens and had had to withdraw to Herat, allowing the Turkmens to occupy Nishapur unopposed. See Meisami, *Persian Historiography*, pp. 99–100.

129 This is Qarakhanid prince Böritegin, son of the Ilig Naṣr b. 'Alī, and later better known in the sources as Ibrāhīm Tamghach Khān (d. 460/1068); he was from the Western branch of the family whose possessions were centred on Transoxania. At this time, however, Böritegin had recently escaped from custody of his enemies, the sons of his distant kinsman 'Alītegin, and had come, via a stay in Uzgend/Özkend, to the upper Oxus region, where he had gathered together a force of the predatory Kumījīs and Kanjīna Turks of the Buttamān mountains region (see above, Part Three, n. 49) and was harrying the Ghaznavid dependencies of Wakhsh and Khuttal. See Barthold, *Turkestan*, pp. 300–1; Pritsak, 'Die Karachaniden', pp. 36–7.

130 See above, n. 34. Ḥabībī in his text, p. 202 n. 1, quotes a verse of Farrukhī on Maḥmūd's earlier meeting there with the Qarakhanid Yūsuf Qadïr Khān.

131 The Sultan's invasion of Transoxania was undertaken at the worst time of the year for weather, the winter months of 430/1038–39, as his advisers had pointed out but to no avail. Whereas Bayhaqī's account does not conceal the terrible hardships endured by the army, Gardīzī relates the episode in a comparatively neutral fashion; the expedition was in fact a disaster, achieving nothing and diminishing Mas'ūd's prestige. See Barthold, *op. cit.*, pp. 301–2; Meisami, *op. cit.*, pp. 77, 100–1.

132 The operations against this bandit chief are described in detail by Bayhaqī; see Bosworth, *The History of Beyhaqi*, Vol. 2, pp. 241–3.

133 The Yabghu here is clearly the Seljuq Mūsā Yabghu, successor in this title to his close kinsman Arslān Isrā'īl (whom Maḥmūd had imprisoned in India towards the end of his reign, see Nāẓim, *Sulṭān Maḥmūd of Ghazna*, pp. 63–4) holding this title in rivalry with its original holder amongst the Oghuz, the ruler in Jand, see above, n. 10. The problems regarding the various holders of the title are discussed by Cahen, 'Le Malik-nâmeh et l'histoire des origines seljukides', pp. 53–5. Here in this passage of Gardīzī, Mas'ūd seems here to have regarded Mūsā Yabghu as nominal head of the Seljuqs (it was to him that the Sultan had the Turkmens' severed heads delivered, see below), although insofar as there was any central direction at all amongst the Seljuqs, it was Ṭoghril Beg and Chaghri Beg who in practice exercised this. See Bosworth, *The Ghaznavids*, pp. 244–5.

134 *āncha mā khwāstīm ba-kard amīr khwud ba-kard.*

135 There is thus no mention by Gardīzī of the several months' occupation of Nishapur by the Seljuqs, whose arrival there is described in detail by Bayhaqī.

136 Mas'ūd's forces had reoccupied Nishapur towards the beginning of 431/end of 1039 and opening of 1040, see Bosworth, *op. cit.*, p. 251.

137 Following Ḥabībī, *ū-rā andar na-yāft.*

138 The people of the towns and cities of northern Khurasan like Bāward/Abīward and Sarakhs were clearly despairing of securing any protection from the Sultan against the Seljuqs, and were making their own terms with the Turkmens. The most notable instance of this was the ease with which Nishapur passed temporarily under Seljuq control in 429–30/1038–9 (an episode unnoted by Gardīzī but described in detail by Bayhaqī; see on this Bosworth, *The Ghaznavids*, pp. 244, 252ff.). See also *ibid.*, pp. 264–5.

139 Bayhaqī relates that 500 defectors from the Ghaznavid side had joined the Seljuq group of Yīnāliyān (i.e. those under the leadership of Ibrāhīm Ināl) at some point before the battle of Dandānqān, and that before this, former troops of Ghaznavid commanders whom Mas'ūd had vindictively hunted down and killed, such as his uncle Yūsuf b. Sebüktegin, the Ḥājib 'Alī Qarīb, Eryārūq, Ghāzī, etc., had joined the Turkmens.

140 This was one of the decisive battles in the history of the eastern Islamic world, for the way was now open for the Seljuqs to sweep westwards, confront the powers of western Persia like the Kakuyids and Buyids, and establish the Great Seljuq sultanate, whilst the Ghaznavids, whilst still a great power, were forced to concentrate their vision eastwards to northern India. Bayhaqī has a very detailed account of the course of the Dandānqān battle, see *The History of Beyhaqi*, Vol. 2, pp. 309ff. See also Meisami, *Persian Historiography*, pp. 102–4.

141 Thus in Ḥabībī's text, *ihmāl warzīda*; Nazim has *iḥtimāl warzīda* 'had been wavering and uncertain'.

142 Bosworth, *The Later Ghaznavids*, pp. 9, 139.

143 Bayhaqī's narrative shows, however, that several of the Sultan's advisers were against this retreat to India and thought that the situation in eastern Afghanistan could be held, see *ibid.*, pp. 15–16,

144 *Ibid.*, pp. 9–13. The exact location of Hupyān (if this is the correct vocalisation of the name) is uncertain; see *ibid.*, pp. 12–13.

145 Bayhaqī calls these disruptive elements, in what is now eastern Afghanistan, Khalaj; these were almost certainly Turks but may well have become mingled with Afghan tribesmen, i.e. Pashtuns. See above, Part Three, n. 104, and Bosworth, *The Later Ghaznavids*, pp. 13–14 and n. 27, where it is said that the first mention in Islamic sources of Afghans appears to be in the *Ḥudūd al-'ālam*. However, we now have mention of *abagano*, *abgano*, pl. *abaganano*, from some two centuries earlier in the recently discovered letters in the Middle Iranian Bactrian language from the Rōb/Ro'b and Gūzgān regions of northern Afghanistan (information from Professor N. Sims-Williams, and cf. above, Part Two, n. 18).

146 See on these places, Bosworth, *The Later Ghaznavids*, pp. 16–17.

147 In Bayhaqī this fortress is named as Naghar.

148 Barthold, *Turkestan*, p. 303; Bosworth, *op. cit.*, pp. 14–17. It is at this point that the ninth volume of Bayhaqī's *Mujalladāt* ends, so that Gardīzī's narrative assumes a particular importance as the sole contemporary source on the end of Mas'ūd's sultanate.

149 This is modern Marigala, in a pass of the low hills separating Attock from Rawalpindi; Mas'ūd had thus just crossed the Indus at Wayhind when his troops mutinied. See Bosworth, *op. cit.*, pp. 19, 140.

150 *Ibid.*, pp. 20, 140.

151 Text in the two mss., *dīnawar*, as also in Bayhaqī. Peshawar has been conjectured as a possible reading, but Ḥabībī, p. 205 n. 3, suggests that we should read *d.n.pūr*, *d.n.būr*, this being a site near the later Jalālābād, and this is more plausible; Jūzjānī, in his *Ṭabaqāt-i nāṣ irī* (see above, Part One, n. 112) says that the battle took place in Nangrahār, i.e. in this same region of the middle Kabul river valley. Dunpūr is in fact known as a town, the resort of merchants, from the *Ḥudūd al-'ālam*, tr. Minorsky, pp. 63, 72, 92, being placed on the opposite bank of the Kabul river from Lamghān, cf. comm. p. 252. The town is mentioned, in a later form, in the *Bābur-nāma*, and its name is possibly from the Sanskrit *Udyānapūra.*

152 This *du'ā* or invocation of long life for 'Abd al-Rashīd implies that Gardīzī was writing his history during that Amir's reign, i.e. between ?440/1049 and 443/1052, thus confirming the lauding by Gardīzī of 'Abd al-Rashīd as reigning monarch in the texts of Nazim, pp. 61–2, and Ḥabībī, p. 174, above.

153 It would be interesting to know the circumstances in which 'Abd al-Rashīd was present near the battlefield. Did he have supporters of his own with him, and was there perhaps a feeling amongst the Ghaznavid troops that he, as son of Maḥmūd and the eldest representative of the family, had a superior claim to the succession? Mawdūd obviously felt a strong need to conciliate him. But despite Mawdūd's promises to him in return for his neutrality in the struggle, 'Abd al-Rashīd was after the battle arrested and imprisoned by Mawdūd during the whole of the latter's reign; see Bosworth, *The Later Ghaznavids*, pp. 23, 25.

154 For the battle, which took place in Rajab or Sha'bān 432/March or April 1041, see Bosworth, *op. cit.*, pp. 22–4, 140, and for Mawdūd's vengeance on Muḥammad and his supporters after it, *ibid.*, pp. 24, 140.

SELECT BIBLIOGRAPHY

Note. This bibliography does not include some items which are mentioned only once or so in the text of the book and are of peripheral relevance to Gardīzī's work; but where such items occur in the book, full bibliographical details are given there.

Abbott, Nabia, *Two Queens of Baghdad. Mother and Wife of Hārūn al-Rashīd* (Chicago, 1946).

Ahmad, Nazir, 'A critical examination of Bayhaqī's narration of the Indian expeditions during the reign of Mas'ud of Ghazna', in *Yād-nāma-yi Abu 'l-Faḍl Bayhaqī. Majmū'a-yi sukhanrānī-hā-yi Majlis-i Buzurgdāsht-i Abu 'l-Faḍl-i Bayhaqī, Mashhad, 21 tā 25 shahrīwarmāh 1349*, ed. Mashhad University Faculty of Letters and Human Sciences (Mashhad, 1350/1971), English section, pp. 34–83.

Anon., *Ḥudūd al-'ālam*, English tr. and commentary by V. Minorsky, with a Preface by V.V. Barthold, as *Ḥudūd al-'ālam 'The Regions of the World', a Persian Geography 372 AH–982 AD*, GMS NS XI (London, 1937), 2nd ed. with additional material by the late Professor Minorsky [and with comments by Dr Manuchihr Sotudeh and 'The second series of Addenda' by V. Minorsky], ed. C.E. Bosworth (London, 1970).

Anon. (by Ibn Shādī?), *Mujmal al-tawārīkh wa 'l-qiṣaṣ*, ed. Malik al-Shu'arā' Mīrzā Taqī Bahār (Tehran, 1318/1939).

Anon., *Tārīkh-i Sīstān*, ed. Malik al-Shu'arā' Mīrzā Taqī Bahār (Tehran, 1314/1935), English tr. Milton Gold as *The Tārīkh-e Sīstān*, IsMEO, Serie Orientale Roma, Vol. XLVIII/Literary and Historical Texts from Iran, 2 (Rome, 1976).

Bahār, Mīrzā Taqī, Malik al-Shu'arā', *Sabk-shināsī yā tārīkh-i taṭawwur-i nathr-i fārsī*, 3 vols. (Tehran, 1337/1958).

al-Balādhurī, Aḥmad b. Yaḥyā, *Futūḥ al-buldān*, ed. M.J. De Goeje as *Liber expugnationis regionum* (Leiden, 1866).

Barthold, Wilhelm (V.V. Bart'old), *Turkestan down to the Mongol Invasion*, GMS N.S. V (London, 1928), 3rd ed. with an additional chapter, ed. C.E. Bosworth (London, 1968).

Bayhaqī, Abu 'l-Faḍl, *Tārīkh-i Mas'ūdī*, English tr. C. Edmund Bosworth as *The History of Beyhaqi (The History of Sultan Mas'ud of Ghazna, 1030–1041)*, 3 vols. (New York, 2009).

al-Bīrūnī, Abū Rayḥān, *al-Āthār al-bāqiya 'an al-qurūn al-khāliya*, ed. Eduard Sachau (Leipzig, 1878), English tr. E. Sachau as *The Chronology of Ancient Nations* (London, 1879).

——, *Taḥqīq mā li 'l-Hind*, English tr. E.C. Sachau as *Alberuni's India. An Account of the Religion, Philosophy, Literature, Geography, Chronology, Astronomy, Customs, Laws and Astrology of India about AD 1030*, 2 vols. (London, 1910).

Bosworth, C. Edmund, 'The early Islamic history of Ghūr', *CAJ* VI (1961), pp. 116–33, reprinted in C.E. Bosworth, *The Medieval History of Iran, Afghanistan and Central Asia*, Variorum Reprints, Collected Studies Series CS 56 (London, 1977), no. IX.

——, 'The titulature of the early Ghaznavids', *Oriens* XV (1962), pp. 210–33, reprinted in *The Medieval History of Iran, Afghanistan and Central Asia*, no. X.

——, *The Ghaznavids, their Empire in Afghanistan and Eastern Iran 994:1040*, History, Philosophy and Economics 17 (Edinburgh, 1963), 2nd ed. with additional bibliography (Beirut, 1973).

——, 'Early sources for the history of the first four Ghaznavid sultans (977–1040)', *IQ* VII (1963), pp. 3–22, reprinted in *The Medieval History of Iran, Afghanistan and Central Asia*, no. XIII.

——, 'On the chronology of the Ziyārids in Gurgān and Ṭabaristān', *Isl.* XL (1964), pp. 25–34, reprinted in *The Medieval History of Iran, Afghanistan and Central Asia*, no. II.

——, 'Notes on the pre-Ghaznavid history of eastern Afghanistan', *IQ* IX (1965), pp. 12–24, reprinted in *The Medieval History of Iran, Afghanistan and Central Asia*, no. XIV.

——, *Sīstān under the Arabs, from the Islamic Conquest to the Rise of the Ṣaffārids (30–250/651–864)*, IsMEO, Centro Studi e Scavi Archeologici in Asia, Reports and Memoirs XI (Rome, 1968).

——, 'The armies of the Ṣaffārids', *BSOAS* XXXI (1968), pp. 534–54, reprinted in *The Medieval History of Iran, Afghanistan and Central Asia*, no. XVII.

——, 'Abū ʿAbdallāh al-Khwārazmī on the technical terms of the secretary's art. A contribution to the administrative history of mediaeval Islam', *JESHO* XII (1969), pp. 113–64, reprinted in *Medieval Arabic Culture and Administration*, Variorum Reprints, Collected Studies Series CS 165 (London, 1982), no. XV.

——, ch. 'The Ṭāhirids and Ṣaffārids', in *The Cambridge History of Iran. Vol. 4. The Period from the Arab Invasion to the Saljuqs*, ed. Richard N. Frye (Cambridge, 1975), pp. 90–135.

——, ch. 'The early Ghaznavids', in *The Cambridge History of Iran. Vol. 4. The Period from the Arab Invasion to the Saljuqs*, ed. Richard N. Frye (Cambridge, 1975), pp. 162–97.

——, 'The rulers of Chaghāniyān in early Islamic times', *Iran JBIPS* XIX (1981), pp. 1–20, reprinted in C. Edmund Bosworth, *The Arabs, Byzantium and Islam. Studies in Early Islamic History and Culture*, Variorum Collected Studies Series CS 529 (Aldershot, Hants., 1996), no. XXI.

——, *The History of the Saffarids of Sistan and the Maliks of Nimruz (247/861 to 949/1542–3)*, Columbia Lectures on Iranian Studies 8 (Costa Mesa and New York, 1994).

——, 'Rulers of Makrān and Quṣdār in the early Islamic period', *St.Ir.* XXIII (1994), pp. 199–209.

——, *The New Islamic Dynasties. A Chronological and Genealogical Manual* (Edinburgh, 1996).

——, 'Notes on some Turkish names in Abu 'l-Faḍl Bayhaqī's *Tārīkh-i Masʿūdī*', *Oriens* XXXVI (2001), pp. 299–313.

——, 'Further notes on the Turkish names in Abu 'l-Faḍl Bayhaqī's *Tārīkh-i Masʿūdī*, to appear in *Festschrift for Dr Farhad Daftary* (London, 2010).

——, 'The appearance and establishment of Islam in Afghanistan', in *Islamisation de l'Asie centrale. Processus locaux d'acculturation du VIIe du XIe siècle*, ed. E. de la Vaissière, Cahiers de Studia Iranica, 39 (Paris, 2008), pp. 97–114.

Bosworth, C. Edmund and Sir Gerard Clauson, 'Al-Xwārazmī on the peoples of Central Asia', *JRAS* (1965), pp. 2–12, reprinted in C.E. Bosworth, *The Medieval History of Iran, Afghanistan and Central Asia*, Variorum Reprints, Collected Studies Series CS56 (London, 1977), no. XX.

Bowen, H., 'Notes on some early Seljuqid viziers', *BSOAS* XX (1957), pp. 105–10.

Cahen, Cl., 'Le Malik-nâmeh et l'histoire des origines seljukides', *Oriens* II (1949), pp. 31–65.

Clauson, Sir Gerard, *An Etymological Dictionary of Pre-Thirteenth Century Turkish* (Oxford, 1972).

Crone, Patricia, *Slaves on Horses. The Evolution of the Islamic Polity* (Cambridge, 1980).

Crone, Patricia and Luke Treadwell, 'A new text on Ismailism at the Samanid court', in *Texts, Documents and Artefacts. Islamic Studies in Honour of D.S. Richards*, ed. Chase F. Robinson (Leiden, 2003), pp. 37–67.

Czeglédy, K., 'Gardīzī on the history of Central Asia (AD 746–780)', *AOHung* XXVII (1973), pp. 257–67.

Daniel, Elton L., *The Political and Social History of Khurasan under Abbasid Rule 747–820*, Bibliotheca Islamica (Minneapolis and Chicago, 1979).

Doerfer, Gerhard, *Türkische und mongolische Elemente im Neupersischen, unter besonderer Berücksichtigung älterer neupersischer Geschichtsquellen, vor allem der Mongolen- und Timuridenzeit*, Akademie der Wissenschaften und der Literatur, Veröffentlichungen der Orientalischen Kommission, Bd. XVI, XIX–XXI, 4 vols. (Wiesbaden, 1963–75).

Eisener, Reinhard, *Zwischen Faktum und Fiktion. Eine Studie zum Umayyadenkalifen Sulaimān b. 'Abdalmalik und seinem Bild in den Quellen* (Wiesbaden, 1987).

Fedorov, Michael, 'The Khwarazmshahs of the Banū 'Irāq (fourth/tenth century)', *Iran JBIPS* XXXVIII (2000), pp. 71–5.

Frye, Richard N. ch. 'The Sāmānids', in *The Cambridge History of Iran. Vol. 4. The Period from the Arab Invasion to the Saljuqs*, ed. Richard N. Frye (Cambridge, 1975), pp. 136–61.

——, *Bukhara, the Medieval Achievement*, 2nd ed. (Costa Mesa, 1996).

Gelpke, Rudolf, *Sulṭān Mas'ūd I. von Ġazna. Die drei ersten Jahre seiner Herrschaft (421/1030–424/1033)*, Inaugural Dissertation . . . der Universität Basel (Munich, 1957).

Gibb, Hamilton A.R., *The Arab Conquests in Central Asia* (London, 1923).

Golden, Peter B., *An Introduction to the History of the Turkic Peoples. Ethnogenesis and State-Formation in Medieval and Early Modern Eurasia and the Middle East*, Turcologica Band 9 (Wiesbaden, 1992).

Halm, Heinz, 'Fatimiden und Ghaznawiden', in *Studies in Honour of Clifford Edmund Bosworth. Vol. I. Hunter of the East: Arabic and Semitic Studies*, ed. Ian R. Netton (Leiden, 2000), pp. 209–21.

Ḥamza b. al-Ḥasan al-Iṣfahānī, *Ta'rīkh Sinī mulūk al-arḍ wa 'l-anbiyā'* (Beirut, 1961).

Hodivala, S.H., *Studies in Indo-Muslim History. A Critical Commentary on Elliot and Dowson's History of India as Told by its Own Historians*, 2 vols. (Bombay, 1937–57).

Ibn Ḥawqal, Muḥammad b. 'Alī, *Kitāb Ṣūrat al-arḍ*, ed. J.H. Kramers, 2 vols. (Leiden, 1938–9), French tr. J.H. Kramers and Gaston Wiet as *Configuration de la terre*, Collection UNESCO d'œuvres représentatives, série arabe, 2 vols. (Paris, 1964).

Ibn Isfandiyār, Muḥammad b. Ḥasan, *Tārīkh-i Ṭabaristān*, partial English tr. E.G. Browne as *An Abridged Translation of the History of Ṭabaristán Compiled about AH 613 (AD 1216) by Muḥammad b. al-Ḥasan b. Isfandiyár*, GMS II (Leiden and London, 1905).

Ibn Khallikān, Aḥmad b. Muḥammad, *Wafayāt al-a'yān*, ed. Iḥsān 'Abbās, 8 vols. (Beirut, 1968–72), English tr. Baron McGuckin de Slane as *Ibn Khallikan's Biographical Dictionary*, 4 vols. (Paris, 1842–71).

Kaabi, Mongi, *Les Ṭāhirides au Ḫurāsān et en Iraq (IIIème H./IXème J.-C.)*, 2 vols. (Tunis, 1983).

Kennedy, Hugh, *The Early Abbasid Caliphate. A Political History* (London and Totowa, N.J., 1981).

Kraemer, Joel L., *Humanism in the Renaissance of Islam. The Cultural Revival during the Buyid Age* (Leiden, 1986).

Lassner, Jacob, *The Shaping of 'Abbāsid Rule* (Princeton, 1980).

Lazard, Gilbert, *La langue des plus anciens monuments de la prose persane*, Études linguistiques II (Paris, 1963).

Le Strange, Guy, *The Lands of the Eastern Caliphate. Mesopotamia, Persia, and Central Asia from the Moslem Conquest to the Time of Timur*, Cambridge Geographical Series (Cambridge, 1905).

Løkkegaard, Frede, *Islamic Taxation in the Classic Period, with Special Reference to the Circumstances in Iraq* (Copenhagen, 1950).

Madelung, Wilferd, ch. 'The minor dynasties of northern Iran', in *The Cambridge History of Iran. Vol. 4. The Period from the Arab Invasion to the Saljuqs*, ed. Richard N. Frye (Cambridge, 1975), pp. 198-249.

al-Maqdisī, Muḥammad b. Aḥmad, *Aḥsan al-taqāsīm fī ma'rifat al-aqālīm*, ed. M.J. De Goeje as *Descriptio imperii moslemici*, BGA III² (Leiden, 1906), partial French tr. André Miquel as *La meilleure rēpartition pour la connaissance des provinces* (Damascus, 1963).

Marquart, Josef, and J.J.M. de Groot, 'Das Reich Zābul und der Gott Žūn vom 6–9 Jahrhundert', in *Festschrift Eduard Sachau zum siebigsten Geburtstage gewidmet von Freunden und Schülern*, ed. Gotthold Weil (Berlin, 1915), pp. 248–92.

Martinez, A.P., 'Gardīzī's two chapters on the Turks', *AEMAe* II (1982), pp. 109–217.

Meisami, Julie S., *Persian Historiography to the End of the Twelfth Century* (Edinburgh, 1999).

Minorsky, Vladimir, *Sharaf al-Zamān Ṭāhir Marvazī on China, the Turks and India*, Royal Asiatic Society, James G. Forlong Fund Vol. XXII (London, 1942).

——, 'Gardīzī on India', *BSOAS* XII (1947–9), pp. 625–40, reprinted in *Iranica. Twenty Articles/ Bīst maqāla-yi Mīnūrskī*, Publications of the University of Tehran no. 775 (Tehran, 1964), pp. 200–15.

Mottahedeh, Roy, ch. 'The 'Abbāsid caliphate in Iran', in *The Cambridge History of Iran. Vol. 4. The Period from the Arab Invasion to the Saljuqs*, ed. Richard N. Frye (Cambridge, 1975), pp. 57–89.

Narshakhī, Muḥammad b. Ja'far, *Tārīkh-i Bukhārā*, English tr. Richard N. Frye as *The History of Bukhara. Translated from a Persian Abridgement of the Arabic Original by Narshakhī* (Cambridge, Mass., 1954).

Nāẓim, Muḥammad, *The Life and Times of Sulṭān Maḥmūd of Ghazna* (Cambridge, 1931).

Omar, Farouk, *'Abbāsiyyāt. Studies in the History of the Early 'Abbāsids*, publication subsidised by the University of Baghdad No. 104 (Baghdad, 1976).

Peacock, Andrew C.S., *Mediaeval Islamic Historiography and Political Legitimacy. Bal'amī's Tārīkhnāma*, Routledge Studies in the History of Iran and Turkey (London and New York, 2007).

Pritsak, Omeljan, 'Die Karachaniden', *Isl.* XXXI (1953–4), pp. 17–68, reprinted in O. Pritsak, *Studies in Medieval Eurasian History*, Variorum Reprints, Collected Studies Series CS 132 (London, 1981), no. XVI.

Rásonyi, Láslo and Imre Baski, *Onomasticon turcicum. Turkic Personal Names as Collected by László Rásonyi*, Indian University Uralic and Altaic Series, Vol. 172, 2 vols. (Bloomington, Ind., 2007).

Ray, H.C., *The Dynastic History of Northern India (Early Mediaeval Period)*. 2 vols. (Calcutta, 1931–6).

Sadighi, Gholam-Hossein, *Les mouvements religieux iraniens au IIᵉ et au IIIᵉ siècle de l'Hégire* (Paris, 1938).

Scarcia Amoretti, B., ch. 'Sects and heresies', in *The Cambridge History of Iran. Vol. 4. The Period from the Arab Invasion to the Saljuqs*, ed. Richard N. Frye (Cambridge, 1975), pp. 481–519.

Shaban, Muhammad A., *The 'Abbāsid Revolution* (Cambridge, 1970).

Sharon, Moshe, *Black Banners from the East. The Establishment of the 'Abbāsid State – Incubation of a Revolt*, The Max Schloessinger Memorial Series, Monographs II (Jerusalem, Leiden, 1983).

——, *Black Banners from the East II. Revolt. The Social and Military Aspects of the 'Abbāsid Revolution*, The Max Schloessinger Memorial Series, Monographs V (Jerusalem, 1990).

Storey, Charles A., *Persian Literature. A Bio-bibliographical Survey. Vol. I. Qur'ānic Literature; History and Biography* (London, 1927–53).

Sümer, Faruk, *Türk devletleri tarihinde şahis adları*, ed. Turan Yazgan, 2 vols. (Istanbul, 1995).

al-Ṭabarī, Muḥammad b. Jarīr, *Ta'rīkh al-Rusul wa 'l-mulūk*, ed. M.J. De Goeje *et al.*, 15 vols. (Leiden, 1879–1901), English tr. *The History of al-Ṭabarī, an Annotated Translation. Vol. XXIV. The Empire in Transition. The Caliphates of Sulaymān, 'Umar, and Yazīd AD 715–724/AH 97–105*, tr. David S. Powers (Albany, 1989); *Vol. XXVII. The 'Abbāsid Revolution. AD 743–750/AH 126–132*, tr. John A. Williams (Albany, 1985); *Vol. XXVIII. 'Abbāsid Authority Affirmed. The Early Years of al-Manṣūr AD 753–763/AH 136–145*, tr. Jane D. McAuliffe (Albany, 1995); *Vol. XXX. The 'Abbāsid Caliphate in Equilibrium. The Caliphates of Mūsā al-Hādī and Hārūn al-Rashīd AD 785–809/AH 169–193*, tr. C. Edmund Bosworth (Albany, 1989).

Tor, Deborah G., *Violent Order: Religious Warfare, Chivalry, and the* 'Ayyār *Phenomenon in the Medieval Islamic World*, Istanbuler Texte und Studien, Band 11 (Würzburg, 2007).

Treadwell, W. Luke, 'Ibn Ẓāfir al-Azdī's account of the murder of Aḥmad b. Ismā'īl al-Sāmānī and the succession of his son Naṣr', in *Studies in Honour of Clifford Edmund Bosworth. Vol. II. The Sultan's Turret: Studies in Persian and Turkish Culture*, ed. Carole Hillenbrand (Leiden, 2000), pp. 397–419.

——, 'The account of the Samanid dynasty in Ibn Ẓāfir al-Azdī's *Akhbār al-duwal al-munqaṭi'a*', *Iran JBIPS*, XLIII (2005), pp. 135–71.

Walker, John, *A Catalogue of the Muhammadan Coins in the British Museum. Vol. I. A Catalogue of the Arab-Sassanian Coins (Umaiyad Governors in the East, Arab-Ephthalites, 'Abbāsid Governors in Ṭabaristān and Bukhārā)* (London, 1941).

Wellhausen, Julius, *The Arab Kingdom and Its Fall*, English tr. Margaret G. Weir (Calcutta, 1927).

al-Ya'qūbī, Aḥmad b. Abī Ya'qūb, *Kitāb al-Buldān*, ed. M.J. De Goeje, BGA VII (Leiden, 1892), French tr. Gaston Wiet as *Les pays* (Cairo, 1937).

Yāqūt b. 'Abdallāh al-Ḥamawī al-Rūmī, *Mu'jam al-buldān*, 5 vols. (Beirut, 1374–6/1955–7).

Zarrīnkūb, 'Abd al-Ḥusain, ch. 'The Arab conquest of Iran and its aftermath', in *The Cambridge History of Iran. Vol. IV. The Period from the Arab Invasion to the Saljuqs*, ed. Richard N. Frye (Cambridge, 1975), pp. 1–56.

INDICES

1. Persons, peoples, tribes

ʿAbbās b. Dāwūd 65
ʿAbbās b. Jaʿfar b. Muḥammad b. al-Ashʿath 37
ʿAbbās b. Shaqīq (? Shafīq) 60
ʿAbda b. Qadīd 33
ʿAbdallāh b. ʿAbbās, governor in Sistan
ʿAbdallāh b. ʿAlī, ʿAbbāsid, uncle of the caliph al-Saffāḥ 23, 29, 30
ʿAbdallāh b. ʿĀmir b. Kurayz 2, 13, 14, 15, 16–17
ʿAbdallāh b. Ḥumayd b. Qaḥṭaba 34
ʿAbdallāh b. Khāzim 13, 16, 19
ʿAbdallāh al-Laythī 17
ʿAbdallāh b. Muḥammad b. ʿAbd al-Razzāq 94
ʿAbdallāh b. Muḥammad b. Ṣāliḥ Sagzī 47, 48
ʿAbdallāh b. Muḥammad b. ʿUzayr, Samanid vizier 74 77
ʿAbdallāh b. Samura al-Umawī 16
ʿAbdallāh b. Ṭāhir, Tahirid amir 26, 44–5
ʿAbdallāh b. Zubayr 18, 19
ʿAbd al-ʿAzīz b. Nūḥ (I), Samanid 65, 74
ʿAbd al-ʿAzīz b. al-Walīd, Umayyad 21
ʿAbd al-Ghaffār b. Ṣāliḥ Ṭālaqānī 32
ʿAbd al-Jabbār b. ʿAbd al-Raḥmān 32
ʿAbd al-Malik b. Marwān, Umayyad caliph 19, 20
ʿAbd al-Malik (I) b. Nūḥ (I) al-Rashīd, Samanid amir 65–7
ʿAbd al-Malik (II) b. Nūḥ (II), Samanid amir 78–9
ʿAbd al-Raḥmān b. Abzā al-Khuzāʿī 16
ʿAbd al-Raḥmān b. Jabala 40
ʿAbd al-Raḥmān the Kharijite 47
ʿAbd al-Raḥmān Nīshābūrī 39–40
ʿAbd al-Raḥmān b. Nuʿaym al-Ghāmidī 24
ʿAbd al-Raḥmān b. Ziyād 18
ʿAbd al-Rashīd b. Masʿūd, Ghaznavid sultan 1, 5, 112–13
ʿAbd al-Salām b. Muzāḥim 26
ʿAbd al-Ṣamad b. ʿAlī b. ʿAbdallāh, ʿAbbasid 29
ʿAbdūs, Abū Saʿd 104
Abu ʾl-ʿAbbās ʿAbdallāh b. Muḥammad b. Nūḥ b. Asad, Samanid 54
Abu ʾl-ʿAbbās Aḥmad b. Ḥamūya 61
Abu ʾl-ʿAbbās al-Faḍl al-Ṭūsī 36
Abu ʾl-ʿAbbās Muḥammad b. Ṣulūk 56
Abū ʿAbdallāh, Afrīghid Khwarazm Shah 76
Abū ʿAbdallāh b. ʿAlī b. al-Layth, Saffarid 55
Abū ʿAbdallāh b. Ḥafṣ, Ghāzī 70–1
Abū ʿAlī b. Isḥāq 63
Abu ʾl-ʿAskar, Maʿdānid of Makrān 103
Abū ʿAwn ʿAbd al-Malik b. Yazīd 29, 33, 34–5
Abū Bakr al-Khabbāz 59
Abū Bakr al-Ṣiddīq, Rightly-Guided caliph 13
Abū Dāwūd Khālid b. Ibrāhīm, *naqīb* 26, 28, 31–2
Abu ʾl-Ḥārith b. Abu ʾl-Qāsim 63
Abu ʾl-Ḥasan Aḥmad b. Muḥammad 55
Abu ʾl-Ḥasan Naṣr b. Isḥāq 56
Abū Jaʿfar, Samanid, nephew of al-Muntaṣir 83
Abū Jaʿfar Ghūrī 58
Abū Jaʿfar Ṣuʿlūk 55, 58
Abū Jaʿfar Ziyādī 69–70
Abū Kālījār, Ziyārid 105

Abu 'l-Khaṣīb, Ḥājib 31
Abū Manṣūr Aflaḥ b. Muḥammad b. Khāqān 47
Abū Manṣūr Muḥammad b. ʿUzayr, Samanid vizier 65, 66
Abū Muslim al-Khurāsānī 2, 3, 4, 27–31, 34
Abu 'l-Najm b. ʿImrān, *naqīb* 26
Abū Naṣr b. Aḥmad b. Abī Zayd 73, 76
Abū Nuʿmān 34
Abū Saʿīd Bakr b. Mālik 65–6
Abū Saʿīd Shaybī 73
Abū Salama al-Khallāl 29
Abū Ṭalḥa Jaʿfar b. Mardānshāh 64
ʿAdī b. Arṭāt al-Fazārī 23
ʿAḍud al-Dawla Fanākhusraw b. Rukn al-Dawla, Buyid amir 70, 72
Aḥmad, brother of Bars 63
Aḥmad b. ʿAbdallāh 55
Aḥmad (I) b. Asad, Samanid amir 53
Aḥmad Darāz 51
Aḥmad [b.] Ināltegin or Yināltegin 5, 103, 106–7
Aḥmad (II) b. Ismāʿīl al-Shahīd, Samanid amir 54, 55–6
Aḥmad b. Jaʿfar, amir of Khuttalān 63
Aḥmad b. Manna 49
Aḥmad b. Manṣūr b. Qarategin 69
Aḥmad b. Muḥammad, Ghaznavid 113
Aḥmad b. Muḥammad b. ʿAbd al-Ṣamad, Ghaznavid vizier 104, 108, 111, 112
Aḥmad b. Mujīb 47
Ahmad, Nazir 9
Aḥmad b. Nūḥ (I), Samanid 65
Aḥmad b. Sahl 54, 57–8
al-Aḥnaf b. Qays 14
ʿAlā' b. Ḥurayth, *naqīb* 26
al-ʿAlawī, Ḥasan b. Ṭāhir 87
ʿAlī b. ʿAbdallāh b. al-ʿAbbās, ʿAbbasid 28
ʿAlī b. Abī Ṭālib, Rightly-Guided caliph 16
ʿAlī Dāya, Abu 'l-Ḥasan, Ḥājib 101, 102, 111
ʿAlī b. ʿĪsā b. Māhān 2, 38–9
ʿAlī b. Judayʿ al-Kirmānī 28
ʿAlī b. Kāma 72
ʿAlī b. al-Marzubān 65–6
ʿAlī b. Masʿūd (II), Ghaznavid sultan 5
ʿAlī b. Qadīr Rāḥūq (?) 91
ʿAlī Qarīb b. Il Arslān 91, 99, 100, 102
ʿAlī b. al-Qāsim 69
ʿAlī Quhandizī 109
ʿAlī b. Sharwīn 51
ʿAlī b. Yaʿqūb b. Muḥammad b. ʿAmr b. al-Layth, Saffarid amir 55–6
ʿAlītegin b. Hārūn or Ḥasan Bughra Khān, Qarakhanid 93, 95
Alptegin Bukhārī 88–9
Alptegin, Ḥājib 66, 67–8, 74
Altuntāsh, Ḥājib, Khwarazm Shah 85, 89, 93
al-Amīn, Muḥammad, ʿAbbasid caliph 2, 3, 36, 38, 53
ʿĀmir b. Ḍubāra 28
ʿĀmir b. Ismāʿīl 29
Amīrak Ṭūsī 77
ʿAmr and ʿĪsā, sons of Aʿyan, *naqībs* 26
ʿAmr b. al-ʿĀṣ 16
ʿAmr b. al-Layth, Saffarid amir 2, 49–51, 54, 58
ʿAmr b. Muslim 22
ʿAmr b. Yazīd al-Azdī 38
ʿAmr b. Zurāra al-Qasrī 26
Anandpāl, Ānandpāla, Hindu king 85
Aparwīz, Khusraw (II), son of Hurmuz, Sasanid emperor 23
Ardashīr Bābakān, Sasanid emperor 13
Arends, A.K. 8–9
Arslān Jādhib 83, 85, 96, 98
Asad b. ʿAbdallāh al-Qasrī 24, 25–6
Ashʿath b. Muḥammad al-Yashkurī 69
Ashnās 51
Ashras b. ʿAbdallāh 25
ʿĀṣim b. ʿAbdallāh al-Hilālī 25
Aslam b. Zurāra al-Kilābī 18
Ayāz b. Aymaq or Uymaq 101, 102
Azd 32
ʿAzīz b. Nūḥ, Samanid 44

Bābak Khurram-dīn 44
Badr al-Kabīr 50
Bahār, Malik al-Shuʿarā' 6
Baḥīr b. Warqā' 19
Baḥr b. Dirham 24
Bājī Rāy, Hindu king 84
Bajkam, Khuttalī commander 63
Bajkam Mākānī 60
Bakr b. al-ʿAbbās, *naqīb* 26
al-Balʿamī, Abū ʿAlī Muḥammad b. Muḥammad, Samanid vizier 67, 69
al-Balʿamī, Abu 'l-Faḍl Muḥammad b. ʿUbaydallāh, Samanid vizier 59, 60
Bānha b. Muḥammad b. M.l.l.y, 106–7
Bānījūr 40
Barāz b. Māhūya 15, 16
Barāz-banda b. B.m.rūn, claimant to be Ibrāhīm b. ʿAbdallāh al-Hāshimī 32
al-Barghashī, Abu 'l-Muẓaffar Muḥammad b. Ibrāhīm, Samanid vizier 77, 78

al-Barmakī, Abu 'l-Qāsim al-'Abbās b. Muḥammad, Samanid vizier 78
Bārs, Samanid commander 54
Barthold, W. 7
Bassām, *mawlā* of the Banū Layth 15
Bayhaqī, Abu 'l-Faḍl 1, 4, 5, 6, 9–10
Bāyjūr 63
Bāytūz 72
B.b.dāḥ (?) 68
Begtughdï, Ḥājib 105, 106, 110
Begtuzūn 74, 77, 78
Bhīmdeva, Hindu king 97
Bihāfarīd 4, 28–9
Bilgetegin, Ḥājib 95
al-Bīrūnī, Abu 'l-Rayḥān 1
Bīsutūn b. Wushmgīr, Ziyārid 64
Böritegin, Ibrāhīm b. Naṣr, Qarakhanid 108
Bosworth, C.E. 10
Budayl b. Warqā' 19
Buḥayj, Ibn 83
Bukayr b. Wishāḥ 19
Bukhār-Khudāh 29

Carmathians, Bāṭinīs, Ismā'īlīs 86, 87, 100
Chaghānī, Abū 'Alī Aḥmad b. Muḥammad b. al-Muẓaffar 60, 61–6
Chaghānī, Abū Bakr Muḥammad b. al-Muẓaffar b. Muḥtāj 55, 60
Chaghānī, Abū Manṣūr Naṣr b. Abī 'Alī 64
Chaghānī, Abu 'l-Muẓaffar 'Abdallāh b. Abī 'Ali Aḥmad 63–4
Chaghrï Beg Dāwūd, Seljuq chief 106, 108–9
Chakraswāmī, Hindu idol 86–7
Chandra Rāy, Hindu king 90
Czeglédy, K. 6

al-Ḍaḥḥāk b. Qays al-Fihrī, Kharijite 27
Dārā b. Qābūs, Ziyārid 75, 78
al-Dāmghānī, Abū 'Alī Muḥammad b. 'Īsā, Samanid vizier 73
Dāwūd b. al-'Abbās b. Hāshim b. Bānījūr 47
Dāwūd b. Naṣr, amir of Multān
Dāwūd b. Yazīd b. Ḥātim 37
Daypāl Haryāna, Hindu king 107–8
Dhimmīs 25
Dhūbān the Astrologer 40
Ḍirār b. Ḥuṣayn al-Ḍabbī 21
Durayd b. al-Ṣimma 17

Epifanova, L.M. 9
Ertegin, Ḥājib 111, 113
Eryārūq, Ḥājib 103

al-Faḍl b. Muḥammad b. Ṣāliḥ Sagzī 47, 48
al-Faḍl b. al-Rabī' 40
al-Faḍl b. Sahl 33, 40, 41, 43
al-Faḍl b. Yaḥyā al-Barmakī 37–8
Fādūspān, *dihqān* of Nishapur 28
Fā'iq Khāṣṣa 70, 72–4, 75, 77, 78
Fakhr al-Dawla 'Alī b. Rukn al-Dawla, Buyid amir 73, 76, 77
al-Fārisī, Abū Muḥammad 'Abd al-Raḥmān b. Aḥmad, Samanid vizier 73
Fragner, Bert 2

Ganda, Hindu king 90–1, 92
Gardīzī, Abū Mursil Manṣūr b. Aflaḥ 1, 102
Gardīzī, Abū Sa'īd 'Abd al-Ḥayy 1ff., 81
Ghālib, uncle of al-Ma'mūn 33
Ghālib b. Ustādsīs 41
Ghassān b. 'Abbād 41, 51
Ghāzī, *ākhur-sālār* 85
Ghāzī, Ḥājib 99
Ghiṭrīf b. 'Aṭā' al-Kindī 36, 37
Ghuzz, Oghuz, Turkmens 83, 98–9, 104, 105, 106, 109ff.

Ḥabībī, 'Abd al-Ḥayy 7–8
al-Hādī, 'Abbasid caliph 36
Ḥafṣ b. Manṣūr al-Marwazī 38
Ḥafṣa bt. Sahl 58
Ḥājj Aḥmad, mu'addil 44
al-Ḥajjāj b. Yūsuf 15, 18, 20–1
Ḥakam b. 'Amr al-Ghifārī 17
Ḥakam Ṭālaqānī 35
Ḥakīm Bukhārī 34
al-Ḥākimī, Abu 'l-Faḍl Muḥammad b. Muḥammad, Samanid vizier 61, 62
al-Ḥamūlī, Abu 'l-Ḥusayn b. Muḥammad, Samanid vizier 178
Ḥamūya b. 'Alī 57, 59
Ḥamza b. Ādharak 38–9, 43
Ḥarb b. Ziyād 32
Hardat, Hindu king 89
al-Ḥārith b. Surayj 25, 27
Harthama b. A'yan 39–40
Hārūn or Ḥasan Bughra Khān, Qarakhanid 73
Hārūn b. Sulaymān, Abū Mūsā, Ilig Khān, Qarakhanid 74
Ḥasan b. 'Alī b. Abī Ṭālib 16
Ḥasan-i Būya, Rukn al-Dawla Ḥasan, Buyid amir 64–5, 65–6, 68–9, 70
Ḥasan b. Ḥumrān 33
Ḥasan b. Pīrūzān 65
Ḥasan Uṭrūsh, 'Alid 56

Ḥasan b. Zayd, ʿAlid 46, 48
Ḥasanak, Ḥasan b. Muḥammad Mīkālī 103
Ḥātim b. al-Nuʿmān al-Bāhilī 14
Hephthalites 14, 17
Hind bt. Muhallab 20
Hishām, Umayyad caliph 24–6
Hodivala, S.H. 9
Ḥuḍayn, Kharijite 37
Ḥumayd b. Qaḥṭaba 33–4
Ḥusayn b. ʿAlī b. ʿĪsā 38–9
Ḥusayn b. ʿAlī al-Marwazī 55, 56, 57, 59
Ḥusayn b. ʿAlī b. Mīkāʾīl 105
Ḥusayn b. Maʿdān, Maʿdānid of Makrān 103
Ḥusayn b. Muʿādh 34, 35
Ḥusayn b. Ṭāhir, Saffarid 72
Ḥ.ykān (? Jaykān) the Qurʾān-reader 49

Ibn al-ʿAmīd, Abu ʾl-Faḍl, Buyid vizier 65
Ibn al-ʿAmīd, Abu ʾl-Fatḥ, Buyid vizier 70
Ibn al-Ashʿath, ʿAbd al-Raḥmān b. Muḥammad 20
Ibrāhīm and Yaḥyā, sons of Zaydūya 55
Ibrāhīm b. ʿAbdallāh, al-Imām, ʿAbbasid 27, 29
Ibrāhīm b. Abu ʾl-Ḥasan 63
Ibrāhīm b. Aḥmad, Tahirid retainer 48
Ibrāhīm b. Aḥmad (II), uncle of Amir Nūḥ (I) b. Naṣr (II), Samanid 59, 62
Ibrāhīm b. Alptegin, Ḥājib 66
Ibrāhīm b. al-Ashtar 18
Ibrāhīm b. Jibrāʾīl 38
Ibrāhīm b. Ṣāliḥ al-Marwazī 47
Ibrāhīm b. Sīmjūr 61, 62
Ibrāhīm b. al-Walīd (I), Umayyad caliph 27
Ibrāhīm b. Zaydūya 55
ʿIkrima, *mawlā* of ʿAbdallah b. al-ʿAbbās 15
Īkūtegin Ḥājib 109
Il-Mengü 77
Ilyās b. Asad, Samanid 53
Ilyās b. Isḥāq b. Aḥmad (II), Samanid 57
Inanch Ḥājib 74
ʿĪsā b. ʿAlī b. ʿĪsā 39
Isḥāq b. Aḥmad (II), Samanid 57
Ismāʿīl b. Aḥmad (I), Samanid 4, 51, 53–5, 58
Ismāʿīl b. Ḥammād 44
Ismāʿīl b. Naṣr (II), Samanid 61
Ismāʿīl b. Sebüktegin, Ghaznavid 77–8
Ismāʿīl b. Ṭoghān 70

Jabūya, in Farghāna 37
Jaʿda b. Hubayra al-Makhzūmī 16
Jaʿfar b. Baghlāghuz (?) 50–1
Jaʿfar b. Ḥanẓala 26
Jaʿfar b. Muḥammad b. al-Ashʿath 37
Jaʿfar b. Sh.mānīqwā (?) 63
Jaʿfar b. Yaḥyā al-Barmakī 38
Jahm b. Ṣafwān 27
Jarīr b. Yazīd al-Bajalī 30–1
Jarrāḥ b. ʿAbdallāh al-Ḥakamī 23
al-Jayhānī, Abū ʿAbdallāh Muḥammad b. Aḥmad (? b. Muḥammad), Samanid vizier 57, 60
al-Jayhānī, Abū ʿAbdallāh Aḥmad b. Muḥammad, Samanid vizier 70
Jaypāl, Jayapāla, Hindu king 84
Jhats 97–8
Jibrāʾīl b. Yaḥyā 34, 35
Judayʿ b. ʿAlī al-Kirmānī 27
Jumhūr b. Murār 30
Junayd b. ʿAbd al-Raḥmān 25
Justān b. Wahsūdān, Justānid ruler in Daylam 54
Jūzjānī, Minhāj al-Dīn 8

Kābul Shāh 47
Kāmgar 58
Khalaf b. Aḥmad, Saffarid amir 72, 76, 82, 84
Khalaj 76
Khālid b. ʿAbdallāh al-Qasrī 19, 24, 25–6
Khālid b. al-Walīd 13
Khāqān of the Turks 25
Khārākhuruh, ruler of Ushrūsana 38
Khārija, partisan of al-Muqannaʿ 35
Kharijites, Ḥarūrīs 27, 38–9, 43, 44, 47
al-Khaṭṭāb b. Yazīd 32
Khātūn, ancestress of Bukhār Khudāt 17, 18
Khāzim b. Khuzayma 32–3
al-Khujistānī, Aḥmad 49
al-Khunāmatī, Abu ʾl-Faḍl Muḥammad b. Aḥmad, Samanid vizier 78
Khurāsha b. Sinān, Kharijite 38
Khuzāʿa 32
Krishna, son of Bāsdīv 89
Kulchandra, Kulachand 89
Kumījīs 63

Lāḥiz b. Qurayẓ, *naqīb* 26
Layth b. Saʿd 41
Lazard, Gilbert 6

al-Mahdī, ʿAbbasid caliph 32, 34–6, 38

Mahdī, in Chaghāniyān 64
Mahdī, son of Muḥsin 47
Maḥmūd b. Sebüktegin, Ghaznavid sultan 4, 5, 76, 77–8, 81–100
Maḥmūdiyān or Pidariyān 5
Māhrūy 83
Majd al-Dawla, Rustam b. Fakhr al-Dawla, Buyid amir 99, 103
Majdūd b. Mas'ūd (I), Ghaznavid 105, 108
Mākān b. Kākī 60
Mākān b. Kākī, son of 65
Malik, Raḥīm Riḍāzāda 8
Malik b. Dīnār 18
Malik b. al-Haytham, *naqīb* 26
al-Ma'mūn, 'Abdallāh, 'Abbasid caliph 2, 3, 33, 38, 43–4, 53
al-Ma'mūn (II) b. al-Ma'mūn (I), Abu 'l-'Abbās, Khwarazm Shah 88
al-Ma'mūn (I), Abū 'Abdallāh, Khwarazm Shah 76
Manāt, goddess 96–7
Manṣūr b. Aḥmad (II), Samanid amir 59
Manṣūr b. 'Alī 57
Manṣūr b. Bayqarā, Abū Naṣr 66
Manṣūr b. Isḥāq, Abū Ṣāliḥ, Samanid 54, 55–6
Manṣūr (I) b. Nūḥ (I) al-Sadīd, Samanid amir 67–70
Manṣūr (II) b. Nūḥ (I), Samanid amir 77–8
Manṣūr b. Qarategin 62, 64
Manṣūr b. Yazīd 38
Marājil, mother of al-Ma'mūn 33
Mardāwīz b. Ziyār, Ziyārid amir 60
Maris 83
Martinez, A.P. 6
Marwān (II) b. Muḥammad, al-Ḥimār, Umayyad caliph 27, 29
al-Marwazī, Ḥafṣ b. Manṣūr 2, 38
Marwazī, Sharaf al-Zamān Ṭāhir 7–8
Maslama b. 'Abd al-Malik, Umayyad 23
Mas'ūd (I) b. Maḥmūd, Ghaznavid sultan 1, 5, 89, 97, 101, 102–11
Mas'ūd (II) b. Mawdūd, Ghaznavid sultan 5
Mas'ūdiyān or Naw-khāstagān 5
Mawdūd b. Mas'ūd (I), Ghaznavid sultan 4, 5, 107, 111, 112–13
al-Maymandī, Abu 'l-Qāsim Aḥmad b. Ḥasan, Ghaznavid vizier 5, 103, 104
Māzyār b. Qārin 44–5
Meisami, Julie 3–4
Mengütirek, Ḥājib 102
Mihrān, *mawlā* of 'Ubaydallāh b. Ziyād 15
Mīkālī, Abū Naṣr Aḥmad b. 'Alī 71
Milḥān Gūyānī 14
Minorsky, V. 7–8, 9
Mu'addal b. 'Alī b. al-Layth, Saffarid amir 55
Mu'ādh Faryābī 35
Mu'ādh b. Muslim, forbear of the later Mu'ādhīs 15
Mu'ādh b. Muslim, governor of Khurasan for al-Mahdī 35
Mu'āwiya b. Abī Sufyān, Umayyad caliph 16, 17, 18
Mu'āwiya b. 'Ubaydallāh 32
Mu'ayyid al-Dawla, Abū Manṣūr 'Alī b. Rukn al-Dawla, Buyid 72
Muḍar 19, 27
al-Mufaḍḍal b. al-Muhallab 20
al-Muhallab b. Abī Ṣufra 17, 18, 20
Muḥammad b. al-'Abbās, 'Son of the Grave-Digger' 55–8
Muḥammad b. 'Abd al-Razzāq, Abū Manṣūr 66–8
Muḥammad b. 'Abd al-Ṣamad 54
Muḥammad b. 'Abdallāh b. Khāzim 19
Muḥammad b. Aḥmad, Abu 'l-'Abbās 63
Muḥammad b. Aḥmad b. Farīghūn, Abu 'l-Ḥārith 70, 76
Muḥammad b. Ajhad 57
Muḥammad b. 'Alī al-Imām, 'Abbasid 23–4, 26
Muḥammad b. Bishr 49–50, 51
Muḥammad b. Ḥamīd/Ḥumayd al-Ṭāhirī 43–4
Muḥammad b. Hārūn 54
Muḥammad b. Hurmuz, Mawlā Ṣandalī 55–6
Muḥammad b. al-Ḥusayn b. Muṣ'ab, Tahirid 41
Muḥammad b. al-Ḥusayn b. Mut, Abū Manṣūr 77
Muḥammad b. Ibrāhīm al-Ṭā'ī 88
Muḥammad b. Maḥmūd, Ghaznavid sultan 5, 89, 97, 100–2, 103, 111–13
Muḥammad b. al-Muhallab b. Zurāra al-Marwazī 57
Muḥammad b. al-Munawwar 8
Muḥammad b. Naṣr (II) b. Aḥmad (II), Samanid 62
Muḥammad b. N.w.la 47
Muḥammad b. Ṭāhir (II), Tahirid 46, 47–8
Muḥammad b. Ṭoghān 61
Muḥammad b. Zayd b. Muḥammad, 'Alid 54
al-Muhtadī, 'Abbasid caliph 46

Muhtājids 2
Mujāshiʿ b. Masʿūd 17
Mukhallad b. Yazīd b. al-Muhallab 22, 23–4
al-Muktafī, ʿAbbasid caliph 50, 54, 55
al-Muntaṣir, ʿAbbasid caliph 45–6
al-Muntaṣir, Abū Ibrāhīm Ismāʿīl, Samanid amir 82–3, 84
al-Muqannaʿ 4, 34–6
al-Muqtadir, ʿAbbasid caliph 55
Murār b. Anas 29
Mūsā b. Kaʿb, *naqīb* 26
Mūsā Yabghu, Seljuq 109
Muṣʿab b. Ruzayq 35
Muṣʿ ab b. al-Zubayr 19
Musayyab b. Zuhayr 35–6
Muslim b. Saʿd b. Aslam 24
al-Mustaʿīn, ʿAbbasid caliph 46
al-Muʿtaḍid, ʿAbbasid caliph 50, 51, 54
al-Muʾtaman b. al-Rashīd, ʿAbbasid 40
al-Muʿtamid, ʿAbbasid caliph 46, 48–9
al-Muʿtaṣim, ʿAbbasid caliph 44–5
al-Mutawakkil, ʿAbbasid caliph 45, 46
al-Muṭīʿ, ʿAbbasid caliph 66, 69
al-Muttaqī, ʿAbbāsid caliph 60
al-Muwaffaq, ʿAbbasid 48–9
al-Muzanī, Abu ʾl-Ḥasan Muḥammad b. Muḥammad, Samanid vizier 72–3

Narshakhī 4
Naṣr, *sharāb-dār* 64
Naṣr b. Aḥmad (I), Samanid amir 53–4
Naṣr (II) b. Aḥmad (II) al-Saʿīd, Samanid amir 56–60
Naṣr b. ʿAlī, Arslān Ilig, Qarakhanid 77, 78–9, 82–3, 86
Naṣr al-Mukhtārī 50
Naṣr b. Nūḥ (I), Samanid 65
Naṣr (Naḍr) b. Ṣāliḥ 47
Naṣr b. Sayyār 3, 24, 26–8
Naṣr b. Sebüktegin, Ghaznavid 78, 82–3, 92
Naṣr b. Shabath 43
Nazim, Muhammad 7, 9
Nubāta b. Ḥanẓala 28
Nūḥ b. Asad, Samanid 41, 53
Nūḥ (II) b. Manṣūr (II) al-Raḍī, al-Riḍā, Samanid amir 70–7
Nūḥ (I) b. Naṣr (II) al-Ḥamīd, Samanid amir 60–5

Ögretmish 54

Peacock, Andrew C.S. 5
Pīrūz, *mawlā* of Ḥuṣayn b. Mālik al-ʿAnbarī 15
Pīrūz b. K.b.k 47

Qābūs b. Wushmgīr, Ziyārid amir 72
al-Qādir, ʿAbbasid caliph 77, 82, 97, 102, 103
al-Qāhir, ʿAbbasid caliph 59
Qaḥṭaba b. Shabīb, *naqīb* 26, 27–9
al-Qāʾim, ʿAbbasid caliph 2, 3
Qarategin al-Isfījābī 59
Qawām al-Dawla b. Bahāʾ al-Dawla, Abu ʾl-Fawāris, Buyid 87
Qays b. al-Haytham al-Sulamī 14
al-Qazwīnī, Aḥmad b. Muḥammad b. ʿAlī 62
Qazwīnī, Mīrzā Muḥammad 7
Qitā Khān 97
Qutayba b. Muslim al-Bāhilī 21–2
Qut-tegin, treasurer 63, 66

Rabīʿ b. al-Ḥārithī 17
Rabīʿ b. Ziyād 15
Rabīʿa 27
al-Rāḍī, ʿAbbasid caliph 60
Rāfiʿ b. Harthama 50
Rāfiʿ b. al-Layth b. Naṣr b. Sayyār 39–40
Rajāʾ b. Ḥaywa al-Kindī 20
Rājyapāl, Rājyapāla, Hindu king 90
Rām, Rāma, Hindu king 87, 108
al-Rashīd, Hārūn, ʿAbbasid caliph 36–40
Ratbīl/Zunbīl 20, 47
Raverty, H.G. 8
al-Riḍā, ʿAlī b. Mūsā, Eighth Imām of the Shīʿa 41
Rustam b. Farrukh 13
Ruzgānī, Abū Isḥāq 63

al-Saffāḥ, Abu ʾl-ʿAbbās, ʿAbbasid caliph 29–31
Safīd-jāmagān 'Wearers of White' 4, 31–2
al-Ṣāḥib Ibn ʿAbbād, Buyid vizier 76
Sahl b. Ḥamdān 50
Sahl b. Hāshim 58
Saʿīd b. ʿAbd al-ʿAzīz 24
Saʿīd b. ʿAmr al-Ḥarashī 24
Saʿīd b. Bashīr 36
Saʿīd Ḥarashī 35, 36
Saʿīd Jawlāh 32
Saʿīd b. Manṣūr b. Yazīd 38
Saʿīd b. ʿUthmān b. ʿAffān, Umayyad 18
Salama, mother of al-Manṣūr 31
Salama b. Muslim 35
Sālār b. Shīrdīl 69
Ṣāliḥ b. ʿAbd al-Raḥmān 15

al-Sallāmī, Abū ʿAlī al-Ḥusayn 2, 3
Salm b. Aḥwaz 26
Salm b. Ziyād 18–19
Sāmān Khudā 53
Sawwār 53
Sebük-eri 58
Sebüktegin, Ghaznavid 4, 74–7
Seljuqs 93ff., and see Ghuzz, Oghuz, Turkmens
Shādān, son of Masrūr 49
Shaddād b. Khālid al-Asadī 17
Shahrākīm b. Sūriyal 105
Shahriyār b. Zarrīn-kamar 69
Shamardal b. Warqā' 19
Shāpūr Dhu 'l-Aktāf, Sasanid emperor
Sharaf al-Dawla Shīrzīl b. ʿAḍud al-Dawla, Buyid amir 73
Shaʿrānī, Abu 'l-Ḥasan 45
Sharīk b. Shaykh al-Mahrī 29
Shaybān the Kharijite 27
Shēr or Shār, of Gharchistān 87
Shīʿa 26
Shibl b. Ṭahmān, *naqīb* 26
al-Shiblī, Abū ʿAbdallāh Muḥammad b. Aḥmad, Samanid vizier 67
Shūkpāl. Sukhapāla, Hindu king 86
Sīmjūrī, Abū ʿAlī Muḥammad b. Muhammad 72ff., 76–7, 86
Sīmjūrī, Abu 'l-Ḥasan Muḥammad b. Ibrāhīm 65, 66, 68–9, 71ff.
Sīmjūrī, Abu 'l-Ḥusayn b. Abī ʿAlī Muḥammad 77
Sīmjūrī, Abu 'l-Muẓaffar Muḥammad b. Aḥmad 74
Sīmjūrī, Abu 'l-Qāsim ʿAlī b. Muḥammad 78, 83, 84
Sīmjūrī, Abu 'l-Qāsim b. Ibrāhīm 73–4, 75

Tāhartī 87
Ṭāhir (II) b. ʿAbdallāh b. Ṭāhir (I), Tahirid amir 45–6, 49
Ṭāhir b. ʿAlī 55
Ṭāhir b. al-Faḍl, Abu 'l-Ḥasan 74
Ṭāhir b. Ḥafṣ 47
Ṭāhir (I) b. al-Husayn, Tahirid amir 3, 39, 40–3
Ṭāhir b. al-Ḥusayn b. Ṭāhir 47
Ṭāhir b. Khalaf b. Aḥmad, Saffarid 76
al-Ṭāʾiʿ, ʿAbbasid caliph 70
Ṭalḥa b. ʿAbdallāh al-Khuzāʿī 18
Ṭalḥa b. Ruzayq, *naqīb* 26
Ṭalḥa (I) b. Ṭāhir (I), Tahirid amir 43
Tamīm 21
Ṭarkhūn, king of Sogdia 20
Tāsh, Abu 'l-ʿAbbās, Ḥājib, Samanid commander 70, 72–3
Tāsh Farrāsh, Ḥājib, Ghaznavid commander 103
Tegin the Treasurer 86
Tilak, commander in India 107
Ṭoghrïl Beg, Seljuq chief 110
Trilochanpāl, Trilochanapāla, Hindu king 87–8
Tūlakī, Abu ʿAlī Muḥammad b. al-ʿAbbās 69–70
Tūztāsh 83

ʿUbaydallāh b. Sulaymān 50
ʿUbaydallāh b. Ziyād 17–18
ʿUmar b. ʿAbd al-ʿAzīz, Umayyad caliph 23–4
ʿUmar b. Hubayra 24
ʿUmar b. Jamīl 37, 38
ʿUmar b. al-Khaṭṭāb, Rightly-Guided caliph 13, 23
ʿUmayr b. Aḥmar al-Yashkurī 15
Umayya b. ʿAbdallāh 19–20
Umm al-Ḥasan bt. ʿAlī b. Abī Ṭālib 16
ʿUqba b. Salm 35
Usayd b. ʿAbdallāh 33
Ustādsīs 4, 33
al-ʿUtbī, Abu 'l-Ḥusayn ʿAbdallāh b. Ahmad, Samanid vizier 71–2
al-ʿUtbī, Abū Jaʿfar Muhammad b. al-Ḥusayn, Samanid vizier 66, 69, 70
al-ʿUtbī, Abū Naṣr Muḥammad b. Abd al-Jabbār 1, 4, 5
al-ʿUtbī, Ahmad b. al-Ḥusayn/al-Ḥasan 63
ʿUthmān b. ʿAffān, Rightly-Guided caliph 14, 15
ʿUthmān b. Nahīk 31
ʿUthmān b. ʿUmāra b. Khuzayma 37

Wakīʿ b. Abī Sūd al-Ghudānī 21–2
Wakīʿ b. al-Dawraqiyya 19
al-Walīd (I) b. ʿAbd al-Malik Umyyad caliph 20, 21
al-Walīd (II) b. Yazīd, Umayyad caliph 26–7
al-Wāthiq, ʿAbbasid caliph 45
Wushmgīr b. Ziyār, Ziyārid amir 60, 64, 68–9

Yabghu, of Jand 83
Yaḥyā b. Aḥmad (II), Samanid 59
Yaḥyā b. ʿAlī b. ʿĪsā 38
Yaḥyā b. Asad, Samanid 53

Yaḥyā b. Mu'ādh 37, 40
Yaḥyā b. Muḥammad b. Yaḥyā al-Dhuhlī 49
Yaḥyā b. Zayd b. al-Ḥusayn, 'Alid 26–7
Yamanīs 27
Yaqṭīn b. Mūsā 30–1
Ya'qūb b. al-Layth, Saffarid amir 2, 46–8
Yazdajird (III) b. Shahriyār, Sasanid emperor 14, 58
Yazīd (II) b. 'Abd al-Malik, Umayyad caliph 24
Yazīd b. Abī Muslim 20
Yazīd (I) b. Mu'āwiya, Umayyad caliph 3, 18
Yazīd b. al-Muhallab 20–1, 22–3
Yazīd b. 'Umar b.Hubayra 27, 28, 29
Yazīd (III) b. al-Walīd (I), Umayyad caliph 27
Yazīd b. Yaḥyā 34
Yughur Khān 97
Yuḥannā, physician 68
Yūsuf [al-Barm] Thaqafī 35
Yūsuf b. Isḥāq, Abū Manṣūr, Samanid vizier 66, 67, 70
Yūsuf b. Naṣr b. Sebüktegin, Ghaznavid 92
Yūsuf Qadïr Khān, Qarakhanid 4, 5, 94–5, 108
Yūsuf b. Sebüktegin. 'Aḍud al-Dawla, Ghaznavid 97, 102

al-Zawzanī, Abū Sahl Muḥammad b. al-Ḥusayn 89
Ziyād b. Abīhi 17
Ziyād b. Ṣāliḥ 29

2. Places

Ahwāz 48
Āmul, in Gurgān 69, 104, 105
Āmul-i Shaṭṭ, Āmūy 36, 51, 61, 74, 83
Andarikh, near Ṭūs 76
'Arafāt 15
Argūy, in Gurgān 27
Armenia 95
Arrajān 65
Asadābād, near Nishapur 25
Astarābād 38, 69, 72, 105
'Ayn al-Shams 29
Ayqān 62

Baghdad 33, 35, 39, 40–1, 48, 51, 53, 60, 103
Bādghīs 13, 17, 26, 33, 38, 72, 73
Balkh 13, 16, 17, 26, 32, 33, 39, 47, 59, 63, 68, 77, 78, 82, 85, 86, 93, 97, 100, 107–8, 111
Balkhān Kūh 104
Baran, fortress in India 89
Bardha'a 94
Barghund, fortress 111
Bārī 90
Basand 64
Basra 14, 16, 20, 23
Bāward, Abīward 8, 36, 68, 83, 85, 96, 98, 104, 109–10
Bhatinda, Bhāṭiya 84–5, 97
Bhīmnagar 86
B.nāwad-Kōt (?). fortress 111
Bukhara 4, 17–18, 34ff., 53, 56ff., 62ff., 72ff., 77–9, 83
Busht, near Nishapur 28
Būṣīr 29
Bust 17, 47, 55, 74, 87, 98, 101
Bustān Banī 'Āmir 15
Būzgān 82
B.y.h (?) 72

Chāch, Shāsh 53
Chaghāniyān 2, 38, 63, 64, 66, 93
Chāh-i Asad (?) 37

Dahak 84
Damasus 21
Dandānqān 5, 110
Darghān 83
Dayr al-'Āqūl 48
Dayr al-Jamājim 20
Dīdī-Rū, fortress 111
Dīnārzārī defile 99
Dīnawar 37, 44
Dunpūr 112

Egypt 29, 103

Faḍlābād, in desert of Āmūy 36
Farāwa 96, 98–9
Farghāna 21, 29, 36, 44, 53
Farhādhān, near Nishapur 47
Fars 13–14, 48, 49
Fāryāb 25, 27
Firabr 56

Ganges river 90
Ganj Rustāq 17, 73
Gardīz 47, 74, 77
Gharchistān 87
Ghazna, Ghaznīn 4, 47, 74, 77, 78, 82, 84ff., 96–112
Ghūr 110
Ghūrak, fortress 86
Gīrī, fortress 111
Gurgān 22–3, 28, 46, 47–8, 54, 59, 60, 65, 68, 69, 72, 73, 82, 99
Gurgānj 74, 86
Gūzgān(ān) 22, 25, 35, 76, 84, 89, 100, 109
Gwalior 92

Hamadan 40
Hānsī 107–8
Hawzān, on the Murghāb 59
Hazārasp 88
Herat 13, 17, 19, 33, 36ff., 47, 48, 55, 57, 70, 75, 76, 78, 82, 84, 85, 89, 102, 109
al-Ḥīra 30
Ḥiṣār, in India 84
Ḥulwān 28, 30–1
Hupyān 111, 112

Īlāq 63
India, Hindūstān, Indians 9, 80, 82, 84, 96, 97, 103, 106–8, 110–11
Indus river 97
'Irāq-i 'Ajam 2, 13, 24, 81, 101
'Irāq-i 'Arab 2
Iron Gate, in Transoxania 63, 64
Isfahan 27, 28, 60, 65, 100, 104
Isfarāyin 82
Isfījāb, Ispījāb 59, 74
Ispahbad, fortress of, in Sistan 82

Jājarm 65
Jāla (?) 68
Jīranj, near Merv 58
Juḥfa 15
Jumna river 89
Jundīshāpūr 48
Juwayn, Gūyān 14, 38, 65
Jūy-i Mūliyān, at Bukhara 74

Ka'ba 96
Kabul 16, 20, 21, 33, 37, 47, 74
Kālanjar 92
Kandasan pass 48
Kārūkh 47
Kashghar 94
Kashmir 85, 87, 88, 92, 104
Katar steppe or plain 86
Kāth, Madīnat Khwārazm 76, 88, 89
Khabūshān 68
Kharjang 63
Khartang, near Samarqand 57
Khmer 95
Khulm 68
Khunāmat, near Bukhara 78
Khurramak Garden, at Nishapur 73
Khuttal(ān) 63
Khwāf 28
Khwarazm 10, 21, 26, 74, 76, 88–9, 97, 104
Kish 20, 21, 34, 75
Kirman 13–14, 17, 87
K.m.kānān, in Chaghāniyān 63
K.r.kān or Qaṣr al-Mujāshi' 17
K.sh.r.w.r, (?) Khewra 86
Kufa 23, 28, 29
Kūhak 83
Kushmayhan 21, 83

Lahore 92, 108
Lōhkōt 88, 92

Mahābar, fortress in India 89
Mākhān, near Merv 28
Makrān 103
Mandīsh, fortress 111
al-Manṣūra 97, 107
Maranj, fortress 111
Mārīkala, *ribāṭ* of 111–12
Marw al-Rūd 19, 20, 25, 27, 35, 85, 110
Mastang 87
Mayhana 8, 110
Maysān 15
Mecca 96
Medina 21
Merv, Marw Shāyigān 13, 15ff., 21, 25, 27, 28, 32, 34ff., 40, 41, 53, 57–8, 62, 68, 75, 82, 108–9
Multān 64, 86, 97, 111
Muttra, Mātūra 89–90

Nahrawāla 96
Nakhshab 21, 39, 62, 63, 75
Nandana 87–8
Nasā 21, 22, 61, 68, 69, 73, 85, 98, 105, 109
Nawshad, at Balkh 47
Nāy-Lāmān, fortress 111
Nibāj 15
Nihāwand 28
Nishapur or Abarshahr 14, 26ff., 44, 45, 47ff., 57ff., 63ff., 67ff., 73ff., 78, 82, 84–5, 101–2, 105
N.m.kh.k.n 68
Nukhayla 15
Nūr valley 91
Nuwajkath (? Numijkath) 34
Nuwākath, citadel 34
N.z.n of Bāward 109

Oxus river 5, 17, 18, 33, 51, 59, 61, 63, 64, 67, 83, 85, 86, 95–6, 108

Panjwāy 47
Parwān 74
Peshawar 84
Pūshang 13, 35ff., 47, 72, 76

Qādisiyya 13
Qanawj 89–90
Qarnīn 46
Qaṣr Mujāshi', see K.r.kān
Qīrāt valley 91
Quchqār-bāshī 74
Quhistān 14, 36, 38, 39, 70, 73
Qūmis(h) 14, 21, 60

Ramal Samm (?) 48
Raqqa 42
Ray 21, 29, 48, 54, 55, 60, 61, 64, 66, 69–70, 73, 76, 99–100, 104
R.khnā 62
Rukhwad, Rukhūd, al-Rukhkhaj 47, 55, 102
Rūyān 48, 69

Sabzawār 39
Sālūs, Chālūs 69

Samarqand 18, 21, 25, 34, 35, 39, 40, 41, 51, 53, 57, 62, 63, 73, 77, 83, 94
Sanām, fortress 34
Sarakhs 14, 41, 62, 73, 78, 82, 85, 96, 104, 110
Sarastī 104–5
Sārī 60, 105
Sāsind river 84
Sāwa 28
Shābahār, near Kabul 37
Shādyākh, at Nishapur 48
Shāhbahār, at Ghazna 93
Shahrazūr 37
Shūmān 64
Ṣiffīn 16
Simingān 63
Sind 107
Sing, near Merv 62
Sistan or Nīmrūz 13, 15, 17, 18, 20, 37, 39, 46–7, 49, 55–6, 57, 70, 72, 80, 82, 84, 85, 93, 97
S.n.k.r 34
Sogdia 18, 20, 36, 39, 83
Somnath, Sūmnāt, Somanātha 96–7
S.p.n.danqān (?) 105
Sūnīpat, fortress 107

Ṭabaristān 44, 46, 54, 56, 60, 65, 66, 69, 95, 105
Ṭabas, Ṭabasayn 13–14, 36, 76
Tākīshar 91
Ṭālaqān 19, 25, 27, 33, 35
Ṭāq, fortress in Sistan 84
Ṭawāwīs 35
Tegīnābād 102
Thānesar 86–7
Tigris river 48
Tirmidh 26, 63, 64
Transoxania 3, 13, 18, 36, 37, 40, 50, 54, 93, 95, 108
Tukhāristān 13, 28, 63, 68
Tūlak 69–70
Ṭūs 14, 19, 28, 41, 67, 76, 96, 98, 99, 102, 105, 109

Ūq, Ūk, fortress in Sistan 37, 38, 85
Ushrūsana 38, 53
Uzgend 78–9

Wālishtān 84
Wardī 64
Wāshgird 63
Wayhind 84

Zābulistān 1, 47
Zāghūl 20
Zam 32–3, 51
Zamīndāwar 17
Zarang 39, 46, 55–6, 58
Zawzan 28
Zhāsht 63

3. Technical terms

āb-shināsān 15
aḥdāth 48, 68, 72
ākhur-sālār 82
'ayyār, 'ayyārān 15, 45, 80,106

barīd 32
bast-āb 36
bīstagānī 48
bundār 80

dā'ī, dā'iyān 23, 34
dārkhāshāk 92
dawīt-dār 54
dihqān 14, 15, 16, 56
d.y.h.rā 93

fay' 16

Ghiṭrīfī dirhams 36, 37

ḥadd 22

jizya, gazīt 48

kadkhudā 86, 101, 102
kharāj 16
khuṭba 16, 102
khutuww 92

māl-i bay'at 76
marzbān 13, 21
ma'ūnat 68, 72
mūbad, mūbadān 29
mughān 13
muṣādara 61
Musayyibī dirhams 36
mutaqanna'iyān 36
muṭṭawwi'a 48

namāz 28
naqīb 26

qa'adiyān, qa'ada 39

ṣāḥib-i shuraṭ 55
sarāy-parda 90
sarhang 21
sharāb-dār 62

ta'aṣṣub 24, 74

uwaysī 92

wakīl-i dar 66

zarrād-khāna 90

4. Book titles

Asrār al-tawḥīd fī maqāmāt al-shaykh Abī Sa'īd, of Muḥammad b. al-Munawwar 8
al-Āthār al-bāqiya 'an al-qurūn al-khāliya, of al-Bīrūnī 1

Kitāb Kharāj Khurāsān, of al-Marwazī 2, 38
Kitāb al-Qunī 44

Ṭabaqāt-i nāṣirī, of Jūzjānī 8
Taḥqīq mā li '-Hind, of al-Bīrūnī 1
Tārīkh-i Mas'ūdī, of Bayhaqī 10
Ta'rīkh Wulāt Khurāsān, of al-Sallāmī 2